Practical Puppetry A–Z

A Guide for Librarians and Teachers

CAROL R. EXNER

McFarland & Company, Inc., Publishers

Jefferson, North Carolina, and London

Photographs by Elizabeth Wright.

LIBRARY OF CONGRESS CATALOGUING-IN-PUBLICATION DATA

Exner, Carol R., 1944–
Practical puppetry A–Z : a guide for librarians
and teachers / Carol R. Exner.
p.   cm.
Includes bibliographical references and index.

ISBN 0-7864-1516-9 (softcover : 50# alkaline paper)

1. Puppet theater — Encyclopedias.   I. Title.
PN1972.E86   2005   791.5'3'03 — dc22   2005010590

British Library cataloguing data are available

Cover photograph ©2005 Photodisc

Manufactured in the United States of America

*McFarland & Company, Inc., Publishers
Box 611, Jefferson, North Carolina 28640
www.mcfarlandpub.com*

To my husband, Frank, Little Bear,
with thanks for his unflagging support

Acknowledgment

Nancy Renfro—teacher, librarian, artist, and publisher—was an inspiration to everyone who has sought to reach children through puppetry. Beginning in the 1970s, she was an advocate for the use of puppets in the library and in the classroom, feeling that puppetry was a natural way to reach children.

At the time, puppetry was not a technique commonly associated with curricula or even book talks. On top of that, puppets could be expensive, ruining the marginal budgets of librarians and teachers everywhere. If puppetry was to be useful in the library and the classroom, it had better be inexpensive and easy to implement.

So Nancy Renfro began to publish books on puppetry, first with traditional publishers, then on her own in conjunction with educators and librarians who used puppets in their work. Because she felt that puppetry should be accessible to all, she focused on "junk puppets" because they were cheap, the materials were available everywhere, and they made puppetry available to children, the handicapped, and the less affluent. Junk puppets also stimulated the imagination and relied on the creative impulse. Anything could be a puppet! It all depended on your point of view.

Nancy Renfro is no longer with us, and her books are hard to come by. If your interest is in making, using, and getting into the essence of puppets, make the effort to search out these books. You, your work, and the children and adults you work with will be the richer for it. Thank you, Nancy Renfro, for all that you have given us!

And thanks to Elizabeth Wright, my patient photographer. This book is much better for her efforts.

Contents

Preface

I wrote this as the kind of book I would like to buy. As a somewhat experienced puppeteer, I was interested in trying new techniques and broadening my technical base for performance. As an advanced beginner, I wanted to work on my presentation techniques to make my puppets more expressive. And as a children's librarian, I wanted to present puppetry to children as an exciting, expressive, creative way to tell a story.

This book can benefit people who work with children and those who are interested in beginning puppetry or who want to expand their puppetry knowledge base. It is meant to be an aid to research, an idea starter, and a curiosity tickler.

If you have always wanted to try shadow puppetry, for instance, you might want to know a little about the cultures that use shadow puppetry. Then you might want to be led to some books that would give you ideas for trying out shadow puppetry. The titles of suggested books at the end of each entry will lead you to the bibliography with its annotations, which in turn will give you information about the recommended books. Reading the annotations will help to refine your choices and point you toward the first title to try. For example, if you're a classroom teacher interested in shadow puppetry, you might gravitate to Wisniewskis' *Worlds of Shadow*, a book written for teachers. The same title might also appeal to a health worker with a minimum budget and small amount of equipment space who wants to use puppets to involve children in learning about healthy living.

Puppetry is an exciting, flexible, malleable art form which can engage the creative forces of children or adults. Puppetry is elastic; it needn't be perfect (whatever that is).

Not only can puppets tell a story, they can be used to enhance the curriculum, present an idea or a concept in a compelling way, or teach any number of necessary skills. Children and adults presenting a puppet play are given a sense of their own inventive power.

1

Let this book entice you into the world of puppetry — or bring you farther into that world if you've already taken some first steps. I didn't work with puppets until my interview for my job in a public library. "Bring your puppets or whatever," said my boss-to-be. My predecessor had been a notable puppeteer. What was I to do? I borrowed a hen puppet, threw together some chicks, and did "The Little Red Hen." I got the job.

Slowly, I became acquainted with puppets and simple puppet plays, got a stage of my own, and began to feel really comfortable with puppets. Now I'm ready for something more, and this book is the fruit of my curiosity and research. I invite you to come along and see what I've discovered. You may just find that technique, stage, or concept you've always wanted to try but didn't know where to look. As shown in the bibliography, there are more puppet books than you may have ever known existed — enough for a lifetime of puppetry.

Advertising *see* Business of Puppetry: Advertising and Marketing

African Puppetry

Through the long history of Egypt, the use of puppets in religious services in the temples was commented on by Greek historians and travelers. Today, however, puppetry in Africa is most likely to be part of a public festival. These festivals may have a civic or religious theme, and puppetry is just a part of the whole display. African puppetry seems to be a product of the many influences which have come to it through traders and other cultural influences. While puppetry has been used in the far past as religious expression and entertainment, today it is used as an educational tool to tell people about health issues, especially aids information.

In traditional African public festival gatherings, puppeteers—along with musicians, dancers, jugglers, and storytellers—wait until a crowd gathers around them to begin their show. The crowd wanders in and out, pauses to listen, and then moves on to something else. The puppets are also often used by storytellers to amplify stories told to the assembled crowd.

The purpose of these stories is to tell the history of the tribe of place, the reason for the festival, or the works and deeds of gods or heroes. The puppets act as visual aids in the telling of the story and may be worked by strings or rods, or a fully detailed puppet figure can be posed and manipulated by hand. Traditional puppets are carved by local people both above and below the Sahara. However, with the advent of television, puppeteers are taking on the look of *Sesame Street* and similar programs. These modern puppeteers are used by various agencies to teach about the dangers of AIDS and other health crises. Puppetry is and remains a vital force in Africa in the cultural life of all the people.

Bell, John. *Strings, Hands, Shadows: A Modern Puppet History.* Detroit: The Detroit Institute of Arts, 2000.
Doney, Meryl. *Puppets.* New York: Franklin Watts, 1995.

American Indian Puppetry

Although the Indians of North America are embracing puppetry as a way to tell the legends and history of their people, it is not widely known that at least two tribal groups—the totem pole peoples of the northwest and the Hopi of the southwest—used puppets in their ceremonies and storytelling.

In each case, the puppets are thought to have grown out of that which already existed. In the case of the peoples of the northwest coast, it was the mask which already existed, often in a jointed form as elaborate as any Bunraku puppet. (*See* Bunraku.) Beaks of bird masks clack open and shut, and frequently, the mask opens to show the inner spirit of the mask. It is not a big step from a jointed mask to a mask with a body to a puppet. Museums have artifacts showing this transition as well as puppets from these tribes.

Puppets of many societies have been given a divine origin, so it is not surprising to find that these American Indian puppets were not used as children's toys but as figures illustrating the tribal stories. In the long houses of the clans, marionette strings could be run down from the beams of the houses and operated by hidden puppeteers, although they certainly would not have thought of themselves as puppeteers. They were participants in sacred drama (just as the ancient Egyptians or the medieval French monks surely felt that they were participating in the continuance of sacred tradition, not the performance of secular drama). Winter was the time for telling stories, and surely this was also the time for sacred puppet drama as well.

In the southwest, the Hopi used puppets in ritual dramas concerned with the corn cycle. Figures of humans and animals were used as well as masks. The dramas were performed inside, most likely in a kiva, a sacred space. The dramas were exciting, using a number of sound effects as well as marvelous effects with the puppets. These dramas were important to the success of the corn crop and were treated with all the seriousness which they deserved.

The use of marionettes and other puppet forms in these two societies were treated as a part or an extension of secret societies whose task it was to advance the cycle of the year and ensure the health of the people as well as the success of crops and the hunt by performing rites and ceremonies which were known only to the members of the societies. These people were entrusted with the important task of performing the necessary rituals in the proper manner at the proper time to ensure the continuance of the society. In this way, the puppets of the tribal peoples of North America join a long line of historical religious practice, where the hopes of humans join with the flow of nature to continue living happily and successfully on the earth.

Baird, Bil. *The Art of the Puppet*. New York: Macmillan, 1965.

Apron Stages

An apron stage is one which is worn as a cover-up and which can be used in any storytelling situation. The apron stage can either be a body cover with scenery painted or sewn upon it or an actual apron. An apron stage is meant to be portable and informal for use in schools, libraries, festivals, and other child-friendly situations.

Body-Covering Stage

One apron-stage idea was developed by Nancy Renfro. It is a circular covering pulled over the head with slits for the arms to stick through at various points. The design is that of a circle divided into quarters with the sections representing four seasons, four geographical areas (mountains, seashore, city, and country), or various fairy tale scenarios (forest, castle, cottage, town). The choice is yours, depending on the stories you tell. The material should be something with a medium drape, such as a summer skirt-weight or pants material. Lightweight felt might do, but it could also be very hot.

Because this stage is designed to be worn by a sitting person, the body covering stage is useful for performers sitting in wheelchairs or those who are temporarily unable to stand.

Apron-Shaped Background Stage

The apron-shaped background for puppetry has either a dark or black background and pockets which can hold puppets, scenery pieces, accessories, cue cards, or whatever. It is shaped like a standard butcher's apron and made of felt with pockets added or turned up at the bottom. Scenery panels can be buttoned or attached with Velcro to the apron at chest level if you feel comfortable with that idea. Felt is used for the apron because items made of, or backed with, Pellon or flannel will adhere to the felt easily.

By using a black background, the puppeteer taps into the Bunraku idea of wearing dark clothing to fade into the background more effectively. (*See* Bunraku.) If you can't wear black clothing successfully, the black of the apron creates the same effect without needing to wear black all the time or to change your clothing frequently. The puppeteer simply slips the apron on over regular clothes and goes from there.

When I use my apron stage, I sometimes untie it and spread it out since that seems to make the placement of the figures easier for me without looking down and breaking eye contact all the time.

If you have no access to felt-by-the-yard or if your favorite apron is made of any other material — denim and canvas being the most popular — a small

One design for an apron stage from Nancy Renfro. This is a plain butcher apron with button-on scenery which can be changed by the puppeteer.

"stage" or viewing area can be made from a rectangle of craft felt and buttoned or Velcroed onto the apron. While this will not be as expansive as an entire work area of felt, there may be other advantages which will make it worth the puppeteers while to use.

MATERIALS

- A pre-made butcher-style apron in a dark color of felt with pockets if possible.
- Cloth for adding pockets. (remnants of colorful cotton cloth or a color that blends in with the dark background)
- One 9" × 12" felt rectangle to just fill in the bib area of the apron and sit nicely above the pockets and below the top of the apron
- Thread to match the cloth
- Velcro strips or buttons to fasten on the felt rectangle

- Sewing machine or needle and thread. Scissors. Measuring tape. Straight pins
- Pencil or tailor's chalk that contrasts with the pocket material

ASSEMBLY—THE POCKET OR POCKETS

1. Wash, dry, and iron any *non*-felt cloth.
2. Measure the area for your pocket or pockets. Include allowance for seams on three sides and a folded finished edge on the side that remains open.
3. Fold the pocket cloth in half, right sides together, and iron.
4. Mark the size of the pocket on the pocket cloth with pencil, tailor's chalk, or straight pins.
5. Cut out the pocket.
6. Sew around three sides of the pocket leaving one side open; turn the pocket right side out and iron smooth.
7. Fold in the seam allowance on the open side of the pocket, and sew it with a basting thread. Be sure to leave the opening.
8. Pin the pocket to the apron with the open side on top.
9. Sew a narrow top seam all around the three sides of the pocket, attaching it to the apron.
10. If the pocket is long, divide the length into two or three sections and top stitch those down. If you have room, sew in a narrow pocket to hold a pen or pencil.

ASSEMBLY—THE FELT "STAGE" AREA

1. Decide if you want to attach the felt with buttons or Velcro strips. If you want to leave the felt on the apron rather than taking it on and off, use Velcro strips to detach the felt when washing the apron.
2. If you use buttons, mark their placement and make button holes in the apron. Attach the buttons to the back of the felt.
3. If you use Velcro strips, sew the Velcro firmly in place on the apron. Use tacking or running stitches to attach Velcro to the scenery.

Hunt, Tamara, and Nancy Renfro. *Puppetry in Early Childhood Education.* Austin, TX: Nancy Renfro Studios, 1982, pp. 61–68.

Armatures

An armature is a support on which something can be built. We often think of it as being a wire mesh frame, usually made of chicken wire, which reduces

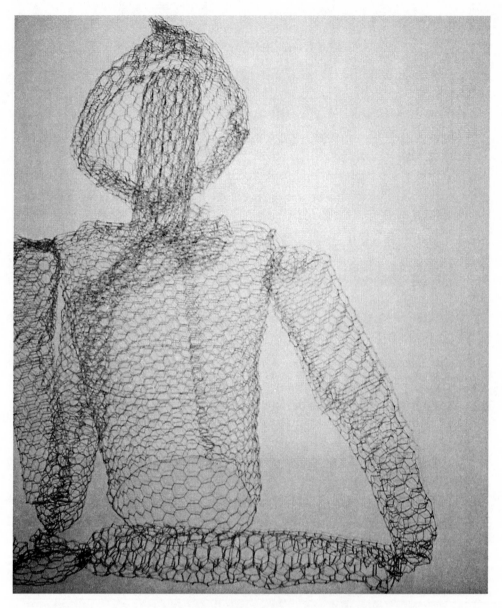

An armature for a giant puppet is made of chicken wire. The puppet will be worn on the shoulders when finished; the hands will be operated by rods.

the weight of a project. However, an armature can also be a rod or tube upon which a puppet head is built, or it can be the wires upon which a hand is modeled. An armature can be made of many things, but it is always a support for something else.

The simplest armature is the rod or tube on which a puppet head is built. Clay is placed on the armature, and the puppet head molded around it. Papier-mâché can then be placed over the clay, and a puppet head created from that. All the while, the clay is supported by the armature, which becomes a stand on which the papier-mâché is allowed to dry. The armature can be placed within some support, such as a bottle or vase, or inserted into a base while the papier-mâché dries. (*See* Papier-Mâché.)

Small items, such as hands, are often most easily sculpted over a wire armature. I like the wire twisted back on itself to give something for the molding material to adhere to. Experiment until you find what you feel is best. (*See* Hands.)

Larger items, such as large animal heads and giant puppets, can be made on an armature to decrease the weight of the puppet yet give form to it. By using chicken wire with molding material laid over it, you will have a sturdy, yet light-weight, product. Make the armature smaller than the size you plan the puppet to be, and build up on it. Decide whether you will have many layers or have wrinkles in the finished puppet, each of which necessitates using a much smaller armature. In contrast, if you will have just a few layers of molding material, the armature will be almost the size of the finished puppet. (*See* Giant Puppets.)

The molding material you lay over the chicken wire can be tissue dipped in glue and lightly formed on the mold, cloth soaked in glue or plaster, or papier-mâché mash or strips laid on a base of some other material to keep it from falling through the wide mesh of the chicken wire. The tissue paper can be either a base layer which will then be covered with papier-mâché mash or strips, or the tissue can be the modeling material itself from which a mold will be created. Plaster-soaked modeling gauze, which can be purchased at craft stores, can also be used as a modeling material, but it will be heavier. Consider what you are ultimately going to use the puppet for, and work accordingly.

In making a large puppet with an armature, make sure that the pole carrying the puppet and the armature on which the puppet is built are firmly attached to one another. Slippage is not desirable! Another alternative is to have a mounting into which the pole can fit attached to the armature. This will make the armature easier to work with. (*See* Giant Puppets.)

Armatures are essential to puppetry, whether it is the support on which the clay for a puppet head is molded or the large form on which a giant puppet will grow. Whenever you are considering weight reduction in puppet construction, an armature will assist your design and manufacture.

Fling, Helen. *Marionettes: How to Make and Work Them.* New York: Dover, 1973.
Flower, Cedric, and Alan Fortney. *Puppets, Methods and Materials.* Worcester, MA: Davis Publ., 1983.

Assistants

Puppet assistants are special puppets used to introduce story times, puppet shows, or other events. The leader always uses the same puppet assistant and becomes identified with it. The puppet assistant lives in a special place and always comes out from and goes back to that special place.

A puppet assistant is a great way to get used to using a puppet even if you don't want to do puppet plays. The puppet assistant doesn't have to have a voice; it can pantomime its reactions, or it can whisper in your ear after which you can tell the children what the puppet assistant has told you.

You can carry on conversations with the puppet assistant which introduce the theme of the story time or other event.

You: Have you ever ridden in an airplane?

P.A.: No, I haven't. I think it would be exciting to fly through the air and visit other places.

You: Well our stories today are all about traveling in an airplane. You should listen with the boys and girls!

P.A.: Oh, I will! Are we going to exotic, far away places or somewhere closer to home?

And so on. Have a short talk to introduce the day's topic, and then let the puppet assistant return to his or her special place by your chair.

A puppet assistant can be especially useful if you are tackling difficult subjects such as sibling rivalry, bullying, or the loss of a pet. The puppet assistant can give voice to the fears and concerns of the children without involving them directly and putting them on the spot. In this way, the puppet assistant may allow children to express emotions to parents that they might not have otherwise known how to talk about.

Your puppet assistant should have a special place where it lives while you are going on with story time or the lesson at hand. If you can, make the special place for your puppet assistant match its character. A rabbit, bear, or an owl might live in a tree. A fish could have its own bowl decorated with ocean scenes. And a bookworm would, of course, live in a book and pop out from between the pages to talk to the children. As you can tell from the descriptions, the special place is a hiding and resting place; while in it, the puppet is not seen by the children.

Little ones will probably try to come up and look in the special place for the puppet that is hiding there. If you have quite a few little ones, have a smaller puppet assistant and put it in the pocket of your story time apron. (*See* Apron Stages.) A mouse, a small turtle, or a book worm sock puppet would be great for this. The puppet would not even have to talk, just respond to what you are saying; of course, the appearances would be brief!

A puppet assistant is a great accompaniment for story times and for introducing special classroom segments for younger children. Any work with children is made more fun with a puppet assistant, and it gets the children's attention

"Miss Lulabelle" in her hollow stump tree house. Miss Lulabelle is a stuffed toy. Her tree-stump house is built on a chicken-wire armature covered with painted, unprinted newsprint.

right away. If you've never thought of using puppets before, a puppet assistant is a great way to get started!

Hunt, Tamara, and Nancy Renfro. *Puppetry in Early Childhood Education.* Austin, TX: Nancy Renfro Studios, 1982.
Minkel, Walter. How to Do "The Three Bears" with Two Hands: Performing with Puppets. Chicago: American Library Association, 2000.

Atlanta Center for Puppetry Arts

The Atlanta Center for Puppetry Arts was founded in 1977. It moved into its current home in 1978 with Jim Henson and Kermit the Frog assisting at the ribbon-cutting ceremony. The Center is the creation of its founder and director, Vincent Anthony, an experienced puppeteer. He saw a need for a central site devoted to furthering an interest in all areas of puppetry and supporting and educating puppeteers. The Center may be found at Center for Puppetry Arts, 1404 Spring Street at 18th, Atlanta, GA 30309. Their web site is http://www.puppet.org/.

The Atlanta Center for Puppetry Arts not only acts as a major venue for all sorts of puppetry performances, it also supports education of the public and of puppeteers through its many programs. Their interactive museum of puppetry, called "Puppets: The Power of Wonder," is an award-winning presentation of the world of puppetry from many countries, times, and artists.

Educational programs help the public and professional puppeteers become more educated about the world of puppetry. More than 100,000 children and their teachers plus interested adults attend the Center's puppet-making programs. The Center's volunteer and internship programs assist puppeteers and potential puppeteers entering the world of professional puppetry.

The Atlanta Center for Puppetry Arts is a nonprofit organization. Memberships are available, and donations are always welcome.

Audiences

Bil Baird, the master puppeteer and popular historian of puppetry, says that real puppetry requires a puppet, a puppeteer, and an audience. It is the audience which sets the puppet show apart from playing with dolls or action figures.

Audiences for puppet plays come in all ages and all varieties of sophistication. They may look forward to the slapstick of a Punch and Judy play or a more sophisticated production of opera, Shakespeare, or contemporary drama. The audience is drawn into the action of the play and participates in the creation of the magic of puppetry.

Puppeteers from all over attest to the fact that both children and adults are convinced that puppets hanging on the wall are moving, that puppets without mouths can talk, and that the puppet rather than the puppeteer expresses the personality, action, and dialogue of the play.

In Europe, adult audiences have experienced sophisticated puppetry for centuries. Americans still think of puppetry as something for children. But the growth of professional, traveling puppet troupes in America and educational centers such as the Atlanta Center for Puppetry Arts are creating a more-sophisticated audience for professional puppetry. (*See* Atlanta Center for Puppetry Arts.) The phenomenal success of *The Lion King* stage play with its use of masks and gigantic puppets is one indication of an adult acceptance of more sophisticated puppetry.

As interest in puppetry as an art form continues to grow and is supported by college programs, grants, and public funds, the audience for puppetry will continue to grow, be educated, and be willing to support the work of a growing body of American professional puppeteers. Thus, the audience will rise to its proper place as the impetus for greater creativity and exposure of professional puppet troupes.

Bag Puppets

Bag puppets are simple puppets usually made from lunch bags. They are often a child's first introduction to making puppets. The fold on the bottom of the bag makes a perfect "mouth" when the hand is inserted into the fold. Simple movement makes the mouth move and the puppet appear to talk.

The bag puppet is a "junk" puppet made from found materials. The bags used are usually the plain brown ones that children take their lunches in to school. A mouth, some eyes and maybe some arms are added. Personality can come from hair, clothes, or any other additions which the puppet maker thinks will add to the character of the puppet.

Bag puppets are not always easy to manipulate. They are bigger than even an adult's hand and tend to slide around due to the slick finish of the paper. Sometimes the fingers cannot truly fit into the bag flap to make the "mouth" move without using something which will provide traction for the fingers.

On the other hand, bag puppets are easy to make and to personalize. Even very young children of four or five can get the idea of creating a character on a bag. They are used to creating people and faces in their artwork. Now they can create a character they can make come alive on their own.

Bear

Pilgrim

Superhero

Robot

Paper bag puppets from Nancy Renfro. These designs show that the inexpensive paper lunch bag can be converted into all sorts of puppets for any number of inexpensive productions. The flap mouth need be moved only a fraction for it to appear to be talking.

Paper bags do come in sizes smaller than lunch bag size, but buying a lot from a wholesaler might cost more than you want to spend as well as the problem of storing all those bags in your art supplies cabinet. Check around with the stores you do business with and see if they will sell small numbers of small bags or let you go in with them on their next order.

Some puppeteers and actors have taken the brown paper bag and created performances of great humor and sophistication. Let's face it: brown paper bags—the ubiquitous grocery bags—are cheap and plentiful. If you find the right store, the bags may have one side without markings. The puppeteer now becomes more than an actor; the puppeteer now becomes the puppet!

Other "junk puppet" specialists such as Nancy Renfro have taken the brown paper bag, turned it inside out, and created hand puppets from them. The face is painted onto the bag which is then stuffed to fill it out. The neck is cinched in with thread, cord, or anything which will hold the neck in place. A body can then be added, perhaps made from another paper bag. And behold: you have a perfectly good, expressive puppet made out of inexpensive, even free materials.

Renfro also makes a puppet out of small letter envelopes. While you are scouting your local shops for small bags, see if any stores have paper bags without the fold on the bottom. These can be made into envelope puppets by creasing the bottom of the bag to form a mouth and adding eyes, eyelashes, hair — whatever your puppet requires.

You can make a wonderful puppet by taking a piece of paper and folding it lengthwise into thirds. Make sure that the paper can fit around your hand. Then fold the paper so that it makes a "W" shape. The two open ends of the "W" fit over the fingers and thumb. The center fold becomes the inside of the mouth. By bending the hand over and attaching facial features, you have made a simple puppet from almost nothing.

Puppets are conveyers of wonder and should be accessible to all, even the youngest and the poorest. A simple bit of paper, the common lunch or paper bag, can become anything in the world a puppeteer could want. All that's needed is a little bit of imagination.

Peyton, Jeffrey L. *Puppetools: Introductory Guide and Your Specialized Applications Manual.* Richmond, VA: Prescott, Durrell, 1986.

Renfro, Nancy: *Puppets for Play Production.* New York: Funk and Wagnalls, 1969.

http://familycrafts.about.com/cs/puppets/index.htm Contains many patterns for kid-friendly puppet making, including bag puppets.

http://www.legendsandlore.com/Sackpuppets.html This is a fine, general-purpose, kid-friendly puppet-making site.

http://www.puppetools.com/v1/frame.html Site of the Puppetools organization. Offers workshops for continuing education credits.

Balinese Puppetry *see* Wayang

Beaks

Beaks are a specialized kind of mouth worn only by birds and monsters. Having a beak could mean that your puppet can talk when the beak moves. It can also mean that the puppet simply has a beak as a part of its identification as a bird and the beak does not move.

Beaks can be sewn from any fairly firm fabric such as felt or anything reinforced with a stiffener such as Pellon. They can also be formed out of craft foam, poster board, or any other stiff material.

Beaks can be sculpted out of clay and covered with papier-mâché. They can also be sculpted from Styrofoam, foam rubber, or wood. (*See* Armatures; Hinges; Papier-Mâché.)

The important thing to remember when creating any beak is its weight. The beak will jut out in front of the head of the puppet. If it is too heavy, it may weigh the head down and distort the puppet or just be unwieldy and hard to work.

As with so many other body parts, when you are creating something which looks like a bird, look for beak-shaped things. Clothespins of either kind, folded paper mouths, or drinking cups cut in half and then formed into a beak shape can become beaks. Card stock or poster board can be folded into diamonds or sculpted into beaks and glued onto the puppet's head. The corners of boxes can also be formed into mouths and shorter beaks. A hinge can be applied, and the mouth can move by means of a rod attached to the lower jaw. (*See* Mask Puppets with Movable Mouths.)

Move the beak or let it stay immobile, whichever you like. Your bird will be that much more charming if you consider the beak as part of your puppet's personality and character. If the bird's character is zany or serious, if you are trying to be realistic or fantastic, remember that the bird's beak does not just sit there; it is as much of the puppet's personality as its eyes, hair, or clothes (or feathers). Its prominence dictates that you take the beak into consideration. It may be the first part of your character that the audience sees. Make it appropriate, keep everything in character, and you'll have a beak your puppet can sing about.

Feller, Ron, and Marsha Feller. *Paper Masks and Puppets for Stories, Songs, and Plays.* Seattle, WA: The Arts Factory, 1985.

Henson, Cheryl, and the Muppet Workshop. *The Muppets Make Puppets!* New York: Workman Publishing, 1994.

Wright, Lyndie. *Masks.* New York: Franklin Watts, c. 1989.

Beginners

If you are a beginner, it is tempting to say that you won't be intimidated by working with puppets, but this isn't necessarily so. People have many preconceived notions about puppets: what they should, and should not, do; how they should sound, react, and move. Some of this comes from their own early puppet experiences or from the things they learned in their education as teachers, librarians, actors, or whatever.

A good rule to remember, especially if you will be working with children as you begin your work with puppets, is: *children don't care about how it "should" be; they just want to see the puppets.*

Walter Minkel, in his instructive *How to Do "The Three Bears" with Two Hands: Performing with Puppets*, says that a good way to begin with puppets and children is to have a puppet friend, assistant, or mascot with you whenever you gather the children together for story time or a similar together time. The puppet lives in a special place — perhaps a box or barrel decorated to carry out a theme — and comes out at the beginning of the group session. It can introduce story time, sharing time, health information time, or whatever you like. The puppet appears briefly, discusses the upcoming event with the leader, and then returns to the special place. (*See* Assistants.) In this way, a librarian can focus on the story theme of the day; the teacher can talk about sharing circle or an upcoming lesson; and a nurse or health worker can lead into a discussion of tooth brushing, washing hands, or healthy eating. The interaction is brief and conversational so that the leader doesn't have to agonize over memorization or the proper words. The leader and the puppet will have a little talk, just as the leader might with another child, and then go into the planned activity.

Another simple approach for the beginning puppeteer is to use a single puppet to introduce the story or theme. For those reading or telling stories, an animal or child puppet which matches the story might be appropriate. The puppet in this case need not even say anything. The storyteller talks about the puppet who goes through some appropriate movements and then retires to enjoy the story along with the children.

An extension of this is the puppet apron or pocket where the librarian, teacher, or any other person working with children has a puppet which comes out and talks to or interacts with smaller children. (*See* Apron Stages.) In a one-on-one situation, if the puppet is inexpensive, it can be used and then given to the child. In this way, the adult introducing the puppet has a chance to teach the child how to use and interact with puppets — that they can be used to tell a story of your liking. Older children can be directed to books on puppets or given a sheet of simple finger puppets to make.

A word about talking directly with your puppet ... go ahead and do it! Again, remember: the children don't care. They will make the leap necessary to tune you out and focus on your puppet. Look at your puppet when it is speaking, and look away from it when you are speaking. This brings audience focus to the puppet when it is talking.

For performance, consider dressing in black or a dark color. This tends to help you in your "disappearing act" and lets the puppet come more to the front, especially when the puppet is dressed in light or bright clothing.

A First Stage Experience

If you are contemplating making a puppet stage and putting on performances on a regular or even an irregular basis, consider one of the simple, inexpensive, disposable stages suggested in this book. (*See* Stages.) Using a doorway, a heavy cardboard box, cardboard three-fold screen, or something equally simple and inexpensive is a good first bet. You don't want to sink a great deal of money into something you may discover you don't care for. In addition, it shows the children that they don't need to spend a lot of money making a puppet theater.

Consider what you will have at your disposal before you commit yourself to a big program of puppet plays. Will you have a human assistant? Will you have to make all your own puppets? Are you thinking of putting on a big play with several acts or are you just going to do five minutes at story time? Remember: go easy on yourself unless you have unlimited imagination, talent, energy, and time. If you have all that, go ahead and have fun!

What I chose to do was begin with five-minute programs at story time based on Aesop's Fables. First of all, Aesop usually uses only a couple of characters—great for those of us who have only two hands! Second, this introduces children to one of the classics of Western literature—the animal fable—and the master of the genre. Third, the tales are very flexible. If you don't have the puppets to do "The Lion and the Mouse," or you would like to give greater exposure to other puppets you might not use so often, try "The Great Orca and the Little Fish!" No puppets for "The Fox and the Crane?" Then try "Dog and Giraffe Do Lunch." The story line stays the same, and you can emphasize the friendship between the two characters and how thoughtlessness can harm that closeness.

As my boss often says: "Go Easy! Burnout from programming is the number one problem for those who work with children." And when you're ready for a bigger stage, check out the ones in this book. You needn't spend a fortune, and you can get pretty much what you want and can afford if you plan for what you want to do with your puppets.

Minkel, Walter. *How to Do "The Three Bears" with Two Hands: Performing with Puppets.* Chicago: American Library Association, 2000.

Renfro, Nancy. *Puppets for Play Production*. New York: Funk & Wagnalls, 1969.
Watson, Nancy Cameron. *The Little Pigs' Puppet Book*. Boston: Little, Brown, 1990.

Body Puppets

The body puppet is a huge, flat, or nearly flat puppet, usually representing a human character, that children can wear. It is meant to be a life-sized character, fully developed, that a child can use in a puppetry situation. It is not a costume but is a puppet which the child wears. The body puppet can be worn by any child, including a child in a wheelchair, a child who is blind or has limited vision, or a child on crutches. Small-motor facility is not involved with the body puppet, so children of all abilities can use it to participate in a puppet play.

Body puppets are the invention of Debbie Sullivan, a professional puppeteer working with the Nancy Renfro Studios. Ms. Sullivan and Ms. Renfro have written that every child, no matter how disabled, should be able to use puppets. Their pioneering work in creating puppets, lesson plans, and puppet corners for all types of situations is designed to bring the joy of working with puppets to all children everywhere.

All children — and adults as well — can enjoy the body puppet. It can be made of any kind of material that is not too heavy and can be folded and manipulated fairly easily. Paper, cloth, or foam rubber are all materials that can be used to good advantage in making a body puppet.

Construction of the body puppet can be quite simple if you are using paper, felt, or some soft material that you will leave in a two-dimensional state. If possible, have the child lie on the floor or stand against a sheet of paper taped to the wall or floor. Draw around the child to create an outline of the real child. If this is not possible, measure the child's height, arm length, and head size to get an idea of how big the child really is. Then draw an outline of a figure that can be used as a pattern.

Color in the outline figure just as it is, and then cut it out. Alternately, the outline can be used to create a pattern for a more elaborately clothed puppet depending on what part the puppeteer will play. Make the puppet smaller than the child so that the top of the puppet comes to the child's nose or chin.

Use bands of paper or cloth to fasten the body puppet to the child at the neck, wrists, waist, knees and ankles. Test to make sure that the child can move easily and safely in the body puppet and that it won't get caught somehow and cause an accident.

If a three-dimensional effect is desired, a soft-sculptured face, hands, and body can be made, rather like making a life-sized, flattened rag doll. The pup-

Panda

slippers

Paper-Bag Body Puppets

Paper bag "Bodi-Puppet" from Nancy Renfro. Any paper bag or large sheet of drawing paper can be transformed into a wearable puppet. The arms are moved by the wearer's own arms and the puppet is worn low enough on the body for the puppeteer to be able to see easily.

pet can then be given clothes, hair and accessories to match its character. The sculpted body puppet is fastened to the child in the same way.

I have seen body puppets made large and worn by adults. Again, this was a puppet, not a costume, and the adult inside had to consider herself as both a manipulator and as an actor. The adult body puppet comes close to the Bunraku characters and yet maintains its uniqueness. (*See* Bunraku.) Unlike the Bunraku puppeteers, who are manipulating the puppet from the outside, a puppeteer working with a body puppet is inside the puppet and causing it to move. There is great possibility for this kind of puppet for those who are interested in experimentation.

Hunt, Tamara, and Renfro, Nancy. *Puppetry in Early Childhood Education*. Austin, TX: Renfro Studios, 1982.
Sullivan, Debbie. *Pocketful of Puppets: Activities for the Special Child with Mental, Physical and Multiple Handicaps*. Austin, TX: Renfro Studios, 1982.

Bottle Heads and Puppets

Plastic bottles can be used to create the heads for rod puppets and marionettes. Bottles with a "waist" can also become the body of a puppet, especially a female one. Because of their light weight and inexpensive cost, plastic bottles can be a puppeteer's friend, and bottles can be used in so many ways.

To find out whether a bottle will be useful as a puppet head or body, you may have to invert the bottle to look at it in a different way. If you have a plastic bottle with a handle, grasp it by the handle, and turn it upside down. Turn it so that the handle is facing you. Now hold the bottle by the cap or with two hands on either side. Does it suggest a face to you with the handle as the nose? Imagine where the eyes would go. What kind of eyes would this bottle head require? If you change the eyes, does the character of the puppet become different?

A tall plastic bottle, such as a one-quart milk or juice bottle, can have its body (now the top of the puppet's head) cut into interesting shapes. By cutting points into the plastic you can make a crown. Cutting off the base of the bottle and cutting the body into strips can make curly hair when the strips are run over the edge of a scissors as you do when curling ribbon. And cutting the plastic into interesting shapes can make an alien or a punk rocker.

Most plastic bottles are a clear-to-gray color. Look for plastic bottles that are already colored. These can make exotic, lively puppets. Because the plastic is slick, paints may not adhere to the surface. I have had uneven success with paints and continue to look for surface finishers to help paint stick to the surface. Watercolor markers tend to bead up on the plastic; indelible markers seem to fare a bit better. Still, they come in a very limited number of colors. Because plastic bottles are available everywhere, are inexpensive and lightweight, it is worth looking around and asking at art and hobby shops for paint that will adhere.

Plastic bottles with "waists," usually dish detergent bottles, have been

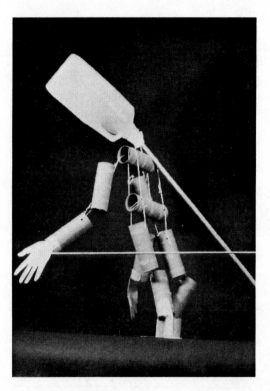

A rod puppet's head may be made from a plastic milk jug. The handle of the jug becomes the nose. The high crown of the jug can either be cut down or built into the design of the costume for the puppet. The rod in the head allows the head to turn, lean, and move expressively.

used for dolls for quite some time. Their human figure appearance lends them to being dressed up as country grannies, Christmas angels, and baby dolls. With some planning, they can be used as puppet forms as well.

The "chest" portion of the bottle, the portion above the "waist," can be cut off just below the "waist" to provide shoulders for a rod puppet which will not have legs. The neck of the bottle will hold the head of the puppet made from papier-mâché or Styrofoam. Arms built on a wire, rope, or chenille stick armature can be run through the "chest" and either allowed to hold a pose or moved with rods or strings. The main rod of the puppet can either be inserted into the neck of the bottle from the bottom or attached to the back of the puppet with duct tape. The puppet's dress should be a long one with an opening in the back for the rod if it is attached at the back. (*See* Rod Puppets.)

As a simple marionette, the bottle's lower part can be shortened a bit so it doesn't clunk on the floor as it's being moved along. The head and arms can be attached as mentioned above. The doll can be dressed in a long gown and a simple control used for the marionette. This control is a single rod — dowel rod, paper towel tube, wrapping paper tube, lath strip, or paint stirrer — with three strings: one each for the head, right arm, and left arm. The marionette moves along by rocking the control gently back and forth. (*See* Marionettes.)

Male marionettes can be made from the same bottles with the bottles cut short and the waist falling more in the regular place. Legs are attached by hot glue at the waist. Shirts should be a bit loose around the waist to hide the bottle underpinnings. The same kind of control can be used for the male puppet. These are simple puppets not meant to make complex movements. Again, they move by a gentle rocking movement of the control. Besides, some of the oldest puppet troupes in India use the same or even simpler controls, so don't worry. You're historic!

Puppeteers don't always have huge funds to call upon when designing their puppets. They want to entertain their children, tell a story well, and send people away happy. Ordinary objects, such as plastic bottles, are used every day and thrown away (or recycled) without a thought. If you work in a school, library, or other child-friendly place, ask parents for donations of plastic bottles. You'll have enough for several plays in short order! Take these bottles and try out some of the suggestions mentioned here. Look in some of the books mentioned in the bibliography. And liberally apply your own imagination. You're sure to have some wonderful creations. When you've made all your puppets, assemble your audience and put on a play! 'Cause the play, not the money, is the thing!

Henson, Cheryl, and the Muppet Workshop. *The Muppets Make Puppets!* New York: Workman Publishing, 1994.
Lade, Roger. *The Most Excellent Book of How to Be a Puppeteer.* Brookfield, CT: Copper Beech Books, 1996.

Box Stages

Reversible Box Stage for Hand Puppets or Marionettes

The following instructions are for a lightweight, serviceable hand puppet or marionette stage which can be made from a refrigerator carton. Cut away a portion of the carton to make a puppet stage. The box is ready for use with hand puppets, or it can be turned upside down for use with marionettes.

MATERIALS

- One refrigerator carton or clothing storage box from a moving company in good condition
- Box cutter or heavy duty craft knife for cutting through the cardboard
- Ruler, yardstick, or tape measure
- Pencils
- Eraser
- Scissors
- Paints, markers, or contact or shelving paper for decoration
- Plain black cloth 1½ times the width of the refrigerator box and 45 inches wide for back curtain
- Sewing machine, needle and thread, or glue gun to make the curtain
- Rod, dowel, or heavy cord to hold up the curtain

ASSEMBLY

1. Find the front of the carton. This is where you will make the stage opening.
2. Open up the box to make cutting easier. This will allow you to lay the box flat while measuring and cutting.
3. Measure 2" starting from the top of the box below the flap. Measure all across the front of the box from side to side, stopping at the folds. Then draw a connecting line which you will use as the cutting line for the top of the stage opening.
4. Measure 2" from each side fold; draw a line for each side.
5. Measure down 2' 6" starting from the line you drew in step 3. Measure all across the front of the box from side to side, stopping at the folds. Then draw a connecting line which you will use as the cutting line for the bottom of the stage opening.
6. Cut away the cardboard for the stage opening. Use the box cutter to cut along the sides of the box and your cutting line.

7. Stand the box up with the stage opening at the top and check the results of your cut. Any problems that are discovered now can be repaired later.

8. Loosely close the box up and step inside. Do you have enough room to move or do you need to leave the box open with the sides angled slightly for easier movement? Either is OK. Is there enough room for your arms to reach up and hold your hand puppets?

9. Get an assistant and turn the box upside down to see how much room you have for marionettes. Don't worry about your feet showing. You will move your back curtain into a marionette performance position later (or you can make a second back curtain).

10. Decorate the outside of your stage. If you want to have a pattern or design on the outside of your theater, choose something that looks good either right side up or upside down. Notice any part of your design, for example, flowers, trees or vines, that may look funny when inverted. Stripes, brick, stone, or a scalloped border around the stage area all look good from both sides.

11. Make the back curtain for your puppet theater. Sew a pocket large enough to accommodate your rod. Sew a narrow hem in the bottom of the curtain. Thread the curtain on the rod.

12. For hand puppets, with the puppet stage at the top of the box, measure 8 inches back from the stage opening and mark on both sides of the box. Cut a hole large enough to accommodate your rod. Hang the curtain. For marionettes, turn the puppet stage so that the opening is at the bottom (in the marionette position). Stand inside the box. Work with the marionettes to estimate the amount of room you will need. Measure that length and mark it on both sides of the box at the top of the marionette theater. Cut holes for the back curtain to accommodate the rod. Hang the curtain.

13. Make curtains for the front of your theater if you want them. Consider how you will open and shut them. A sign announcing the play or an attractive picture placed in front of the stage and removed just before the play begins might serve just as well or even better than curtains. If you do want front curtains, make them as you did the back curtain.

ADDITIONAL CONSIDERATIONS

Consider making a place to hang your puppets. Professional puppeteers hang their hand puppets upside down using rings (attached to the bottom edge of the puppet) and hooks (attached to the theater) while the puppets are not in use. That keeps them ready for use and out of the way. Then you can simply slip your hand into the puppet as if you were putting on a glove, and you're set to perform.

Instead of rings, you could try Velcro with a strip attached to the box by self-sticking adhesive and a dot or square on the puppet. Make sure the Velcro is securely attached to both the box and the puppet.

Also consider making a place to put props and other puppet "stuff." Puppeteers often attach a shelf to the back of their stage and use that for props. They also attach hooks to the shelf for hanging their puppets as mentioned above.

As an alternative to a shelf, you might try a net tray instead. Attach this firmly enough to the box so the net stays open and does not get tangled. The mesh of the tray should be small enough so that small props would not fall through.

You might use your Velcro strip for attaching props as well. Put a Velcro dot or square on the prop and hang it from the theater wall. This might be the easiest solution, but you are the puppeteer and need to make that decision yourself. Work with your theater a while and see what works best for you.

Small Box Stages

The small cardboard box stage sits on a tabletop and is used for hand puppets, finger puppets, or small marionettes. With the attachment of cloth or paper to the stage opening and the use of a back lighting source, the stage becomes a shadow puppet screen. (*See also* Shadow Puppet Screens.)

This is another simple beginner's stage and one that can be used to great effect for practice, for trips to schools or clinics, or for bookmobiles. When used as a marionette stage, the puppeteer will be seen unless a concealing curtain is erected. This is also a great craft experience for older children who bring their own boxes and take home a puppet theater. As such, it could be part of a puppet club's program where children learn to make several puppets and then make their own puppet theater to perform in at home.

MATERIALS

- Large cardboard box, the kind used for televisions or microwaves
- Paint, paper, markers, contact paper or construction paper, and other things for decorating the stage
- Craft knife or box cutter
- Pencils
- Erasers
- Ruler or tape measure
- 1½ yards of 45" material in black or a dark color for the back curtain
- Dowel 3" longer than box width to hang the curtain (or cord) upon
- Sewing machine, needle and thread, or glue gun to make the back curtain

ASSEMBLY

1. Measure and draw a border 2"–3" wide around the front or widest edge of the box depending on your taste and the size of your box.

2. Cut around the edges of the box on the line and remove the center part. Smooth any ragged edges.

3. Cut away the back of the box to provide entry to the stage. If the box seems to be too deep, cut the box down to an 18" depth to provide a more comfortable working space.

4. Decorate the box using paints, contact paper, construction paper or whatever.

5. Make the back curtain by sewing a rod pocket at the top for the dowel and a hem at the bottom of the material.

6. Cut holes in the top side back of the box 1" from the top of the box and at least 6" from the back to hold the dowel.

7. Thread the curtain onto the dowel.

8. Insert the dowel into the holes.

The back curtain can also be hung on a cord and fastened to the back of the box using strapping tape, staples, or even duct tape.

Brown, Jerome C. *Puppets & Mobiles.* Belmont, CA: David S. Lake, 1983.

Lade, Roger, *The Most Excellent Book of How to Be a Puppeteer.* Brookfield, CT: Copper Beech Books, 1996.

Watson, Nancy Cameron. *The Little Pigs' Puppet Book.* Boston: Little, Brown, 1990.

Brush Puppets

Brush puppets build upon the shape of a brush to create a character which is informal and perhaps a bit zany. Brush puppets can be made from any sort of brush, and the handle becomes the control stick.

The important thing about brush puppets is to see the character in the brush or have the character firmly in mind and match the brush to the character. On page 26 of *The Muppets Make Puppets,* there is a perfect example of what I am talking about. The Muppet Workshop folks have made a caricature which they call George and Barbara Brush. George is tall and thin and wears a power tie and glasses. Barbara is topped with a white mound of hair, wears a blue dress and pearls, and has blue beads for eyes. By considering the physical characteristics of George and Barbara Bush, the Muppet Workshop has created a great caricature of this past-presidential couple.

Take a walk in the laundry products isle of your grocery store or visit your local hardware store. Look at the brushes you see there, and imagine what characters they might become. The bristles will become the hair and may determine the character as they did for Barbara Brush. However, you might look at the same brush and see something — or someone — else. Some advertisers have even done a bit of the work for you and turned their brushes or dusters into characters illustrated on the package sleeve. So a scrub brush or a wildly colored feather duster might need just a pair of googly eyes to become a character on its own. Add a mouth or a beak and you're in business!

Creating informal characters such as the ones made from scrub brushes means that you will need to have a supply box of items for features you can apply readily to your new puppet. No need to run around looking for plastic cups, wiggle eyes, chenille sticks, or pom-poms, you will have them right at hand.

If you wish to add arms to your brush puppet, consider chenille sticks with pom-poms for hands. Plastic forks are another possibility for hands and arms. They can either be attached to a chenille stick with the handle of the fork becoming a rod for moving the arms, or the fork can be hot glued to the brush. For a bit more realism, remember to trim the top tine to become the thumb.

Mouths for a brush puppet can be formed from rubber bands, ponytail holders, or paper. Beaks can either be made of paper, cut-down plastic cups, or they can be made with two short pieces of lath hot glued together to form an open beak. Mouths can also be made from a single piece of lath hot glued to a brush which has a long crosspiece. To make the lath fit well onto the brush, you will need to cut the end of your lath at an angle. Use a miter box and saw to achieve this cut.

These two brush puppets are made from feather dusters. The working part of the brush (feathers, bristles, or cotton mop head) becomes the hair, and the handle is the rod of the puppet. These characters are enhanced with jumbo pom-pom and felt eyes and ponytail-holder mouth that can move to simulate talking.

Since the handle of the brush forms the rod which you will hold to manipulate your puppet, your hands will be exposed holding the handle of the brush. You can either accept that, or you can put on a pair of tightly fitting colored gloves which may add to the character of the puppet.

Brush puppets can increase the number of puppets you have with little cost. If you enjoy informality and humor, brush puppets may be just the thing for you!

Henson, Cheryl, and the Muppet Workshop. *The Muppets Make Puppets!* New York: Workman Publishing, 1994.
Renfro, Nancy. *Make Amazing Puppets.* Santa Barbara, CA: Learning Works, 1979.

Bunraku

Bunraku is the puppet theater of Japan that is best known in the west. The nearly life-sized puppets manipulated by visible puppeteers present plays which are centuries old and which eventually influenced popular Kabuki theater styles.

Bunraku is not merely the puppets, but a complex trio of puppets and puppeteers, the chanter who tells the story, and the shamisen player who accompanies the chanter. A shamisen is a three-stringed instrument played with a plectrum or very large pick.

In the middle of the seventeenth century, noted chanter or storyteller Takemoto Gidayu set up his own theater in Osaka, ably assisted by famed theater owner Takeda Izumo and noted playwright Chikamatsu Monzaemon. Chikamatsu is to the Japanese theater what Shakespeare is to English-speaking theater.

Takeda, the theater owner, was an experienced producer of puppet plays and well known among the merchant class. As a result, his new theater was patronized by the increasingly powerful merchants. For them, the new puppet theater was an opportunity to learn the classical Kabuki theater of Japan which had been denied to them because of their low, commoner status.

Chikamatsu, the renowned playwright, preferred writing for the puppet theater because the puppets projected a purer and more refined emotion than human actors could.

In addition, Chikamatsu wrote special plays called *sewamono* for the merchants, chiefly plays of love-suicide or *shinju*. The most famous, *Sonezaki Shinju,* was based on a real-life incident where a courtesan and her lover committed suicide together rather than be parted by society's demands. This led many to commit *shinju* at the time. In a more contemporary vein, the play and its suicide act form a major plot element of the 1950s post-war American film *Sayonara*.

For the west, the most famous element of Bunraku is the visibility of the puppeteer and his assistants. The chief puppeteer operates the head, with all its mechanisms to create and reveal emotions, and the right arm, which handles the samurai's sword, gestures to emphasize emotional states and pick up, carry, or handle objects. The chief puppeteer is the only person to have his face exposed. An assistant puppeteer, dressed all in black and masked, handles the left arm, and an advanced apprentice handles the feet. Each major puppet has three operators who have chosen to work with either male or female puppets exclusively. Apprentices start with simpler puppets representing humorous secondary characters and advance with experience to the more complex major puppets.

Bunraku is centuries old but its future, like that of all traditional arts in Japan and elsewhere in the world, is uncertain. While speaking about the condition of Bunraku today, Matthew Johnson states in his comprehensive article on Bunraku for the puppetry home page that "Bunraku today is enjoying a mild revival.... The popularity of puppeteers Yoshida Tamao, Yoshida Minosuke, and Yoshida Bunjaku helps fill the theaters and the number of younger patrons has begun to rise in recent years. Still, though audiences are important, the aging of the all-important backstage workers — head carvers, costume makers, etc. — and the lack of people to take their place poses an increasing problem for the future of this 300-year-old art form."

Another problem for Bunraku is the static form of the plays. According to Mr. Johnson, the last great Bunraku play is thought to have been written at the end of the eighteenth century. Still, there is always hope. The first new Noh play in many centuries was produced a few years ago, a ghost play dealing with the contemporary theme of organ transplants. Perhaps new playwrights will come along to translate contemporary themes to the Bunraku stage as well.

Bunraku-Style Puppets

The puppets used in Bunraku are around 4' tall and thus nearly life-sized. The puppeteers in the Bunraku theater are visible and manipulate all parts of the puppets.

Some puppeteers use Bunraku-style puppets in their theater productions or incorporate elements of Bunraku in their presentations. For instance, one North Carolina puppeteer (Becky Lofgren) uses a single, large puppet (Androgeena) sitting on her lap. Becky dresses in black, making it easier for her to disappear to the audience. She talks with her puppet, but the puppet is the focus of the performance. Anything the puppeteer says is just to prompt responses from the puppet. The puppet is a mouth puppet with a rod on one arm. (*See* Mouth Puppets.)

In another instance, "Dan Dilly Poe," a puppet play for adults, uses many kinds of puppets: rod, shadow, miniature Bunraku, and mouth puppets. The puppeteers are visible to the audience, dressed in black but not masked. Their Bunraku-style puppets, including the central figure of Edgar Allen Poe, are miniatures which are still manipulated by hand, giving the puppets a wide range of flexible and expressive movements.

Another puppeteer (Grian McGreggor of The Ivy Vine Puppet Theater) dresses in a portable stage, places a crown on her head, and disappears into her puppet stage. The puppets she generally uses are simple rod or stick puppets. But they are so full of vigor and the action on stage is so lively that the lack of full articulation is not noticed. The story and the action sweeps the audience along. All manipulation and scene changes are performed in full view of the audience and make perfect sense within the action of the story.

The puppet styles just mentioned are all applications of various elements of the Bunraku theater technique. The use of life-sized or nearly life-sized puppets, dressing in black, the use of a visible story teller, the placement of the puppeteer in full view of the audience, and the visible manipulation of the puppet by the puppeteer are all Bunraku elements skillfully applied by individual puppeteers to achieve a style or approach to puppet story telling.

CONSIDERATIONS FOR BUNRAKU-STYLE PUPPETRY AND PUPPETS

If you wish to use a life-sized or nearly life-sized Bunraku-style puppet in a production, you will need to have sufficient puppeteers to manipulate it and all the large-sized puppets you may have in your play. This may be a good solution where there are many more children signed up for your puppet club than expected.

The puppet will need three people to operate it as with a traditional bunraku puppet: one for the head and right arm, one for the left arm, and one (perhaps two) for the feet and legs. This will require an elevated performance space and a slightly smaller than life-sized puppet.

The materials selected for the Bunraku-style puppet should be light in order to prevent the manipulation of the puppet from becoming difficult or exhausting. Cardboard and cardboard tubes, plastic bottles and tubs, foam rubber tubing, garden sticks or lightweight dowels should all be considered in combination as possible materials for your puppet. Lightweight cloth, tissue paper, or even paint applied directly to the puppet-making materials, can be used for clothing. Accessories should be similarly light.

The basics needed for the puppet are material for the head; a box-like shape for the torso; limbs of equal length, jointed at knee and elbow; and simple hands and feet. The puppet is held and supported at the torso with a rod extending into the body area to turn the head. The action of the right arm is guided either by the puppeteer's hands or a lightweight rod; hands or another rod guide the left arm. The feet are manipulated by hands either holding the feet or using flaps attached to the shoes.

Making Bunraku-Style Puppet

This bunraku-style puppet is made of cardboard tubes with either a plastic milk carton or a mask for the head. This is meant to be a beginning form to practice with and to build upon. By dressing the puppet in lightweight materials, its character can be changed. By using a mask, the puppet can be given a more fanciful, even mythological form.

MATERIALS

- A selection of cardboard tubes: toilet paper rolls, paper towel, and wrapping paper tubes

- String or brown paper to join the tubes together
- Tag or poster board and corrugated cardboard pieces or a selection of light-weight boxes to make the torso and head
- Optional for the head: an empty quart plastic milk or juice jug or a lightweight box
- Optional for the rod operating the head: dowel rod no more than ½" in diameter or use a wrapping paper or paper towel roll
- Poster board or foam cone board for hands and feet
- Markers
- Newspaper
- Pencil
- Rulers
- Scissors
- Craft knife
- Glue
- Brads
- String

ASSEMBLY

1. Outline a figure using the items you have. Estimate arm and leg lengths to get an idea of how the puppet will go together. If you want to use the plastic milk carton or lightweight box for the head, try it in place to check its proportion to that of the rest of the figure.

2. As an alternative to step 1, use newspaper to make a size mock-up for the head and torso. Use these as a pattern to create the front of the torso box and front and back of the head.

3. If you are using a mask for the head, create it now or make a rehearsal stand-in for the mask using poster board.

4. Mount the head on a tube or dowel by inserting it in the box or milk carton. Use the scissors or craft knife to cut a hole in the bottom of the box. If you are making a rounded box head out of poster board or cardboard, create a hole for the head control in the same way.

5. Using string or brown paper and glue, make joints to hold the tubes together.

6. Join the arms to the torso box with a joint made of string or cardboard washers and brads.

7. Join the legs to the torso box using a joint made of string.

8. Use poster board or foam core board to make hands and feet. Join these to the arms and legs.

9. If you want to use a lightweight rod to manipulate the arms, attach these to the forearm tubes.

10. Attach rods or flaps to the feet to manipulate them and make the puppet walk.

Baird, Bil. *The Art of the Puppet.* New York: Macmillan, 1965.

Bell, John. *Strings, Hands, Shadows: A Modern Puppet History.* Detroit: The Detroit Institute of Arts, 2000.

Lade, Roger. *The Most Excellent Book of How to Be a Puppeteer.* Brookfield, CT: Copper Beech Books, 1996.

http:.//www.sagecraft.com/puppetry/definitions/Bunraku.hist.html The puppetry home page's article on the history of Bunraku by Matthew Johnson.

http://www.ultra-k.com/bunraku/english/intro.html A page on Bunraku published by The Yomiuri Shimbun Osaka Head Office (1998).

http://candy.alacarte.co.jp/~oichni06/Pi+intre.html Japanese web page called "Café de Bunraku Fan." The page has an interesting presentation of the organization of a Bunraku performance as a double triangle structure, including the relationship between the puppets completing the action, the chanter telling the story, and the shamisen player providing the background music. The page also has a number of interesting photographs of Bunraku puppets.

http://www2.justnet.ne.jp/~kitayogorou/ The web page of Mojihisadayuh, a Bunraku chanter. This is a most informative page, illustrating the crucial work of one of the central figures of a Bunraku performance.

Business of Puppetry

Getting Started in Business

A puppetry troupe is usually a small business of less than 100 employees. Yours may be very small: You. If you have never taken any business courses before, this might be a good time to consider taking some or reading up on the intricacies of the small business. Up until now, you may have been focusing on the mechanics, design, or construction of puppets and puppetry. Now you're thinking about becoming a theater company, and you need to know some important things.

The first is what do your state, county, and city require of a small business? Usually, it's only a license which may cost nothing or may cost a small amount of money. Check with the reference department of your local public library about doing business in your state. Frequently, they will also have books about just that topic which will cover all the things required of the business person and their business in your state.

The second thing you need to know is a good accountant, especially if you're just starting out. An initial consultation will most likely not cost very much and won't take too long. Our accountant's advice was to save all receipts as you're starting out. Even if it's for glue and string, save those receipts! They are the proof to the government that you've paid the money you say you have to begin your business. Those start-up expenses will come off your taxes once you begin to make an income.

The third, but far from final, thing is a list of considerations: managing your business's finances, marketing, employee relations, and financing your business. You will want to have a business plan for your business—where are you, what resources do you have, and where do you want to go with those resources. This is the business part of being a puppeteer which is not always covered in school or the books you may read.

If you have no background in business, take a look at your library's business book shelves. There is such an interest in entrepreneurship these days that "starting your own business" should be in its own category! There is *The Portable MBA in Entrepreneurship* by William D. Bygrave and Andrew Zacharakis. It's good and complete, but its thickness may deter you from reading it. A more manageable beginning might be Bernard Kamoroff's *SmallTime Operator*, a collection of advice and forms from an accountant and advisor to small businesses. The book is in its umpteenth printing, I think, and is still a great starting point for the small business person.

As you read, you will begin to formulate a list of questions which fall under the topic "business" as opposed to puppet construction, script writing, costume and scenery and the like. What taxes are you required to pay? Do theaters fall into a different category of business? You're self-employed. What does that mean for you and your finances? How do you hire someone? When you've hired that person, what are you legally required to do for that person? How do you calculate someone else's paycheck?

If you have online access, go to any of the large portals and check out the "business" category. Yahoo, Lycos small business, HotBot, and About.Com all had small business categories and information on things like business plans, accounting, and marketing. The Lycos small business site is a good place to start for the basics, and the About.Com site is another good starting point because it has an arts/crafts section. This is a matter of personal preference. Check on your own to see what is best for you.

Another place to look is your local junior college. I know. You're sick and tired of college. But these courses are designed for the adult who is interested in starting a business. They are designed for information, not academic credit, so there are usually no tests, just lots of information. Try them out and see what you can find!

Although there is never an end to all the information you can find on starting a small business, a final suggestion is going to be to turn to your state or local arts or humanities department. See if they have workshops on small business skills for the artist, grant writing courses, or any information you might need. Make an appointment with someone and sit down and talk. Tell them of your needs and plans, and see what they have to say. Dress in your best and bring your puppets in your briefcase! Who knows what might happen?

Talk with other puppeteers, too. You hope to be able to support yourself, but you need to make a name for yourself. If you're young and have no ties or responsibilities, you can plan to live out of your van if you really have to. If you're older and thinking about starting a puppet company, you may have to treat it as a part-time business until you can build up enough of a clientele where you can think of going it alone.

From the other side of the fence, if you are a teacher, librarian, or social worker involved with children, you may have the steady job but need a way to get out and build up an audience for your work. Think about what it is that you want to do with your puppetry. Do you want to perform? To use it as a creative door for children and youth? Perhaps you want to find some balance between making and doing, between having an audience and being a director? There may be many possibilities for you if you begin to ask questions about what you can do in your present position and where you might be able to take your dream within your system.

This discussion only points the way; it doesn't provide an entire course. It is only the beginning, but it is an important one. As artists, we get carried away with the desire to create beauty and wonder and take that out to the world. Unfortunately, we must also think of the nuts and bolts of being a business in whatever way that business presents itself.

Start with where you are and the assets you have. Consider where you would like to be — not in the traditional five or ten years, but what you would like to be doing with the skills you have acquired for yourself. Work from that starting point and map out the trip from where you are to where you would like to be. At each point along the way, list the skills or talents you will need to accomplish the task at that point on your journey and list how you might acquire those skills. You may not know right now, but at least you will be thinking about it. The best part is that you can begin this trip right now! What are you waiting for?

The Iron Triangle

The Iron Triangle is a concept I picked up in library graduate school from management teachers John Lubans and Sheryl Anspaugh. Their contention was that the library was always part of a triangle: library–patrons–county management, for instance. This triangle, in its constituent parts, was unshakable, as if it were made of iron. There may be several iron triangles in the life of an organization, but they are always there, and their relationships must be observed and balanced if all is to go well in that area or if the tensions in that area are to be understood.

For a puppeteer, the basic iron triangle is puppet–puppeteer–audience. If you change one point of the triangle, the whole triangle changes. Let us say that you, as a puppeteer, have always played to children's audiences, but now, for whatever reason, you want to reach an older, more-adult audience with more-adult, serious themes. As the puppeteer, do you eliminate your entire, established audience? Or do you find a way to appeal to two audiences? Do you change the thematic material of your stories to present the new ideas which have become so important to you, perhaps appealing to both adults and children at the same time?

The iron triangle becomes tricky when funding is concerned. There's the puppeteer–the puppet company (even if it's just you)–and the funding agency. If the "funding agency" is whoever comes to the theater door and pays for a ticket, you have only your audience to please, and you hope that over the years you will build up a clientele to support your efforts. They may even become contributing supporters with fancy titles to assist you in your work through their charitable donations.

If real funding agencies get involved, say grants or contracts with schools and so on, you may find yourself having to meet a whole new set of criteria which the funding agency sees as fulfilling its particular goals. You and they must be very clear on what these goals are and what fulfillment of these goals means to the agency as well as to you.

The iron triangle is a useful device for seeing a situation in a new light. I have not even begun to explore all the ways in which it can work for you as a way to see what is going on around you in your work and professional life. However, I do know this: If I want to spend more time on my puppets at work, I had better square it with my boss and with my clients (the children and their parents who come to my library), or I'm going to be in trouble. Puppets–boss–clients: see how it works?

On the other hand, if I can show that puppetry will bring in a wider age range of children to our programs or that we can have a wider variety of programs (while all the time getting my regular work done and serving the kids and their parents in a reference way), I will have satisfied my boss and kept the regular clientele happy. I may have to make some adjustments to my schedule, but I will satisfy all the points on the triangle and keep them balanced, not tense and full of friction.

Try out the iron triangle and see if it works for you. You may find it to be the answer to all your management questions; or you may chuck it in the round file. Not every management solution fits everyone, but this one may do the trick for you! Try it!

Management

"Management" is a catch-all for all the extra-creative activities you have to do for your puppet troupe. These can be very creative as well, just in a different fashion. They include formulating a mission statement and a business plan, accounting and record keeping, promoting and marketing, training employees and establishing relations with them, and being a transportation specialist. We will deal with some of these in this section. The following sections will discuss record keeping and advertising and marketing.

A mission statement and business plan states the purpose of your troupe and its plans for the future. It takes finances into account, but it is not of itself accounting. It requires that you know who you are as a puppeteer and what you want to accomplish in the short run, say the next five years.

Employee training and relations means you are responsible for making sure that your employees know how to do their jobs and that you are aware of their morale on the job. For most puppet troupes, it means making sure that you — the chief and only puppeteer — got a good night's sleep so that you can drive safely to today's show. It also means that you must take the time to take advantage of learning opportunities which come your way.

For a few troupes, however, employee training means that manipulators must be trained, musicians hired, and lighting and sound technicians found for your troupe. Are all these people to be paid? Or will they be trained volunteers or interns who make a dedicated group of puppet manipulators working under one or two professionals? These are management decisions which only you can make, and they depend upon your mission or vision for your puppet company and the robustness of your financial and business statements.

Being a transportation specialist may involve tearing down everything and putting it in the van, or it may mean designing a portable stage which can be taken to schools, auditoriums, and other venues away from your main theater. It may involve having a puppet theater in a specially designed van or trailer which opens up to present your show. Whatever you decide, you need to fit your transportation to your needs. Not everyone can tour in a 1955 Checker Cab the way George Thoroughgood and the Destroyers do. But hey! You'll find what you need and may be able to deduct it from your taxes as a business expense.

Ultimately, whatever you do managerially comes back to *you* and what *you* want to do as a puppeteer. Management is usually not covered in school or talked about in puppetry books, so you may have to do a great deal of self-educating, but it will be all to the good because you are an excellent puppeteer who loves puppetry and wants to stay in business. To do that, you need some business smarts. Management knowledge is out there. All you need to do is go grab it!

Record Keeping

Records of all kinds are useful to a small business person, especially one as involved with the arts as is puppetry. Everyone knows that a business needs to have records of income and expenditures. Not everyone realizes, however, that there are other sorts of records which will be as useful to the traveling puppeteer as orderly account books.

Check with your accountant. (Yes, you should have one; you will be surprised just how helpful they can be, especially when you are getting started.) Find out what sort of records to keep. When in doubt, save all receipts, and keep a time line of expenditures and income. Find out what can be taken off of taxes for business expenses and how the laws have changed from year to year. All of this is important at tax time, but an analysis of your finances can also show you where you need to tighten up or spend more.

Check your public library's business section for books on keeping records for small businesses. A bit of research now will prevent headaches later. Also, the library may have a copy of Bernard Kamoroff's *Small Time Operator*, an accounting book for all people with a small business. Check it out! It's a gem and has been in publication for many years and many editions.

Another record you should be keeping is that of the puppets you make and the shows you put on. Take pictures of all puppets in an individual play plus stills of various parts of the play. These can be used in advertising, but they also form a history of your puppet troupe. Keep scripts, original recordings of dialogue and music, and the photographs of your puppets and copies of their plays together in one place, ideally apart from the rest of the business. If you have videos of a performance, workshop, or other presentation, keep those together as well. Again, they are the record of your business and may become useful if you wish to seek financing for your future endeavors.

It may sound paranoid to suggest keeping copies of records, scripts, photographs, recordings, and videos in a place separate from your business. But the *New England Opera Theater* lost everything in a fire. Only a few photographs remained of their beautiful puppets, and those were posted on their web site so that people could see what they had been at one time. Fire, flood, tornadoes— all manner of troubles can happen to a puppet company. With separate records kept in storage, there are at least records of what had been in the event of the worst, and they can help rebuild after a time of trouble.

Another record you may want to keep is an inventory of supplies. This could be a detailed record of your musical albums or a note to remind yourself that you are running out of pom-poms or pipe cleaners. If your business is small enough, an inventory of everything is probably not necessary. A large company might want to keep track of supplies, though.

Another reason for keeping detailed records is for the future. Many notable puppeteers' works have been lost simply because they lived before video recording made permanent records cheap and possible for all. Their puppets may remain; still photographs may have been taken; but the plays or acts in which they performed were lost, and so their work is lost to posterity. It can never be enjoyed or duplicated. That is truly sad and, in this age of copiers, video, and digital cameras, quite unnecessary.

A final record you may want to keep is a journal of the road. Which play dates were enjoyable and which were not? Which paid on time and which were … er … troublesome? Which ones enjoyed subtle humor and which ones preferred slapstick? This is not to create a record of sites to encourage or avoid; it is, however, a record to give you some idea of your own comfort with various places and various productions. It is as much a journal of your own reactions to your own work as it is anything else. As such, you may find it totally unnecessary. On the other hand, it may give you something for reflection and a report to yourself on your enjoyment of your own profession. You may also make notes to yourself on the development of your puppets, styles, and techniques, ideas for new plays or skits you would like to do, as well as a running record of your own development as a puppeteer.

There are all sorts of records, and I have probably not even touched on all the ones you could keep. On the other hand, unless you truly enjoy writing and keeping records, you most likely want to keep paperwork to a minimum. There will be records—the ones for tax purposes, of course—which you will not be able to avoid keeping. Others mentioned are records you owe to your profession and to yourself. All are valuable. Take some time to make note of your work so that you may prevent becoming an ephemera of time as so many other puppeteers and their puppets have become. Remember that you are an ancestor of puppeteers to come!

Advertising and Marketing

When you are just starting out, letting people know who you are is vitally important. This is called advertising and marketing, and it can take up quite a bit of your time. Without it, however, people will not know who you are, and the play dates will not appear as frequently as you would like. Following are some things you must do before requests for them come in.

Have business cards made up. They are inexpensive and can be included with all your fliers, notices, press packages, and so on. Carry them with you.

Design a flier to trumpet this year's program of plays. If you have a color picture of your puppets, include that, too. Your flier should have the name of your company and how to contact it. Names of productions with dates, times, and locations of performances should be correct and prominent.

Get some really good pictures of you and your puppets both in color and in black-and-white glossies. You will use these everywhere, and the black-and-whites will be for newspapers.

Have someone design a web page for you. Use the name of your puppet company in the URL (address) if you can. This may be an expense, but it will be worth it to say to prospective clients that they can find further information on your web site. This may also be one of those things to check out at your junior college.

You will be asked what your price will be for one school or a group of schools or library branches. Know in advance what you will charge. Try to find out what the going rate is as well. Is it $350, $400, or $250? You need to know. You may also want to add "plus mileage." The gas can add up quickly.

Offer something extra. For instance, tell the library or the school system that you will throw in a puppet-making workshop for teachers and librarians if they can cosponsor your puppet theater.

Find out in advance what the summer reading program theme will be for your state, and devise something which will fit in with that theme. States usually know a year in advance and don't mind telling a prospective performer.

Develop a mailing list of schools and teachers, libraries and librarians, camp directors, newspapers, and others you will want to notify about your activities and program offerings.

If you alternate between a school season and an "at home" in the theater season, spell this out in a flier and mail it to your list of prospects.

If you offer a special puppetry camp during the summer or are available to offer one, make this information available.

Contact any and everyone whenever you have a new puppet presentation to offer.

Advertising and marketing are a part of the business of being a puppeteer. In the very old days, puppeteers put up posters or distributed broadsides letting people know that they were putting on a show. They might bang cymbals, play a fanfare on a trumpet, or cry out that a play was just about to begin. In some way, the news has to get out about what it is that you do and that you are available for performances. Advertising is just one of the things that small business people have to do, and this is true for nonprofits— schools and libraries, that is— as well as those who earn a living doing puppetry. The copy doesn't have to be snappy, but it does have to inform. It doesn't have to be expensive; it just needs to look good and be displayed prominently. While you are learning everything else about puppetry, give advertising a try. It will make all those other efforts pay off in increased bookings and exposure.

Adler, Elizabeth W. *Print That Works: The First Step-by-Step Guide That Integrates Writing, Design, and Marketing.* Palo Alto, CA: Bull Publishing Co., 1991.
J.K. Lasser Institute. *How to Run a Small Business.* New York: McGraw-Hill, 1994.

Richman, Peter. *The Insider's Guide to Growing a Small Business: Straight Advice from One Who's Been There*. New York: Macmillan Spectrum, 1996.

Sullivan, Robert. *The Small Business Start-up Guide*. Great Falls, VA: Information International, 2000.

http://www.bizmove.com/ A complete small business site covering all aspects of running a small business including marketing.

http://business.lycos.com/ Lycos small business site covers marketing. Check out their site for other aspects of running a small business.

www.ama.org/ Putting "small business" in their search engine brought up three publications on marketing.

Cardboard Boxes

Boxes are really useful in puppetry, especially in making toy theaters. (*See* Box Stages; Toy Theaters.) However, it is not always possible to find a box of the right size when you want it. Being able to make a box of the precise size you need is a great asset for a puppeteer. Poster board is about the weight of most commercial shoe boxes, so you should be able to construct all the boxes you need without waiting for a trip to the shoe store.

Another advantage of making a box to suit the job is the ability to make the box all in one piece. There is no need to make a lid unless you really need one. The box you create for a puppet theater can be made all in one piece with the openings created as a part of the assembly process.

To make a pattern for a box, first determine the size of box you need. For instance, if you wish to make a finger puppet theater but do not have a box of the right size, take measurements of your own body to determine the correct size.

1. Measure the width of your hand across its widest part including the top of the thumb. Add 2" to this measurement for "wiggle room."

2. Then measure the length of your arm from the inside of your elbow to the tip of your longest finger with the palm of the hand facing you. You may need some assistance with this. These two measurements will give you the length and width of your box.

3. For the depth of the box, measure the length of your longest finger from the base of the knuckle to the tip of the finger. Add 1".

The box's dimensions will then be the length (arm-to-finger measurement) by the width (hand measurement) by the depth (longest finger knuckle-to-tip measurement). Draw three length-by-width rectangles (four if you want a box top). Draw two width-by-depth rectangles. Drawing these rectangles on paper will produce a pattern with all of the sides of the box joined together in a strip (plus a flap joined to the top of one of the sides if you created the top of the box).

To glue the box together, add a 1" tab to one of the long and one of the short sides of the box pattern. Slant the sides of the tab inward. These tabs will fold over and be glued to the inside of the sides and top of the box.

Determine the size and position of the stage opening. When you have the pattern the way you want it, cut out the pattern, place it on the poster board, and trace around it. Cut out the box with a craft knife and straightedge or with scissors. You can create decorations now, especially if you are painting them on.

Use the back of a scissors, knife blade, stick, or other blunt object to make a crease along the folds of the box. Gently fold along the creases for the sides and top of the box as well as the tabs. Glue the tabs into place and let dry. And there you have it! A box of your own making!

Mauriello, Barbara. *Making Memory Boxes*. Gloucester, MA: Rockport Publishers, Inc., 2000.
Owen, Cheryl. *Making Decorative Boxes for Gifts, Storage and Display*. Newton Abbot, Devon, UK: David & Charles, 2002.
Renfro, Nancy. *Make Amazing Puppets*. Santa Barbara, CA: Learning Works, 1979.

Cardboard Tube Sliding-Mouth Puppets

Simple talking puppets are fun to make. These include the simple moving jaw puppet and the elastic mouth for rod and stick puppets. (*See* Mouths; Pony-tail Holder Movable Mouths.) The cardboard tube sliding big-mouth puppet is easily made from a cardboard tube and a sleeve which fits over it and slides up and down. The mouth is painted on and becomes larger or smaller as you move the sleeve up and down over the tube.

MATERIALS

• Large or small cardboard tube or oatmeal box
• Poster board or other light cardboard
• Stapler
• Tape
• Scissors or craft knife
• Pencils
• Eraser
• Paint and paint brushes or markers
• Glue or glue gun
• Scraps of cloth, paper, and yarn to make clothing and hair
• Paint stirrer, dowel rod, or cardboard with which to make a rod to move the inner sleeve up and down

1. Take the poster board and wrap it around the core tube. Make sure that the poster board fits snugly over the tube and that the ends of the poster board overlap enough to fasten together but still move easily. Mark this overlap point.

2. Trim the poster board to size.

3. Tape or staple the poster board. Test for ease of movement of the poster board sleeve over the tube.

4. Draw a face on the core tube, including the top of the mouth and an extension downward to the base of the core tube. This will become the ever-expanding mouth. Color in the face and the mouth on the core tube.

5. Draw a "U" shape on the sleeve. Make sure that the upward legs of the "U" match the downward mouth extension on the core tube.

6. Remove the sleeve. Color in the mouth "U."

7. Cut out the poster board inside the "U." This is how you will see the rest of the mouth as it extends.

8. Cut out arms and hands from poster board.

9. Paint the arms to match the costume of the puppet or cover the arms with the same fabric.

10. Glue the arms onto the sleeve.

11. Finish off the costume, wig, and other essentials of the puppet.

12. Take the paint stirrer, dowel, or stick cut from cardboard and attach it to the base of the core tube with glue, masking tape, or staples.

13. Slip the core tube into the sleeve. Move the core tube up and down with the rod and see how the mouth can become bigger and bigger.

14. Find some music, assemble your puppets and an audience and put on a concert!

Henson, Cheryl, and the Muppet Workshop. *The Muppets Make Puppets!* New York: Workman Publishing, 1994.

Renfro, Nancy. *Puppets for Play Production.* New York: Funk & Wagnalls, 1969.

Cereal Box Puppets

Cereal boxes are great sources of puppet material. They come in three sizes: the standard, rectangular cereal box (which comes in two or three sizes itself); the small, individual-serving rectangular box; and the round oatmeal box, which comes in a small and a large size. These boxes can become the foundation for some interesting puppets.

Rectangular Cereal Box Puppets and Mouths

If you have ever watched the cartoon "Sponge Bob Square Pants," you know that rectangular shapes can become leading characters as easily as any other. Turn your cereal boxes into a family of hand or stick puppets by using decorated boxes of various sizes. (*See* Hand Puppets; Stick Puppets.) If you want to make your boxes into hand puppets, remove the bottom of the box and insert your hand. The mouth can be cut out, and your finger could stick out as a tongue.

Because the box shape is so unusual, you can add legs and feet and it will seem like part of the design. If you want to turn your box puppets into shelf sitters, leaving your hands free to operate the arms or legs by rods, weight the boxes with clay or sand in a plastic bag inserted and taped down firmly onto the inside bottom of the box before the puppet is decorated.

The rectangular single-serving cereal box becomes a wonderful mouth or snout when joined to a body. (*See* Mouths.) Join two boxes together to form a mouth or cut one in half horizontally to form a snout. Glue strips of sandpaper or rubber from a gripping jar opener to provide traction for your fingers. Use cloth or a long sock for the body of the puppet, cutting open the toe of the sock

Cereal box puppet from Nancy Renfro. Any paper bag or large sheet of drawing paper can be transformed into a wearable puppet. The arms are moved by the wearer's own arms and the puppet is worn low enough on the body for the puppeteer to be able to see easily.

to let your hand poke through and hold the box mouth. Fasten the body all around the edge of the box mouth.

Decorate your box puppet any way you want. It can become a dragon, crocodile, alien, or long-snouted monster. Larger boxes can make larger puppets, with the mouth operated by an external rod if necessary.

Round Cereal Box Puppets and Mouths

Round oatmeal cereal boxes can be turned into a variety of puppets. With the consideration of paper tubes of all sizes, round salt boxes, or round boxes of any kind, you can have a variety of puppets in the same manner as the rectangular cereal boxes. Decorate the round boxes and use them as either hand or rod puppets. (*See* Hand Puppets; Rod Puppets.) Weight them as you did for the rectangular boxes and have some more shelf sitters. Round cereal and salt boxes may be turned into big-mouth puppets with the addition of a sliding sleeve. (*See* Cardboard Tube Sliding Big-Mouth Puppets.)

Cereal boxes can also be turned into movable mouth hand puppets by splitting the cereal box in two, joining the two halves with duct tape or another heavy tape, and making a mouth pocket for your hands. (*See also* Mouths.) Make a body and neck and join the neck to the lower half of the jaw. Leave room for your hand to fit through the body and operate the mouth.

Following are directions for using a round box to make a mouth puppet.

MATERIALS

- Medium sized circular cereal or salt box
- Duct, electrical, or cloth tape
- Poster board or cardboard
- Felt
- Glue
- Sock or cloth for the body of the puppet

ASSEMBLY

1. Cut the round box in half horizontally. Join the two halves with a hinge of heavy tape (duct, electrical, or cloth tape).
2. Cover each opening of the box with cardboard or poster board cut so there is room for your hand to enter the mouth.
3. Make a peanut-shaped pattern which is based on the two cereal boxes sitting side by side.
4. Cut the pattern from felt.

5. Glue the felt in place over the cardboard or poster board.

6. Make a slit in the middle of the felt so that you can slip your hand into the mouth pocket and work the two halves of the mouth.

7. Paint and decorate your box however you wish. Let the paint dry.

8. Make a body for your puppet and attach it to the box. Your arm should fit up through the body of the puppet and into the mouth of the puppet.

9. Fit your thumb and fingers into the mouth pockets to work the mouth.

10. Use your mouth puppet in a play or as a puppet assistant.

Henson, Cheryl, and the Muppet Workshop. *The Muppets Make Puppets!* New York: Work-
    man Publishing, 1994.
Hunt, Tamara, and Nancy Renfro. *Celebrate! Holidays, Puppets and Creative Drama.* Austin,
    TX: Nancy Renfro Studios, 1987.
Renfro, Nancy. *Puppets for Play Production.* New York: Funk & Wagnalls, 1969.

Characters

Character creation is one of the central elements of puppetry. An inanimate object must be brought to life by the puppeteer and given a voice and an outlook on the world — which adds up to the puppet's character. If you have never considered this before, think of your friends, relatives, and acquaintances. What elements of their personality add up to their character? Character could also include the way they style their hair or an accessory they always wear. Can you imagine Queen Elizabeth II without a purse or a hat? How about John Wayne without his drawl or Arnold Schwarzenegger without his muscles and accent? They just wouldn't be the same.

Traditional puppets have their characters already established for them by the cultures in which they have arisen. Karagoz, the Turkish shadow puppet anti-hero, is coarse and vulgar, vigorous and clever, heroic and sometimes cowardly all in the same play. He represents the aspirations of the common Turkish man, warts and all. The other characters in the Karagoz plays also have established personalities, and people who know the plays will look for them. (*See* Karagoz.) Similarly, if you go to an Indonesian Wayang Gulek or Chinese shadow puppet play, they will have some similarities with Karagoz but will be as distinct as the puppet's home culture. (*See* Wayang.)

In American and European nontraditional puppet plays, then, the puppet must be given a unique personality. You can practice this by identifying the two or three things that stand out about people you know or see on television or in the movies. Tune in to *Sesame Street* or *Between the Lions* to see how these puppet characters are created. Watch a movie with the Muppets in it or look at some of the old *Muppet Shows*. What are the elements that characterize Kermit the

Frog, Gonzo, Bert and Ernie, or Big Bird? Each of those puppets had to have a character with a personality created for it. What makes them distinct?

Now think about some children's books or common fairy tales you know. What personality traits distinguish the characters you find? Could you translate that into a puppet character? Take the next step and imagine how that character would dress, walk, talk, and so on. If an image is beginning to form in your mind, you might want to make a description or simple sketch of your idea for further reference.

One exercise book which should be in a beginning puppeteer's library is Nancy Frazier and Nancy Renfro's *Imagination: At Play with Puppets and Creative Drama*. This book is full of exercises to help loosen the imagination and think creatively about puppetry. Two of my favorite exercises are: bring a kitchen utensil to life, and what character does this fabric have? In the first, take an ordinary kitchen utensil — a whisk, coffee pot, tea strainer, or what have you — and give it a personality; bring it to life. What would it say and do? What kind of a situation would be normal for this character? The other exercise is to take a swatch of fabric and give it a character. Fake fur, chiffon, a quilt flower print, satin, leather or vinyl — all of them have distinct uses as material so they should be able to have distinct personalities as well. As with the appliances, begin to imagine not only the personality but the situation your fabric character would find itself in. Jot down any notes which seem interesting to you. They could make wonderful new puppet plays for you!

These are just a few beginning ideas for character creation. Once you become accustomed to thinking about character, it will become easier for you. Keep your mind active. Don't slip into stereotyping or typecasting. It may be difficult, but try to make all of your characters special in some way. Not every princess need be sweet and charming. A bit of spice may give your royal character just the touch it needs to become really special. Work at character, and it will begin to work for you in all your puppet plays.

Ackley, Edith Flack. *Marionettes: Easy to Make! Fun to Use!* New York: Lippincott, 1929.

Boylan, Eleanor. *How to be a Puppeteer.* New York: McCall, 1970.

Engler, Larry, and Carol Fijan. *Making Puppets Come Alive: A Method of Learning and Teaching Hand Puppetry.* New York: Taplinger, 1973.

Frazier, Nancy, and Nancy Renfro. *Imagination: At Play with Puppets and Creative Drama.* Austin, TX: Nancy Renfro Studios, 1987.

http://www.sagecraft.com/puppetry/using/character.html See the article "Creating a Puppet Character" by Bill Woodburn.

Chinese Bag Puppet Theaters

In the past China had all the puppet forms which we know: hand puppets, marionettes, rod puppets, and shadow puppets. But the form I love the most, which seems to show the greatest degree of ingenuity, is the bag puppet theater. Everything the puppeteer needs can be carried in a box on the end of a pole, and the theater is no bigger than the puppeteer himself. It is the height of portability, and eventually it found its way to Europe.

The Chinese bag puppet theater is a very old form of street puppetry. The puppeteer ties the bottom of the bag around his knees or ankles and stretches the bag up over his head. The playboard is balanced on the puppeteer's head and he reaches up to work his diminutive hand puppets. The idea of the bag puppet presents the puppeteer with an opportunity to travel wherever the festivals and fairs happen to be. Since everything can be fitted into a box, bag, or satchel, it is easily transportable. So if the puppeteer needs to make a fast getaway for some reason, it is easier than if he had tons of machinery all loaded on a big wagon pulled by a team of horses or donkeys.

Undoubtedly, the puppeteer was a man of the people who knew how to poke fun at the various officials of the village. A conversation with some of the locals would give the puppeteer an idea of the gossip of the village, including who made a good target as well as who it was wise to leave alone. Since the village figures were similar, that is, they were found in all villages, it was easy to insert comic characters wherever the puppeteers went.

Puppeteers were usually welcomed everywhere. Village life was cramped and monotonous. Unless the village were on a post road or near a larger village or town, news was hard to come by. A puppeteer, like a peddler, would bring news of the surrounding countryside and whatever big city news and gossip came his way. As he left, the puppeteer might even be willing to take messages or parcels to the next village he visited.

From time to time, persecutions broke out, and travel was restricted. The first Qin emperor of China slaughtered Confucian scholars and burned books. So puppeteers might have gotten caught up in the net of persecution. Censors might not have liked it if they heard criticism of the emperor or the government in general. A wandering puppeteer had to be careful, but if care was exercised, all would be well.

The Chinese bag puppet must have traveled west to Europe. In Bil Baird's monumental *The Art of the Puppet*, an engraving he labels as one of the first pictures of a puppeteer in Russia shows a bag puppeteer at a fair with the bag around his knees and the playboard on his head, just as his cousin in China would have had it. So the Chinese bag puppet theater became a world traveler, and it comes as no surprise. A smart, compact theater like this would have been a welcome sight at any fair, and the children would have gathered around whether the puppeteer was in Russia or China. It makes you want to go to the fair just thinking about it!

Baird, Bil. *The Art of the Puppet*. New York: Macmillan, 1965.

Clothespin Puppets

Clothespin puppets are nonjointed wooden clothespins or doll pins dressed in costume with a rod attached to move them. These are not the spring clothespins, but are peg-shaped pins with a rounded button at the top and two tines at the bottom. Craft stores also have small flat pins which can be dressed and used in the same way. They can be used in miniature or toy theaters or as substitutes for stick puppets in informal puppetry situations. (*See* Toy Theaters.)

Clothespin puppet costumes are usually made of felt or fabric scraps with notions or trims to make accessories. A wooden bead of suitable size can be glued onto the top of the pin or the rounded top of the pin can become the head. The legs are formed from the stiff tines of the pins. Pipe cleaners, wire, or cord can be used to create flexible or bendable arms. Beads, felt scraps, or cardboard cutouts become the hands.

Before dressing your clothespin puppet, add the rod. This can be done in one of two places. A stiff wire rod can be inserted into the back or between the tines of the clothespin, whichever you prefer. Use a vise or a C-clamp to hold the pin in place while you drill a hole or hammer in a wire rod.

I suggest inserting the rod first and dressing the puppet around it. This will require splitting blouses and shirts if you insert the rod in the back, but I think it is the better way. If you insert the rod after the puppet is dressed, you will have to wrap the puppet in some way to protect its clothes and keep them from shifting while you insert the rod. If the rod slips, it can ruin the costume you've worked so hard to make.

MATERIALS

- Rigid clothespins or doll pins
- Scraps of felt or fabric and trims to make clothing
- Craft sticks to make arms
- Tacky glue or hot glue gun (The tacky glue might be better unless you need the puppets immediately. You may need to move and position the fabric, and hot glue doesn't let you do that easily.)
- Wire rods cut from clothes hangers or purchased at hobby or hardware stores (If you want to bend the wire, use a firm but pliable wire.)
- Drill with a small bit
- Hammer or pair of pliers
- Vise to hold the puppet
- Acrylic paints
- Paint brushes

- Scissors
- Pencil
- (Optional) Plain, unpainted bead or sphere to make a head for your puppet (The bead must be proportional to the pin you are using.)

ASSEMBLY

1. Decide where you want to locate the rod and insert it. If you place the rod between the tines of the pin, you will need to use a vise to hold the pin while hammering the rod in so the clothespin doesn't slip. If you use a drill bit on the back, make sure that it is the same size as or only slightly smaller than the rod.

2. If you want to add a bead for the head, add that once the rod is inserted. Hot glue the bead onto the top of the clothespin.

3. Paint on the facial features. Wait until after the clothes are made to add the hair as the last feature unless the hair is painted on. If so, paint it on now.

4. Add the arms, using pipe cleaners or cord or crafting rigid arms from half portions of craft sticks (popsicle stick size). The craft stick portion becomes both the arm and the hand.

5. Make the clothes. If you want, men's clothing can be painted on. Remember when painting pants to paint between the tines.

6. Add any accessories which will add to the character of the puppet, including wigs and hats as needed.

7. Gather your puppets and put on a play! Experiment with different types of theaters to see which works best.

Renfro, Nancy. *Make Amazing Puppets*. Santa Barbara, CA: Learning Works, 1979.
Renfro, Nancy. *Puppets for Play Production*. New York: Funk & Wagnalls, 1969.

Clubs

The puppet club is a group of young people who are either interested in puppetry generally or are interested in putting on a particular puppet play. The puppet club can be run from a library as part of its youth programming or as a classroom or after-school activity. The activities of a puppet club can vary; the only two constants are that it involves young people and puppets.

The most basic activity for a puppet club is to put on a puppet play. This will take six weeks to two months preparation time with two meetings a week. Since you will have to fight for rehearsal and puppet-making time, two months will never be enough time. This becomes particularly acute in the summer when the puppet club must compete with other summer activities including summer vacations. Still, it is a great activity, and you will be surprised at how wonderfully imaginative the kids can be! Every time we meet to put on a play, I am convinced that it will all be a shambles. Somehow, though, everything pulls together in time, and all is well in the end.

One way to make things a bit easier on everyone is to provide either the puppets or the play. If the play is provided, then the kids make the puppets. If the puppets are provided, then the kids write the play. It can all come together some time at the end of a summer reading program in a special program for admiring parents and friends.

The next level up for the puppet club is to spend time making different types of puppets with the idea that the kids will eventually get together and use these puppets to create a play. This is very difficult to do over a summer unless you make it almost like a camp situation that meets every day for a designated length of time to learn something about puppets. The idea will be to introduce kids to different kinds of puppetry and puppet-making skills with the goal of putting on a play or series of skits at the end of the summer. If you have kids returning year after year, you can have more advanced levels of professionalism as you work.

One activity kids in the puppet club can be involved in is teaching other, younger, children how to work with puppets. If you have a puppet corner, they can supervise the children who come to the puppet corner and guide these younger, inexperienced children in the use of puppets. (*See* Puppet Corners.) This is a real service to your school or library because younger children don't automatically know how to use puppets and, without guidance and instruction, may resort to hitting with the puppets as well as other acts of violence. Children deserve to be able to work with puppets. They take to them naturally, but children don't always know how to use them. The development of imagination and language arts is lost on them unless they are shown how to use puppets. An older child or young adult from the puppet club can be the teacher to younger ones who need to learn how to work successfully with puppets.

A puppet club is a great way for older children and young adults to learn the basic skills of puppetry, learn about making puppets, and learn to put on a puppet play. It can give these children a dramatic outlet and a way to give service to their community by teaching other, younger children puppetry skills. A puppet club is a win-win situation for any school or library that is willing to support it. Seriously consider establishing a puppet club, if not now, then some time in the near future.

Milligan, David Fredrick. *Fist Puppetry*. New York: A. S. Barnes & Co., 1938.
Renfro, Nancy. *A Puppet Corner in Every Library*. Austin, Tex.: N. Renfro Studios, 1978.

Comedy

Comedy is as natural to puppetry as breathing and may be said to be one of the puppet's main reasons for being. Comedy in puppetry has existed so long in spite of all attempts to restrain it. Slapstick, bawdy jokes, lampooning of authority figures—all these are part of puppetry and have very ancient roots.

The roots of European comedy go back to Greek new comedy and the Dorian mime. Near ancient Rome were the Atellan farces. These were rude entertainments reflecting local life. The jokes were raucous and bawdy, full of topical references; the humor was physical, more along the lines of the Three Stooges than serious, classical drama. The characters were memorable and became the stock in trade of later classical comedians and comic writers.

The Atellan farces of Rome built on their Greek roots but never took them seriously. There wasn't much dialogue, and the "script" was rather sketchy. But it included rustic humor and improvisation, songs and dances, and pantomime. There were stock characters here, too, which would feed into the character of Punch. (*See* Punch and Judy.)

Wherever puppets appear, there is room for the clown, the funny scoundrel, the character full of braggadocio, the character who always gets the best of the Devil—in whatever form he may come. Whether his name is Punch, Kasperle, Grimpesulais, or Guignol, the comic puppet character is sure to be found. (*See* Guignol.) At his most basic, he is like Punch—a man of the people, full of fight and ready to take on the whole world. He punctures the arrogant and shows the high and mighty at their worst. He is also violent and crude, resorting to the worst kind of behavior on all occasions. The slapstick and the cudgel are his trademark props, and he uses them with a will.

Our tastes in comedy have changed, we think, from the time of Greek new comedy, and the modern sensibility cringes at the violence of Mr. Punch. But children love the foolishness and meaningless fights between the puppets. Judy isn't dead; she'll be up and tending the baby in time for the next show.

Children between the ages of eight and twelve seem to love the slapstick and violence of Punch and Judy or the Three Stooges. They laugh hysterically at something which might frighten, disgust, or disturb them in any other situation. The puppets and the Stooges are not real; they are cartoon characters and as such are expected to be exposed to all sorts of violence and still survive. It's a bit like the attraction of professional wrestling; we all know that it's choreographed, and it's O.K. since everyone is in on the joke.

The question for the modern puppeteer is how much and how far to go with humor in puppetry for children? Putting on a classic Punch and Judy show would provoke an outcry from parents attending the show and perhaps rightly so. Balancing children's love of slapstick with parents horror of violence is a touchy business!

Humor consists in the exposure of foolishness, as in the drawn-out joke of "The Emperor's New Clothes." It is not until the little child cries out that "The Emperor has no clothes on!" that the joke is exposed, and we can all have a laugh at the Emperor's and the court's expense.

Humor can also be found in off-beat and unexpected situations: a dog barking raucously; a dinosaur appearing where a human character was expected; a serious character wearing a silly costume; and, my favorite, endless and creative snoring.

An unexpected situation can also come from an adult imitating childish behavior, for instance the heroes Cu Chulain or Sigfried having to suck their thumbs in order to access the divine wisdom they possess. And what about "The Golden Goose" with all those adult authority figures trailing out behind the young man and his goose? There's a classic situation of authority being punctured very thoroughly!

So is there any place for slapstick in modern puppetry for children? It depends on the puppeteer and the age of the audience. What do you feel comfortable with? If you don't feel comfortable with slapstick, then don't use it. There are plenty of humorous situations and bits of business for you to use without it. If you are not sure of what I am talking about, look in Hans Baumann's book for the plays involving Kasperle, the Pulcinello of Germany. While the slapstick is greatly toned down, there is still enough to give you an idea of what is meant.

If you are not sure about creating funny business in your puppet plays, first pay attention to what the children laugh at in your plays and use that generously. Second, look in the library at humorous children's books or funny poems. What is the "funny business" going on in the story or poem, and is it something you can use in the future? Third, look at children's television programs and see what is funny there. Programmers know what children find to be funny, so learn from all their high-priced research! Look at *Sesame Street, Between the Lions, Sponge Bob Square Pants,* or any of the other popular children's shows. Record the shows for further analysis, or make notes while you're watching.

Humor and funny business go hand-in-hand with puppetry. From the naughty character of Grimpesulais in the Renaissance miracle plays onward, the puppet is the one who can lighten a serious situation without fear. Use humor liberally and with a generous heart, and you'll find that your audiences and your puppet plays will love it.

Baumann, Hans. *Caspar and His Friends: A Collection of Puppet Plays.* New York: Henry Z. Walk, Inc., 1969.

Concept Puppets

Concept puppets embody the essence of an animal, person, or thing. They *act like* or *represent* something so completely that the audience knows immediately what is being portrayed. A concept puppet is different from a junk puppet in that it does not necessarily look like the thing it is representing. Making a concept puppet is different from giving character to a piece of cloth or an item like a coffee pot. You begin with the character — actually the essence of the character — and give that a form.

For example, my husband, also a librarian, is inordinately fond of insects of all types. He enjoys seeing them, talking to them, and even imitating them. One night as we were talking, I picked up one of those soft, plastic soda holders that have perforations and tear tabs and come all apart by the time you are done removing the soda. I picked up the holder and began to flitter it all around. It landed on his arm and then flittered off, only to land on his ear. Then it flittered off and landed on his glasses. We played this way for some time, and he knew exactly what it was: some sort of flittering, flying thing, probably an insect. It certainly didn't *look* like any recognizable insect. You couldn't look at it and say, "Oh, yes. That's a butterfly/mayfly/moth/bird." But you would know it for a flying creature, probably a small one, that flits hither and thither.

Try making concept puppets with things you have at hand. Flying things are obvious, fun to do, and a great place to start. Try different sorts of flying things: small insect versus large bird; flittering creature versus a soaring one.

Then consider "elephant" or "rhinoceros." They are large and heavy but not necessarily slow, as both can run for short bursts. What is the essence of each animal? Do you want to consider the heaviness of each one? Would you emphasize the ears and trunk of the elephant and the horns and small ears of the rhino?

The application of the concept puppet technique is most often used with the creation of a specific character. Unless it is a well known one — Scrooge from *A Christmas Carol* or the Mad Hatter from *Alice in Wonderland* — you will need to think of the essence of the character of the puppet. Is this character mean, haughty, light hearted, heroic, scholarly? If it has that character, then how does a person with that character walk, talk, look? In short, what is the *essence* or the *concept* of that character, and how will you portray it in the features, stance, and manner of your puppet? What will it wear? What will be its voice to enhance the concept or the essence of that character?

Try making some concept puppets. Run through a list of animals you know and see what you can come up with. Remember: the concept puppet does not look like the thing it represents; it conveys the *essence* of the thing. Have fun! And enjoy the results.

These titles are not in the bibliography. But they illustrate the concept of taking the appearance of one thing to represent the essence of another, I had to recommend them.

Freymann, Saxton, and Elffers, Joost. *How Are You Peeling? Foods with Moods.* New York: Arthur A. Levine Books, 1999.

Any of the books by Freymann and Elffers show what can be done when observation of objects is given free reign. The forms of the fruits and vegetables reflect precisely the emotions the authors are trying to convey.

Steiner, Joan. *Look-Alikes* and *Look-Alikes Jr.* Boston: Little Brown, 1999.

Look closely at the pictures of everyday scenes and places. You will find that these scenes are created from things which have no relation to the real object, yet represent it exactly.

Costumes

Clothing and accessories complete the outward personality of a puppet and act as a visual signal to the audience as to what this character's essential personality might be. Puppetry involves caricature with facial features, clothing, and gesture, providing hints to the audience as to what we will see from these characters in the play that is coming.

Costuming creates the finishing touch that points to the nature of a character. We expect a princess or a queen to be dressed in elegant, royal clothes and perhaps wear a crown. We expect farmers to be dressed in overalls and city folks in suits and ties. But that is where the expectations should stop. Beyond that, you may wander into stereotypes, and that is not a good thing either in puppetry or in daily life. (*See* Stereotypes.)

Think of your puppet. Is it to be a general puppet, part of an ensemble, or is it to have a specific function in a specific play? Did you create the puppet because something about its face or shape appealed to you, or were you aiming for a specific kind of character? These are all questions to answer as you think of a costume for your puppet. If you can draw, you may want to make a sketch of the puppet as you want it to look.

Sometimes a costume is an extension of a design, and the whole puppet presents a picture — refined elegance, rustic simplicity, business type. At other times some part of the physical character may be so important that the costume must take second place, to become a quiet background in order to point to the unusual characteristic.

Take Gonzo of the Muppets. His most outstanding feature is the nose/beak which juts far out from his face and curves down and around toward his mouth. Gonzo is earnest, serious, and innocent — and also from another planet. His nose/beak says that he just doesn't seem to be one of us. If he were to dress in as flamboyant a style as his nose/beak suggests he might, Gonzo would be over the top and totally unbelievable. By dressing him in ordinary dark pants, shirt, and sweater vest, his unusual facial feature stands out, and his innocent yet off-the-wall character comes through easily.

Usually, it's a lot simpler to dress a puppet and takes a lot less soul searching than what I have just discussed. Spend some time in fabric shops imagining what clothes the different types of fabric would make. Visit flea markets and thrift stores to collect trims, old jewelry, and bits and pieces which might add to a costume's appearance. Many times, the creation of a costume and its accessories is a matter of inspired serendipity, but fortunate accidents are helped by having a variety of basic materials at hand.

Another thing to consider is whether or not you will attach the clothes to the puppet's body or give each puppet different clothes and accessories. If each puppet will be a unique and unchanging creation, you can sew or glue the clothes directly onto the puppet's body. Gluing or sewing the clothes to the body happens most often with marionettes and junk puppets but can be true for any puppet. Sewing individual costumes to fit puppet bodies is true for hand puppets only and is time consuming, but it permits greater flexibility in character creation. Having individual bodies dressed in different costumes with interchangeable heads provides yet another solution.

Costuming is as time consuming as creating the puppet's head and body. Careful preparatory work will deliver results that are satisfying to puppeteer and audience alike. Think about your puppet and what character you would like it to portray. Then raid your scrap bag, junk jewelry box, and trims collection to make a puppet that reflects its character in all ways: facial features, hair, and costume.

Doney, Meryl. *Puppets*. New York: Franklin Watts, 1995.
Lade, Roger. *The Most Excellent Book of How to Be a Puppeteer*. Brookfield, CT: Copper Beech Books, 1996.
Lasky, Kathryn. *Puppeteer*. New York: Macmillan, 1985.

Courses

Education for puppeteers is not as hard to come by as it once was. If you have a passion for puppets, you can now find a number of schools for training to help advance your career. Even if you are an OJT puppeteer (on the job trained), there are ways to increase your educational possibilities without returning to school — unless you want to, of course.

Courses of study are discussed elsewhere in this book. (*See* University of Connecticut.) You can also tailor your local college, university, or even junior college's drama or arts programs to give you an emphasis in puppetry arts. Other colleges and universities mentioned on the web site for the Union Internationale de la Marionnette USA (UNIMA–USA) are **California Institute for the Arts** ("CalArts"), Cotsen Center for Puppetry and the Arts, and **Central Washington University**, Department of Theatre Arts. (*See* UNIMA–USA.)

Regular short courses are offered at the **Center for Puppetry Arts** (*see* Atlanta Center for Puppetry Arts); **George Mason University**, Mount Rainier, Maryland; **Northeastern State University**, Theater Department, Tahlequah, Oklahoma; **California Polytechnic State University**, Department of Theater and Dance; **University of California–Santa Cruz**, Theater Arts Department, Santa Cruz, California; **California State University–Sacramento**, Department of Theatre Arts, Sacramento, California; **Dell'Arte School of Physical Theatre Arts**, Blue Lake, California; **Central Washington University**, Puppetry Department of the Theatre Arts, Ellensburg, Washington; and **National Puppetry Conference**, Eugene O'Neill Theater Center, Waterford, Connecticut.

Another source of education for puppeteers is through conferences and other national and local events. The National Festival of Puppetry sponsored by the Puppeteers of America, and the National Puppetry Conference at the Eugene O'Neill Theater Center are two ways to gain education in puppetry. (*See* National Puppetry Conference; Puppeteers of America.) Also, your statewide education or library associations may sponsor puppetry workshops. Finally, there is the National Day of Puppetry sponsored by the Puppeteers of America. (*See* National Day of Puppetry.) Get in touch with the local chapter to see what they are sponsoring.

You may not be able to attend these conferences, schools, or workshops. If you know about them, however, you may be able to persuade your department or funding agency to allow you to attend these educational opportunities. Finally, if nothing works, throw it back in their corner and ask them how you expect to advance to a further level of expertise if you don't get training? Find out what it is that bothers them. You may be able to set up your own workshop and festival to further your own education and that of other puppeteers. (*See* Festivals.) The best of luck to you and your efforts!

www.puppeteers.org/ This is the Puppeteers of America web site.
http://www.sfa.uconn.edu/Drama/Puppetry/HOMEPAGE.HTML This is the University of Connecticut's Puppetry Arts web site.
http://www.unima-usa.org/ This is the UNIMA-USA website.

Craft Clays

There are so many craft clays on the market right now that it would take a separate book to discuss all the various ways of using them. Check your library or bookstore for current titles. Sculpy and Fimo are oven-hardening polymer clays. Celuclay is instant papier-mâché pulp. And Paperclay is an air-hardening papier-mâché clay. In addition, there are a number of other brands of air-hardening clays on the market. (*See* Polymer and Air-Hardening Clays.) All of these products can make wonderful puppets for your puppet theater; unfortunately, these clays cost money, which you or your organization may not have right now.

Craft clays become inexpensive materials if you can make them yourself. Self-hardening clays, inexpensive doughs, and other modeling compounds can be useful for making models, heads and faces, hands and feet. The clays can either be molded by hand or pressed into a mold to make parts for puppets.

Two of the best books I have found on making your own craft clays are MaryAnn F. Kohl's *Mudworks: Creative Clay, Dough, and Modeling Experiences* and John E. Thomas and Danita Page's *The Ultimate Book of Kid Concoctions.* These two books have just about every type of kid mixture you would ever want — and a lot you might hope never to have to use; but that's another story. The books contain a great many versions of recipes for papier-mâché and the paste which is used with it. There are also recipes for various kinds of papier-mâché pulp and how to use them. (*See* Papier-Mâché; Tissue-Mâché.) However, the recipe which may also serve you just as well as papier-mâché is a modeling compound made from sawdust and glue. *Mudworks* calls it "sawdust modeling" and *Kid Concoctions* calls it "woody wood dough." This is a great substitute for making a wooden puppet. Not everyone can carve, after all, and the compound does not need acetone (which is highly toxic and flammable) to soften it as plastic wood does.

I have seen dolls and other figures made of sawdust modeling compound, and they are delightful. The compound can be sculpted or pressed into a mold to a ½" thickness. It takes two to three days to dry and afterward can be sanded and painted as wood can. Repairs are easily made with more compound. Arms and legs can be molded around a wire armature. (*See* Armatures.) Make sure that there is room enough to move the upper and lower portions of the limb easily, or embed screw eyes or fasteners in the compound and join the two sections together after the arm is dry. Paint or leave as is.

Doughs, modeling compounds, and other types of kid art materials can become useful to the puppeteer in a variety of ways. Who knows what will be useful to you until you try it? You may find something wonderful to add to a workshop or a presentation you had never thought of before. So dive right in and try some of these great children's art compounds, and let the little kid inside you have some fun!

Sawdust Modeling Compound

From MaryAnn Kohl's Mudworks, page 93.

MATERIALS

- 1 cup fine sawdust
- Food coloring (optional)

- Jar
- Old newspaper
- 1 cup thin paste or paper paste (see pages 95 and 96 of *Mudworks*)
- Shellac or clear varnish (optional)

ASSEMBLY

1. Mix sawdust with food coloring in a jar.
2. Drain and spread on newspaper to dry.
3. Mix sawdust and paste to thick dough.
4. Knead. If sawdust is coarse, more paste may be needed.
5. Model as with any clay. (Stick bits of dough to a piece with water.)
6. Let dry for 2 to 3 days, or bake at 200° F. for 1 to 2 hours.
7. For a permanent finish, spray with shellac or varnish.

This makes 1 cup. It has a wood grain appearance. It can be sanded for smoother finish.

Woody Wood Dough

From *The Ultimate Book of Kid Concoctions*, page 37.

MATERIALS

- 1 cup clean, well-sifted sawdust
- ½ cup flour
- 1 Tbs. liquid starch
- 1 cup water

ASSEMBLY

1. Mix ingredients together in bowl until a stiff dough is formed. Add extra water if dough is too dry.
2. Allow Woody Wood Dough to dry 2 to 3 days.
3. Use sandpaper to smooth Woody Wood Dough after it is completely dry.

Kohl, MaryAnn F. *Mudworks: Creative Clay, Dough, and Modeling Experiences.* Bellingham, WA: Bright Ring Pub., 1989.

Thomas, John E., and Danita Page. *The Ultimate Book of Kid Concoctions: More than 65 Wacky, Wild & Crazy Concoctions.* Strongville, OH: The Kid Concoctions Co., 1998.

Curtains

Curtains in the theater separate the stage space from the audience. The opening and shutting of the curtains between acts also marks the passage of time and calls attention to the fact that something has ended and soon something else will begin. In the human theater and in large puppet companies, there are people who work with the stage and its elements: lights, sound, music, sets, and curtains. In a small puppet company, especially in the one-person company, you will not have the luxury of a specialist; you do it all.

The more I work with puppets, especially as a one-person puppeteer, the less I like curtains even though I have them on my stage. I always pick the wrong cord and things get confused and difficult, delaying the smooth beginning of my skit. I have found that I much prefer to have a playbill or some filler which the puppets can take down when the play begins, or I have the theater darkened and use the lights coming up to indicate the beginning of the action.

If you do want to use curtains, however, practice with them. Mark the cord to pull the curtain open with some sort of easily seen marker or object. Do the same for the closing cord. Make sure that your puppets can be put on or picked up easily to make sure that all goes smoothly and quickly with the curtain opening.

If you use hand puppets, you may want to have an opening and closing routine where the puppets of the show talk about or mime business for opening and closing the curtains. In other words, make dealing with the curtains a fun part of your play.

If you use marionettes, practice opening the curtains and then picking up the marionettes to begin the play. Seriously consider opening the curtains by hand, not by cord. Decide whether you want to have the marionettes posed on the stage to be discovered when the curtains open or whether you want them to enter after the curtains open. If you pose the marionettes while you open the curtains, you will need a hook or rod to rest the marionettes' controls upon while the curtains are being opened. When the act is finished, the marionettes can be returned to the resting place while you close the curtains.

The curtains I have for my stage are standard pleated curtains mounted on a traverse rod with pulls on one side. Another and better version of this curtain would be no cord but a rod to pull open the curtains. The curtain should be on a traverse-style rod with smoothly operating holders for the curtain pins. The curtains will open in the middle, but the total length of the curtain material should be three times the length of the proscenium opening to provide sufficient fullness. Line the curtains if light shows through.

A simple version of curtains for tabletop and cardboard box theaters can be made from two panels of cotton material, each one as big as the opening in the theater. The curtains are hemmed above and below, with the upper hem forming a casing to string the curtains. Use string or a café curtain rod to mount the curtains. No rod is needed to open and close these simple shades, but the curtains must move smoothly. If you want a valance, attach it firmly to the theater.

Roman Shades

Roman shades are a nice curtain for puppet theaters. The curtain is smooth, just filling the proscenium and leaving both sides open for use. The curtains should be lined unless the material is opaque. On either side of the curtain are lengths of tape with small bone rings attached. These will be the guides for the cords which raise the shades. If the curtains are more than two feet wide, you will need an extra length of tape in the middle of the curtain to insure that the curtain rises smoothly.

The curtain cords (two or three — one for each length of Roman shade tape) are fastened to the rod at the bottom of the shade, threaded up through the rings, and inserted over small pulleys at the top of the curtain. The curtain is opened by pulling on the cord. Since there are no stops as there are with Venetian blinds, the cord must be secured at one side of the curtain. The usual method is to wind the cord around something, but a clamp to hold the cord would do just as well.

The Roman shade needs two hands to operate it: one hand to pull the cords and one to secure it. This means that you may have to raise the curtain, then put on your puppets or pick up the marionette controls. Perhaps you can see why I say that curtains may be more trouble than they are worth. On the other hand, curtains in the theater are traditional, so let's make a Roman shade for your puppet theater.

MATERIALS

- Enough material to fill the proscenium area of your theater plus the same amount of lightweight lining material or fusible interfacing if light shines through the exterior material
- Thread to match the outer cloth
- Enough Roman shade tape to go from the bottom to the top of the shade multiplied by two or possibly three lengths of tape, depending on the width of the proscenium (Remember that a small curtain will only have tape on either end but a larger curtain must have a third length of tape in the middle)
- Enough cord to raise the shade; There should be one cord for each length of tape. Measure from the rod which weights the bottom of the shade to the top of the proscenium, across the proscenium to the side, and down to the bottom of the curtain (The measurement for each cord will be a different length.)
- 3–4 pulleys plus attaching hardware to thread the cord through to make for

easy raising and lowering of the shade (Check with the drapery section of your fabric store or hardware store.)

- Clamps to hold the shade cord plus mounting hardware for the clamps
- Dowel rod or lath to weight the bottom of the curtain
- Lath strip to form the top of the shade and attach the curtain to the proscenium arch
- Nails and screws
- Screw driver
- Pencils
- Tailor's chalk
- Scissors
- Tape measure
- Straight pins
- Sewing machine or needle
- Thread

ASSEMBLY

1. For the material and lining amount, measure the height and width of the opening of your puppet theater. If your proscenium area is wider than 45", you will need to piece material together. Also check the size of the lath or dowel used to weight the bottom of the curtain and form the top of the curtain, and add enough length to accommodate pockets for them and to include a 5/8" hem all around.

2. Cut the material and the lining to the size needed. (*See* step 3 if you are using fusible interfacing.)

3. Sew the lining and curtain material together, right sides together, leaving enough space at the bottom of the shade for your rod or lath. Turn the material right-side out and press it. The cloth must be smooth. (If you use lightweight fusible interfacing, cut it to the size of the curtain. Because it is fused with the material of the curtain, you would not have to have a hem in the sides of the curtain material; and the interfacing itself would provide opacity and stiffness.)

4. Insert the lath or dowel in its pocket and tack it closed using needle and thread.

5. Pin the lengths of Roman shade tape to the back of the curtain, bottom to top, 1½" from the edge of the curtain and just above the rod at the bottom and just below the fastening at the top.

6. Sew the tape in place, using the thread which matches the cloth.

7. Attach the curtain to the theater by screwing or nailing the curtain to the top of the theater's proscenium arch.

8. Attach the pulleys to the theater, one pulley above each piece of Roman shade tape, using appropriate hardware. Attach one extra pulley 3" to the right or left of the shade, depending on which side you will be pulling the cord from.

9. Attach the pull cord to the last ring on each piece of Roman shade tape. Thread the cord through the rings on the tape, then up through the pulley above the tape, then through all the other pulleys which are left above the shade.

10. Let the cord hang down until it reaches the bottom of the curtain. Trim it off at that point.

11. Braid all the cords together so you will have an easily fastened cord for your curtain.

12. Mount the clip which will hold the curtain rod and test it for holding ability.

13. Practice with your curtain to make your entries smooth and professional.

Dioramas

A diorama is a static scene with three different dimensions of depth: near, moderate, and far. The near distance might have grass and palm trees to frame the scene. The moderate distance might have a dinosaur in it. The far distance might have a volcano, mountain, or other dramatic backdrop. The diorama can be built within a box frame, or it can be created out of separate pieces of paper of different lengths which are then joined together to make a scene.

To make a paper diorama, think of a scene. It could be the dinosaur one mentioned above, or it could be a spring scene with sunny blue sky in the far distance, children playing in the middle distance, and a low border of grass and flowers in the near distance. The near distance is the shortest piece of paper, usually 10 to 12" long. The middle distance is 1½" to 2" longer than the near (base) distance. The far distance is 3½" longer than the base distance. When the three pieces of paper are joined together at the edges, the near distance should be flat and the middle and far distances should bow out behind, creating a sense of depth in the scene.

Whenever making a scene such as a diorama, make a mock-up first. This is an example which should give you an idea of whether or not your measurements and general ideas will work or whether they will have to be modified. For instance, the rough measurements given above may be either too large or too small for the needs of your design. The paper may be either too weak or too stiff for your purposes. The mock-up lets you know for sure whether or not your design will work.

When creating a diorama in a box frame, follow similar principles. Make the background large, dramatic, and generalized: mountains, seashore, open sky, or busy city scene. Make the middle ground the focus of the action: tent with campers; bathers at the seashore, trees and a park scene, or children walking down the street of a city. The foreground should be either low, adding an accent, or high at the sides, framing the scene: rocks and a stream, generic seashore things such as sand pails and starfish, trees on either side with low grass and flower border in the middle, street lamps on either side of the scene.

Dioramas can be given a bit of action by mounting a small figure on thin wire, a piece of nylon line, or suspended on thread. In each scene, a bird could be mounted on thin wire or nylon line which is pasted onto the top of the box. Moving the diorama box slightly will cause the bird to appear to fly. In the park scene, a swing could be incorporated into the scene with the swing suspended on threads from the top of the box. Again, a slight movement would cause the swing to move. This is hardly necessary and is not traditional, but it may appeal to you as the diorama's creator.

Another way dioramas can be used is in the planning stages of a puppet play. Backgrounds can be tried out with different kinds of scenery. Finally, the whole drama can be represented in dioramas for enjoyment after the show. Dioramas can remind playgoers of other puppet plays which have been put on by you earlier in the year or in previous years, or they can promote future performances.

Dioramas are wonderful ways to create miniature worlds with depth and drama. Unlike the peep show, the scene is not enclosed and secret but is available for all to see. (*See* Peep Show.) These little pictures can be used to enliven a storytime or decorate a children's program room, or they can set the scene for a larger puppet performance. However you choose to use them, dioramas are a wonderful part of theater your audiences will enjoy.

http://www.amnh.org/nationalcenter/online_field_journal/dr/dr_menu.html This is the diorama portion of the online site of the American Museum of Natural History's Field Journal. There are several dioramas based on real exhibits at the American Museum of Natural History which children and adults can make.

http://familycrafts.about.com/cs/dioramas/ About.com has several links to diorama projects: ocean, favorite book, dinosaurs, and so on. Great for school projects and — of course — for puppetry arts as well.

http://www.princetonol.com/groups/iad/lessons/elem28.html "Easy Dioramas" by Judy Lervolino is the outline of a lesson plan for making dioramas in the classroom. It shows just how easy making a diorama can be.

Directing Puppet Plays

Directors of plays draw all the elements of the play together so that they join harmoniously to produce a work of theater. The director may not be in charge of props, lighting, sound, script, costumes, choreography or scenery, but she must see to it that all those elements come together correctly and at the right time.

For the sake of argument, I will assume that someone else (or you with another hat on) has charge of writing the script, making and costuming the puppets, painting the scenery, recording the music, and working out the lighting. It will be your job as director to see that the puppets have their action blocked out correctly, that the puppeteer or puppeteers are achieving the correct effect with the manipulation of their puppets, that the voices are projecting as they should, that lines are learned or the recording is made and well paced, and that the rehearsal schedule is adhered to. If you are working with child puppeteers during the summer, the rehearsal schedule may be your biggest challenge.

If you are a lone puppeteer and don't have the funds to hire a professional director, try to find someone who can honestly critique your work and give you some idea of what elements need work.

At the first meeting, if there are child puppeteers, make sure the parents attend. Check all calendars for scheduling rehearsals. It is very important that you try to make the parents understand the necessity for knowing accurate dates and having a schedule and sticking to it. Your play date and advertising depend on it.

If you can, go over the script at the first meeting. This will be a first reading. For the child puppeteers, any tough words must be learned or changed. If you are a professional puppeteer working with a director, you should already have a good idea of the script and should be going over it with the director in a reading to detect any barriers to a good story or good story flow. The two of you will need to begin working on pacing as well. An approximate schedule should be in place, at least for the next couple of rehearsal dates.

The professional puppeteer should start rehearsals practicing with stand-in puppets to get the dialogue, voices, and pacing down. The child puppeteers may still be working on the pronunciation and flow of the dialogue. They should begin handling the puppets at the rehearsal table, getting the feel of them if they are hand puppets. If they are marionettes, the children should have practice puppets to work with at home. They will need instruction in manipulating marionettes and time to practice with them.

After the child puppeteers feel comfortable with their puppets, the puppeteers will need to move to the theater. Everyone will want to be back stage at the same time, of course, so the director will become the stage manager at this time, giving the children instructions on where to stand backstage and how to move onto the stage properly.

At some point, the professional puppeteer will feel comfortable with the dialogue, voices, and stage movement and will want to begin using the performance puppets. The introduction of the costumes on the real puppets may occasion some rearranging of movement on stage as well as problems with manipulation.

Smoothing out these rough spots will become the focus of the professional puppeteer's rehearsal. If the dialogue is not prerecorded, there may be issues of timing with the recorded music to work out.

With child puppeteers, slight changes in staging and business may continue almost to the end, and you may wonder if everything will ever settle down. It always does, and the children do a great job. Parents and friends turn out, and everyone has a wonderful time.

For the professional puppeteer, it's show time! The fliers have been sent out, tickets printed, and the children and their parents are crowding into the theater. For the director, it is the culmination of a great deal of hard work. Everyone's reward comes in the smiles of wonder on the faces of the audience members and the applause afterward.

Fijan, Carol, and Frank Ballard with Christine Starobin. *Directing Puppet Theatre Step by Step.* San Jose, CA: Resource Publications, Inc., 1989.
Lasky, Kathryn. *Puppeteer.* New York: Macmillan, 1985.

Disabilities

Disabled persons come in many types and varieties of abilities, but no condition should keep someone from using puppets if they wish to do so. Adaptations can be made to almost all kinds of equipment. With all the puppetry styles available to be used, there has to be something available. This is especially important in a school situation, where participating in school plays is almost an elementary child's rite of passage. I was fortunate enough to see a theatrical version of *The Three Billy Goats Gruff* put on by elementary school students at the North Carolina School for the Blind in Raleigh one year. These children were not only profoundly limited in sight, but many had other conditions which limited them in some ways. Some were in wheelchairs, some had Down's Syndrome, but all had a desire to participate in the school play. The teachers in charge of putting on the play had used a great deal of creativity in adapting roles so that all could participate. Everyone who wanted one had a part to play, and great praise was given to the children who worked so hard to make a success of their experience.

Theater experiences teach more than learning a few lines and being in a costume to do it. First, it makes the participants part of a team working toward a goal. No matter what your condition, that is a great lesson to learn. Pride, self-confidence, and self-esteem are gained through the successful accomplishment of a theatrical production.

Second, theater is not only an artistic experience with painting sets and designing costumes, it is also a language arts experience with the learning of those lines and their interpretation. If children have an opportunity to write or organize the theater experience in any way, they will be adding to their skills in reading, writing, organization of material, and creation of new material.

Third, putting on a play is fun, and who doesn't have a need for fun in their lives? All the children working together may not enjoy every minute of producing their theatrical extravaganza. After all, there are many children's books and stories concerned with the agonies of putting on a school play! However, there are success stories, too, and those should not be overlooked. Try *Amazing Grace*, for instance, or *The Best Christmas Pageant Ever*, or *Nutcracker Noelle*. Each story deals with children putting on a play or ballet, and yes, there are problems which the children are able to conquer by the time the story is over.

Take a look at these entries in this book for some ideas about adaptive puppetry. (*See* Apron Stage; Body Puppets; Masks; Stick Puppets; and Wrist Puppets.) Adaptive puppetry considers the strengths of each child and plays to that.

What, you may ask, about the child who may be a quadriplegic in a wheelchair who is able to do regular school work but unable to move? Here are some ideas you might be able to use. Also ask all the children. They'll come up with some ideas for you, some of which you may be able to use.

If the child is in a motorized wheelchair and can operate it fairly easily, why not draft the chair into the play along with the child? The chair can be decorated and move from one place to another — a mobile scene change. The chair can also cross the stage slowly with a sign announcing scene changes, act changes, wry comments on the action, and so on. There are lots of possibilities, and I challenge you and your budding puppeteers to create possibilities for their classmate.

Play to strengths! Those with limited speech ability but better motor ability can hold a stick puppet or wear a wrist puppet or a body puppet. Participants in wheelchairs don't have to be behind a stage and neither do any of the other participants in the puppet play. Consider putting on a Bunraku-style play using nearly life-sized puppets. (*See* Bunraku.) The participant in a wheelchair can wear black clothes just like everyone else and participate.

Older children and adults who have an interest in puppetry and have the motor and speech skills can choose puppetry styles that play to their strengths. They can use the body covering which doubles as scenery. (*See* Apron Theaters.) They can use a single large puppet sitting on their lap. Finally, they can use one or another variation of a lap stage which fastens onto the wheelchair. The lap stage is a miniature puppet stage — complete with curtain if you wish — which sits across the wheelchair's arms and is clamped or braced in place like a lap desk. Scenery can be attached with Velcro. The scenery can be cut from foam core board, or it can be soft and stuffed. Experiment and see what works best.

What if you're an adult with a disability who is considering the use of puppets for one reason or another? Go for it! There are lots of ideas for different kinds of puppetry in this book, and you can judge which would work best for you. Be realistic in your assessment. If you try many different kinds of puppetry to see what works, you will find the style which is right for you. The children of the world need as many different kinds of puppeteers and puppets as they can get!

Hunt, Tamara, and Nancy Renfro. *Puppetry in Early Childhood Education*. Austin, TX: Nancy Renfro Studios, 1982.
Milligan, David Fredrick. *Fist puppetry*. New York: A. S. Barnes & Co., 1938.
Sullivan, Debbie. *Pocketful of Puppets: Activities for the Special Child with Mental, Physical and Multiple Handicaps*. Austin, TX: Renfro Studios, 1982.

Doorway Stages

The doorway stage is one of the simplest and most portable stages. It consists of one or two spring-tension curtain rods and a length of material that curtains off a doorway and hides the puppeteer. The cloth doesn't need to be hemmed and so can be created without sewing, although hemming makes a neater finish.

Making the Doorway Stage

When making the doorway stage, consider these problems. First, the curtain material must be solid enough so that the puppeteer cannot be seen, but it must not be so heavy that the tension rod's spring will not hold it.

Second, if you are going to use the doorway stage for marionettes, you will need some way to hang a back curtain so the puppeteer's feet and legs cannot be seen. If you are using a narrow hallway, the tension rod may be fine. Otherwise, some alternative hanging method must be found. I have hung back curtain rods from the ceiling with cords and have used long shower curtain tension rods in wider hallways.

Hang the curtain material from sturdy clips between two easels or two chairs if there is no doorway or if the doorway's line-of-sight is wrong.

MATERIALS

- 1 curtain tension rod (2 if you want to make a ruffle or valance at the top of your stage or make a back curtain for marionettes)
- Material 1½ times wider than the door and longer than the puppeteer is tall (Material that is 45" in width is usually good for most doorways. If a dark knit is chosen, no hemming is required, but such material may be heavy and not easy to find.)
- Glue gun and glue sticks if using the nonsewing method
- Sewing machine and thread to match the material if using the sewing method

- Scissors
- Measuring tape or yard stick

ASSEMBLY

1. Measure yourself and add 8" for hem, rod pocket, and leeway. If you want a ruffle or valance at the top of your stage, add an additional 18" to the length of the material to make the ruffle hem and its rod pocket.

2. Measure the width of the doorway you will be using. Most doorways are 24" to 26" in width. The tension rod must fit easily within this space, and the cloth you use should be 1½ times the width of the doorway in order to fill it adequately and hide you behind it.

3. Measure and cut a length of material using the length determined in step 1. If you wanted a ruffle, make sure you have about 18" of material left.

4. Make the rod pocket at one end of the door material. Measure 2" from one end of the material to make the rod pocket. Fold over the 2" and iron in place.

5. Fold under ½" of this material to make a neat hem, press, and sew in place.

6. If you are using the nonsewing method, use your glue gun to lay down a short, thin strip of glue. Fold over the pocket material and press gently into place. Work in short lengths so the glue doesn't dry out. Make sure that the glue is thoroughly dried before putting weight on it.

7. If you want a hem in the curtain material, fold over the material and glue or sew in place using the appropriate method.

8. To make the valance, fold over enough material to accommodate the valance rod. Sew or glue in place using the appropriate method.

9. Thread the curtain (and the valance) on their rods.

10. Check the tension of the rods so the curtain will hang in the doorway. Position the valance rod above the doorway curtain to mark the stage opening, and adjust tension of this rod as well.

11. If you are using your curtain for marionettes, measure the distance from the floor you will need for your stage opening. Place the bottom of the valance (if you have one) at this point, and hang the curtain above it. Fasten your back curtain in place.

12. Let the show begin!

Hunt, Tamara, and Nancy Renfro. *Puppetry in Early Childhood Education.* Austin, TX: Nancy Renfro Studios, 1982.
Watson, Nancy Cameron. *The Little Pigs' Puppet Book.* Boston: Little, Brown, 1990.

Ears

Ears—along with noses, mouths, beaks, teeth, and other facial characteristics—can help establish a character. Like the other facial characteristics, the shape of ears play into our assumptions of how people and animals should look. A clever puppeteer can use these to advantage, either incorporating them into a character or changing the type of ears to make an important statement.

Elephants, for instance, have quite large outer ears which are used to help keep the animal cool. Asian elephants have smaller ears than African ones since it is not quite so hot where they live. But what about an elephant with either really small or really large ears. Remember the Disney cartoon *Dumbo*? Its whole premise was built on the fact of Dumbo's ears were so large they could support Dumbo in flight. All the events in the movie are prompted by those large ears and people's reactions to them.

Puppeteers can use exaggeration as well to help establish a puppet's character. What about a pretty princess with an extra large set of ears or a boy with a too small pair? How would this cause problems for their characters, or would it?

Normally, however, you will just want to find a pair of ears that is appropriate for your character. As with so many of the other facial characteristics, you can keep a collection of potential ears. Knit gloves, felt shapes, pom-poms, and the bowls of spoons are all prime candidates for the ear box.

Sometimes, you may not want to have a pair of ears but just a suggestion that they might be there. In that case, you can have an interesting pair of earrings attached to the head of the puppet where the ears would normally be. People's imaginations will fill in the blanks for you. Other possibilities include covering up the ears with a bandanna, pirate style, or with a large, floppy hat.

Like noses and other body parts, puppets can participate in switching ears around. An animal may envy the large, fanlike ears of the elephant or the large, all-hearing ears of the horse or donkey. A fine puppet play can be built around that.

Just remember that ears should stay in character. Like other facial features, ears should support rather detract from a character. If they are different enough to stand out, it should be for a reason.

Henson, Cheryl, and the Muppet Workshop. *The Muppets Make Puppets!* New York: Workman Publishing, 1994.

Educational Puppetry

Puppetry of all sorts can be used in every classroom in early childhood education. (*See also* Preschoolers' Puppets.) No matter what the ability of the child, puppets can be used to teach and to have fun while doing it. Whether it is colors, letters, parts of the body, simple mathematics or just fun at show-and-tell, puppets can make any classroom a livelier place.

The most basic ways to add puppets to the classroom is to have a class mascot, a puppet corner, and an opportunity for the children to make puppets on a regular basis. (*See* Assistants; Puppet Corners.) A class mascot, or assistant, is a special puppet that helps move the class activities along by introducing various parts of the daily routine. It can help with singing the morning song and reviewing the activities of the day. Show-and-tell, snack time, and clean-up time can begin with a quick chat or song with the class mascot. Class problems and school troubles can also be taken up by the class mascot. Somehow, it's easier for a puppet to introduce a difficult topic to young children, and they listen to what's being said.

A puppet corner in the classroom serves a dual purpose. It has puppets and a stage where children can use puppets to put on plays and skits. It also has materials to make puppets as well. All sorts of scrap materials can be used in this corner. Make sure that there are not only yarns, fabric scraps, paper of all kinds, and basic crafting things like pom-poms and chenille sticks but also tools such as scissors, rulers, and glue.

Making puppets is a wonderful craft project which can tie into many areas of the curriculum. It is also a chance to let imagination take over and find concrete expression. How about making a puppet rainbow or a puppet for the wind or rain? Add in a puppet of the sun, and the whole class can put on Aesop's "The Battle of the Sun and the Wind" with each half of the class being one element or the other. For children who may never have used puppets in an organized way before, a group class activity such as this one can introduce them to cues, beginning puppet manipulation, and the flow of story.

Puppets can be used throughout the curriculum to teach basic subjects such as letter and number recognition, beginning math, color recognition, and language arts. Letter or number puppets can either illustrate the letter and its sound (an ape for the long sound of *a*; ant for the short sound) or numbers (three little birds in a nest to illustrate the number *3*). They can be variations on people puppets labeled with the letter or number which each puppet can introduce and talk about. Puppets made in various colors can help with color identification. Sets of identical shapes, animals, or birds can be colored in by the children or made out of colored construction paper. Cup and stick puppets can be made of cones of colored paper with an item attached to the end of a straw, say a red cup with a strawberry or cherry attached for the color red. (*See* Pop-up Puppets.)

People puppets can be made without faces which must be added or dressed by the children in a circle activity. Larger, flat figures to be used at play tables or at the children's desks can be made for buttoning, lacing, buckling, and all the other activities of getting dressed. Remember to make the skin tone of the figures varied enough to present dolls to children in the class which will look pretty much as they do. In fact, the figures can be completely blank, requiring the children to give them features, hair, clothes—everything. The children can either create the figures on their own, or they can be asked to give the figures clothing, hair, and eyes of specific colors.

Puppets can also assist in teaching children about feelings. In addition to giving the figures features, hair, and clothes, they can also be given features which reflect moods and feelings. A child can give a figure features which reflect the child's own feelings on that day.

In language arts, children can begin to work with story telling and creative theater. Even children who cannot yet read or write can dictate stories or assist in creating an individual or a group story with the class. This story can then be turned into a puppet production with the whole class making puppets, scenery, and props. Remember that everyone can be involved in this production who wants to be involved. (*See* Disabilities.)

Puppets can enrich the curriculum in any classroom. They can be used as a regular feature every day in the classroom, or they can become an occasional bright accent for an older class who may enjoy this foray into theater. Considering all the skills which go into creating a puppet play of any kind, puppets are an ideal vehicle for learning about the history, culture, and folklore of a country or area. If you are a teacher or one who works with children, consider bringing puppets into your work with children. The classroom is an ideal place for puppets. Bring them on in!

Hunt, Tamara, and Nancy Renfro. *Puppetry in Early Childhood Education.* Austin, TX: Nancy Renfro Studios, 1982.
Sullivan, Debbie. *Pocketful of Puppets: Activities for the Special Child with Mental, Physical and Multiple Handicaps.* Austin, TX: Renfro Studios, 1982.

Egg Carton Puppets

Egg cartons are useful things. They can be cut up and used to form parts of puppets, especially noses, ears, and eyelids. The cups can also be used to make teeth for large puppets. Because of this toothy appearance, egg cartons can be used to make scaly or toothy puppets such as alligators, dragons, fanciful beasts, and dimetrodons or other low-legged dinosaurs. I prefer the paper cartons since they will take paint easily. The plastic cartons will take permanent markers, but paint beads up. Colored cartons can be covered with glue and glitter to change the appearance. I usually use the size carton that holds a dozen eggs.

Egg Carton Alligator

MATERIALS

- 5 egg cartons (2 egg cartons cut in half so that each would hold two rows of three eggs, 2 uncut egg cartons, 1 extra carton for spare parts)
- Scissors or craft knife
- White glue or hot glue gun
- Pencils
- Ruler
- Construction paper, card stock or felt
- Glitter
- Ricrac or craft foam
- Muslin or lightweight cotton cloth
- Paints and paint brushes (for paper cartons)

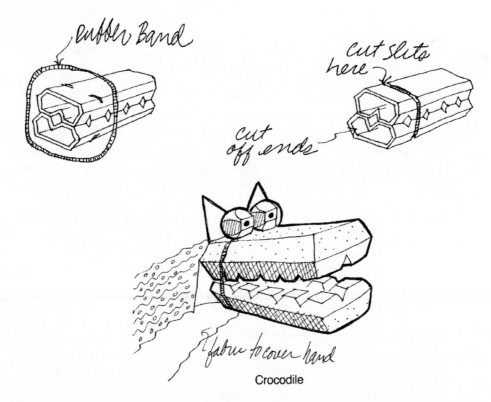

Crocodile

Egg carton crocodile from Nancy Renfro. The two halves of the jaw are joined at the back by a rubber band. The eyes are made from two egg carton cups glued together. And the arm is disguised by a cloth neck.

- Permanent markers (for all cartons)
- 8 toilet paper tubes for the legs
- Felt or cardboard for feet
- 3 to 4 dowel rods ¼" diameter or lightweight gardening sticks
- Paper fasteners or string
- Plastic bone ring

ASSEMBLY

The head is made with the egg cups projecting on the outside. Teeth will be made and added on later. The flat lids of the egg cartons form the inside of the mouth.

1. Glue all cartons shut.
2. Decide whether you will operate the head with your hand. If so, cut off one end of each of two egg cartons; hinge the two cartons with strapping tape or muslin dipped in glue. (*See* Hinges.) Make sure the hinge leaves room for your hand to fit comfortably into the cut ends of cartons and move the cartons easily.
3. Decorate the head, making eyes and nostrils from parts of the egg cartons. Paint and let dry.
4. If you are going to operate the head with your hand, glue ricrac teeth or craft foam teeth to the carton. (*See* Teeth for additional suggestions for making teeth.) Sponge or craft foam is easiest to use when opening and closing a mouth, but you may be able to position your puppet's teeth in a more exposed position and avoid crushing the teeth. In that case, you can use a firmer material.
5. Paint the additional cartons and let them dry. Remember that you can sprinkle glitter onto wet paint.
6. Join the half cartons with strips of fabric or tape.
7. Join three half cartons for the alligator's body.
8. Make legs for your puppet using 2 cardboard toilet tubes per leg. Paint or decorate them first.
9. Make the leg joint in back of the knee.
10. Glue the upper part of the legs to the body so that they are slightly pointed downward toward the ground; the lower leg will dangle and move with the movement of the body.
11. Make felt or cardboard feet and claws and glue them onto the legs.
12. Make the tail by making a tube of poster board and gluing egg carton cups

onto it and painting it to match the rest of the creature or by cutting an egg carton in half and folding the cups over to make a spiky tail.

13. Make your puppet move by fastening rods to the back of the head, two places on the body, and the end of the tail.

14. The mouth can be made to move by one of two methods: (a.) Attach a string to the top middle of the head and thread the string through the near edge of the first body box. Let the string extend down to the head rod and finish the string by attaching a plastic bone ring to it. Pull on the string and the head will move a bit. Remember, you don't need big movement to make a puppet appear to talk. (b.) Moving the mouth by hand requires that the back of the cartons be cut away and the hand inserted into the two cartons. A cover for the hand must be made and the rest of the puppet attached to it and the back of the head. This hand cover can be made using a large sock or a cloth tube sewn to fit.

Dimetrodon

A dimetrodon is an early dinosaur that is very dramatic in appearance. It has a crocodilelike body and a huge saillike fin on its back. For that reason, it is sometimes commonly called a fin-backed dinosaur.

Begin making your dimetrodon by following the steps above to make the alligator/crocodile puppet. Before you attach the sticks, make a pattern for the fin. Take a look at some pictures of dimetrodon in a dinosaur book to get a good idea of what the fins looked like. There were actually several different kinds, so you will have a choice.

MATERIALS

In addition to the materials listed for making an egg carton alligator/crocodile or dragon, you will need:

- Large sheet(s) of paper to make the pattern for the dimetrodon fin
- Dowels or garden sticks to support the fin (Check with your dinosaur book to see approximately how many you will need.)
- Lightweight cloth of a dinosaur color (perhaps olive drab or greenish brown) to make the sail

ASSEMBLY

1. Follow the steps to make an alligator puppet except for attaching the rods.
2. Measure the back of your puppet to see how long the fin will be. Check against pictures.

3. Draw the fin pattern on the large paper.

4. Cut out the pattern and check to see that it fits the puppet and has the right proportions.

5. Pin the pattern to the material and cut it out.

6. Insert the dowels or sticks into the egg cartons and secure with glue.

7. Glue the fin to the dowels and let it dry.

8. Try out your puppet with several children operating it if possible.

Hunt, Tamara, and Nancy Renfro. *Puppetry in Early Childhood Education.* Austin, TX: Nancy Renfro Studios, 1982.

Lade, Roger. *The Most Excellent Book of How to Be a Puppeteer.* Brookfield, CT: Copper Beech Books, 1996.

English Puppetry *see* Punch and Judy

Eyes

Eyes give the finishing touch to a puppet's character. They confirm whether or not the character is silly or serious, youthful or adult. Eyes can be made from almost any material, but they should conform to and reinforce the character you have decided on for your puppet.

A puppet can be nothing *but* eyes. Hobie Ford, a puppeteer from North Carolina, has invented an eye-puppet he called "Peepers." They are two plastic eyes joined by a plastic "U" which fits around the two middle fingers of the hand. He uses these "Peepers" to make an impromptu puppet for interaction with small children and gives them as a gift afterward. A similar eye puppet can be made by pasting large, round stickers on either end of a short piece of wire or pipe cleaner.

In drawing or sculpting a character, the size of the eyes changes the age of the character and is the first element the audience notices about the puppet's face. Children have larger eyes in proportion to their faces than adults do. Making a puppet's eyes larger than usual emphasizes the innocence of the character, even if their character possesses a veneer of sophistication. Miss Piggy of The Muppets is a good example of this.

Shape can also point to the character of the puppet. Large, wide eyes emphasize the innocence of the character unless the eyes are very wide open; then they could show surprise, astonishment, or fear. Eyes that are narrowed and slanted downward show anger; slanted upward, the eyes show weariness. These are, of course, Anglo-American conventions. Try out your ideas for eyes in a drawing or sketch before you make the puppet. Get a second opinion if you have any concerns about stereotyping. (*See* Stereotypes.) When creating eyes for Asian or American Indian puppets, make sure that you are respectful and get the appearance right. The old, cartoonish appearance of Native American, Japanese, and Chinese characters is unacceptable. If you are putting on a play with Asian or American Indian origins, please be careful and respectful.

Fantastic and other-worldly creatures need not have eyes that look like ours. Try another shape: diamonds, for instance, or even two separate shapes. When your ideas begin to get wild, remember the character of your puppet or the character that these eye shapes might signal.

One last idea for consideration when designing the face of your puppet is that your puppet need not have a face at all if it fits the look of your puppets and if your play warrants it. A very modern play or a very dramatic one where the puppets have a stylized appearance could have puppets without faces and eyes at all. Other modern puppets have only eyes and no mouth. Again, these puppets are very stylized.

Some puppeteers have standardized the eyes they make for their puppets. The Muppet characters, for instance, can have eyes made of almost anything, but the pupils must always be slightly crossed, as if focused on something a slight distance away. This underscores their rather goofy appearance and attitude and contributes to the humorous character of all the Muppets.

Paul Vincent Davis, profiled in the children's book *Puppeteer* by Kathryn Lasky, does not seem to use eyes as such. For his production of *Aladdin*, Mr. Davis created molds for his puppets which had eyelids but only a blank space for the eyes. It is a very dramatic concept and reinforces the seriousness of all the characters. Furthermore, it permits the audience to finish the act of creation by imagining the eyes of the puppet.

Yet a third kind of eyes can be seen in *Making Puppets Come Alive* by Larry Engler and Carol Fijan. If you look inside the book at the photographs of the boy and girl puppets, you will notice that the eyes are just black circles which are large in proportion to the face. A careful examination of the picture shows that the eyes are large, flat, and round. This is in keeping with the very innocent character of the puppets. They are supposed to be adults but project the innocence of children. The round, black eyes suit this perfectly.

To see how eyes can act as inspiration, try this interesting exercise. Gather as many pairs of things as possible that you might use for eyes. Don't let your inner critic get in the way; just pick and choose off the top of your head. Gather macaroni shapes, Styrofoam packing peanuts, beads, buttons, the bowls of spoons with the handles broken off, fake fur — anything that you can think of. Make sure that you have large items, such as Ping-Pong balls as well as small items such as pom-poms, beads, beans, and little wiggle eyes. Then imagine the kind of puppet these eyes would fit. If you can, make a sketch of the puppets you liked the best and create them.

You might want to make an eye collection, just bits and pieces paired up to either act as idea generators or to be held for future construction. When you have time, take out your collection and work with it to see what ideas might come. Pair the eyes with different kinds of fabric to create possible characters.

Another interesting exercise: take a piece of fabric — fake fur, leopard print, chiffon, flower cotton — and imagine the kind of character which would go with that fabric. Then find eyes to suit the character. You may find yourself with still more puppets! Even if you don't, the exercise of character creation is a vital one for puppeteers. (*See also* Characters.)

Engler, Larry, and Carol Fijan. *Making Puppets Come Alive: A Method of Learning and Teaching Hand Puppetry.* New York: Taplinger, 1973.
Henson, Cheryl, and the Muppet Workshop. *The Muppets Make Puppets!* New York: Workman Publishing, 1994.
Lasky, Kathryn. *Puppeteer.* New York: Macmillan, 1985.

Festivals

Once a year, the Puppeteers of America have a National Day of Puppetry on the Saturday of the last full weekend in April. (*See* National Day of Puppetry.) That is a great excuse to have a puppetry festival! However, such an undertaking is not for the faint of heart and has to be approached with calendar, to-do list, and pencil firmly in hand. Give yourself a year to plan; you may find that it is just barely enough time.

The first things to decide are what you want to do and where you want to hold it. Since it's April, plan for a rain date or location as well or just plan to hold the festival inside. Begin calling around to find out where you can hold your festival. If you partner with a library or school, you may be able to get facilities for free.

Once you have an idea of what you would like to do, begin to scout around for volunteers who would be interested in working with you. These people will form committees to plan everything from financing to refreshments. They may also know of funding sources that can help sponsor your festival and people who would like to contribute talent.

Considering funding, contact your state's or county's Department of Arts and Humanities as soon as possible. They may be interested in a particular theme or tie-in which would assist you in finding funding. If they are excited about your project, they may even suggest further funding sources or know of people who would be interested in contributing. Who knows? Couldn't hurt.

If you are involved with a school, the art and drama teachers and English or language arts teachers will be the ones you will want to talk to about your project. Not all of them will sign on, but many may. This would be a great focus for the school and will help add clout with funding agencies.

Any talent you invite will need to be contacted well in advance. April is a busy month: National Library Week occurs in April, many states are gearing up for summer reading programs with their talent showcases, and, of course, the National Day of Puppetry is in April, too. Work through your state Puppeteers of America guild for leads on who might be interested in working with you, especially if it's your first year. Contact a number of people, see what their fees are, and see if they are willing to reduce rates or throw in a puppet making workshop — something to give you a little "extra." If you're partnering with the schools, they may be willing to fund part of your puppeteer's expenses if they get a workshop, an extra performance, or something extra in return.

If you haven't done it already, you need to make a checklist. You need performance space. Do you also need tables and chairs? How about a sound system? Refreshments? Recyclables for making puppets? (The school may be able to have a "puppet stuff" drive to get things for you.) Ushers and people to give directions? Parking? Police or Scouts for traffic control? And that's probably the tip of the iceberg!

With a festival this big, you'll want to call the newspapers and the radio and television stations. If you aren't working with the Puppeteers of America, at least let them know what you are doing. If your county's sign policy will allow it, hang a banner advertising your festival and its date. And you'll want fliers everywhere, advertising your event. Maybe the library will make bookmarks to give to their patrons. Ask. They may want to partner with you, too.

What will you do on that day? Make puppets. Have puppet performances. Have strolling puppets. Have an introduction-to-ventriloquism demonstration. Have a parade complete with giant puppets to kick off or wind up or come in the middle of your festival. Have make-and-take tables for demonstrations of different kinds of puppetry. Have storytelling with puppet accompaniment. And how about a puppet show with adults in mind? In short, do just about anything you want to encourage people to enjoy making and working with puppets. Most of all: enjoy yourself and a wonderful, tiring, crazy day filled with the pleasure of puppets and puppetry.

Finger Puppet Theaters

Finger puppets usually perform by themselves. But a cute little theater can be made for them from a shoe box — and everything needed for the performance can be put into the box to be carried with you or used in the puppet corner.

MATERIALS

- 1 large shoe box
- Pencil

- Ruler
- White glue
- Scissors
- Craft knife
- Paints
- Paint brushes or markers
- Poster board
- Paper to cover the shoe box (optional)
- Hot glue gun (optional)

ASSEMBLY

1. If you don't have a box or a box of the right size, make one now of colored poster board. (*See* Cardboard Boxes.) Make sure that you can hold it in your hand easily with room to spare for finger movement. Omit one of the short sides. Make a second long side instead of a lid. Decorate the box before assembly or after, whichever you like.

2. If you use a shoe box, cut away one short side. This is where you will slip your hand into the box, putting it on like a sleeve or long glove.

3. Cut an opening in the upper end of the lid at the height of your hand. This will be your proscenium arch.

4. Glue the lid onto the box.

5. Paint and decorate box.

Wright, Lyndie. *Puppets.* New York: Franklin Watts, 1989.
Wright, Lyndie. *Toy Theaters.* New York: Franklin Watts, 1991.

Finger Puppets

Finger puppets are small finger coverings decorated to look like people, animals, or other characters. Although usually too small to use in theater production puppetry, finger puppets can be used effectively in small-group situations, classrooms, and work with individual children. Finger puppets make fine craft time projects as well.

Traditionally, a finger puppet is made from a covering similar to the finger of a glove. Probably the first finger puppets were made by cutting the fingers from old, worn-out gloves. As with all basic toys, it didn't take long to add a face and some hair, and a tiny puppet was born.

Finger puppets can also be made from a paper ring with a figure mounted on it. The ring is fitted around the finger of the puppeteer who wiggles the finger to make the puppet move and act. Very small children can have the ring fitted around two fingers for a bit more control.

A version of the traditional glove-finger puppet uses the entire glove, with each finger taking on a different character to tell a story:

the three little pigs, a wolf, and a salesman for "The Three Little Pigs"

Cinderella, her two stepsisters, the stepmother, and the prince for "Cinderella"

the little red hen, three farm animals and a miller for "The Little Red Hen" (The chicks who share in the final loaf of bread could be on the fingers of the other hand.)

each finger could have a letter to spell out "BINGO" for the repetitive song (Each time a letter is subtracted, that finger would fold under into the hand. Bingo the dog could be a stick puppet dancing around the letters of his name as the song is sung.)

each finger could be a different related character: farm animals, sailors, space men and so on to act out a made-up story.

The other hand or a stick figure can also be used for additional characters. For instance, a boat for the sailors, a barn for the farm animals, or a space ship for the space men could be mounted on a stick and used with the story.

The characters on each finger can be made from felt, cloth scraps, or pom-poms and either attached to the glove permanently or attached with Velcro dots to make them removable. You may also find special knitting instructions for making gloves with the characters' faces knitted in or chart them on grid paper and knit them in yourself.

By using Velcro to attach characters to a finger puppet glove, you can make a number of interchangeable character sets. A second glove can be used for extra characters or simple scenery, but don't make it too complicated. Simplicity is best with finger puppets. Consider using a snugly fitting glove if it is comfortable. Very loose gloves tend to flop and lose control and sometimes the Velcro becomes entangled.

There is an advantage to having all the characters glued or attached permanently. This tends to thwart loss and make repair less frequent. One glove contains all the characters for a performance, so a trunk full of stories can be created at low cost. Use in front of an apron stage, lap stage, or no stage at all. (*See* Apron Stage; Stages.) Little ones will love them!

Commercial puppet makers are now creating more-complex finger puppets: baby birds, butterflies, flowers, and so on. Even some characters from famous children's books have been turned into finger puppets. Consider the expense versus the amount of use before purchasing. Remember to consider mini-grant money when thinking about purchasing these specialized puppets or any commercially made puppets for that matter. If you have a well-thought-out puppet program whose objectives can be presented to a Friends of the Library, PTA, religious school board, or other sponsoring group, they will be inclined to support the special, one-time purchase of puppets for your program.

MacLennan, Jennifer. *Simple Puppets You Can Make.* New York: Sterling, 1988.
Wallace, Mary. *I Can Make Puppets.* Toronto: Greey de Pencier Books, 1994.

Fist Puppets

"Fist puppet" is an older British term used to describe hand or glove puppets. (*See also* Hand Puppets.) The fist can be used by itself as a puppet and was made famous in the 1950s and 1960s by Senior Wences, a regular performer on the *Ed Sullivan Show*. In this case, Senior Wences used his fist to create a mouth, using the thumb as the movable lower jaw. Lipstick and makeup created a face, and a wig was placed on top of the fist puppet. Senior Wences was an accomplished ventriloquist who gave all his creations different voices and personalities, the most famous being the "talking head" which existed only in a box and made brief appearances for emphasis within the performance. (*See also* Hands as Puppets.)

Bodies can be used for the fist puppet. They can either be made from a pattern or you can purchase a premade body from a craft store. When used as a puppet, the body must be headless. These bodies are predressed and matched with a suitable talking head fist. This permits a great deal of character switching with wigs, bodies, and so on.

A stage for your puppet character is almost unnecessary, although you can have a box or table for your characters to appear on. Whatever stage you use, it should be as simple and uncomplicated as possible.

If you will be sitting next to the stage to talk to the characters, you will need a short, table-height stage. If you are using multiple bodies and wigs, these will need to be laid out in advance behind your stage.

If you are not going to be talking to the puppets or not appearing with them, you will need to have a larger stage for them to use. This can be as simple as a curtain you can sit behind. You can reach underneath the curtain so you can place bodies if they are used and your puppets can perform. You can also use the table as a stage, but will need something to sit behind.

MATERIALS

- Face makeup (from a Halloween set)
- A wig that will fit on the top of your hand

- Head gear such as a scarf or flower or bow for a girl and a doll's baseball cap for a boy character (optional)
- Spirit gum or another light, non-toxic glue for attaching wigs, beards, and accessories

ASSEMBLY

1. Form your hand into a fist with the thumb curled in front of the index finger. Work with your thumb, moving it in and out to make a talking motion.
2. Draw around the thumb and finger with lipstick or face paint to emphasize the mouth. A tongue can be made, when necessary, by sticking a finger from the other hand through the mouth opening.
3. Draw eyes above the mouth with face paint. Make them simple and large so they will be easy to see. Wiggle eyes or buttons can be used, but attach them firmly.
4. Place the wig on your index finger knuckle. Since the wig will not be very big, use spirit gum or another non-toxic, lightweight glue to fasten the wig. If you are using multiple characters, the wigs can be removed and exchanged as necessary.
5. If your puppet has a body, it can be placed on the stage and the head (fist) used to hold it in place. Remember to avoid placing costume frills near the mouth; try to have everything lying flat so the mouth will be easy to see.
6. Use props imaginatively to assist in creating your fist puppet's character. Think of the attitude your character will project and match the accessories to that.

Henson, Cheryl, and the Muppet Workshop. *The Muppets Make Puppets!* New York Workman Publishing, 1994.
Milligan, David Frederick. *Fist Puppetry*. New York: A. S. Barnes & Co., 1938.
Wallace, Mary. *I Can Make Puppets*. Toronto: Greey de Pencier Books, 1994.

Flannel Boards

A flannel board is a basic story time tool. For puppeteers, the flannel board is both a backdrop and a kind of static puppetry or moving storybook, if such things can be. A flannel board is just that: a board covered with flannel or felt to which figures cut from flannel, felt, or Pellon will adhere. The figures are like stick puppets without the stick. They do not move and are placed to form tableaux which illustrate the story being told. A flannel board can also form the backdrop for simple puppetry with stick or finger puppets. Scenery changes can be quick and fairly smooth, making for a more elaborate production.

It is good to have at least two sizes of flannel board: a small one that can be held in the lap like a book, with puppets manipulated from above, and a larger one used like an easel. Both can be made in the same way.

If you have a painting easel, you can make felt backdrops with different themes and attach them to the easel for a puppet backdrop and simple theater. The disadvantage is that it is not particularly portable unless you can collapse and carry the easel.

MATERIALS

- Cardboard or foam core board in the size desired (Look for foam core board used to mount embroidery; it is pre-glued for even adherence.)
- Flannel or felt in a solid color to cover the board and have a 2" overlap all around (Black makes the flannel board figures show up better.)
- Felt to back the board and cover any overlaps of cloth
- For the folding flannel board:

    a yard of grosgrain ribbon for ties

    2" wide cloth tape to form a hinge to join the two halves of the folding flannel board (Duct tape will work in a bind.)
- Glue gun
- Glue for attaching the cloth if you haven't found the pre-glued foam core board

CONSIDERATIONS

Rubber cement forms an even coat and does not soak through but has toxic fumes. Tacky glue applies evenly and does not have toxic fumes but takes a while to dry. More-liquid glues may soak through. Hot glue guns will work well for applying cloth, but work quickly and in small areas at a time. Experiment with an extra piece of board and some spare cloth to see what works.

- Scissors
- Pencil or chalk
- Measuring tape
- Craft knife

ASSEMBLY

1. Measure the board and cut it to the desired size. Remember that if you are making the folding flannel board, take the full size and divide in half.
2. Cut the cloth to size, allowing for a 2" overlap. For a folding flannel board,

cut the cloth in half. Cut the corners from the overlap, allowing for smoother mitered corners.

3. Cut the backing felt the size of the board.

4. If you are using preglued foam core board, remove the backing and slowly pat the cloth in place. You may want an extra pair of hands for this.

5. If using plain board, apply a layer of glue to the board. Then slowly pat the cloth in place. Again, you may want an assistant for this step.

6. Turn the board over and apply glue to a 2" strip around the edge of the board. Gently fold the cloth over and pat into place.

7. Measure the back of the flannel board for the backing cloth.

8. For a folding flannel board: Stack the two boards and measure around the stack in a "U." An area for the hinge joining the two boards is needed, and measuring the boards closed will provide this measurement.

9. For a folding flannel board: Before gluing the backing cloth in place, attach ties to the flannel board by gluing ties in place with a hot-glue gun.

10. Cut the flannel board backing cloth and glue to the back of the flannel board.

11. For a folding flannel board: Glue the backing cloth in place with the boards closed and the ties sticking out. When the glue is dry, measure and cut a piece of flannel matching the inside of the flannel board and glue in place. This will make the inside hinge for the flannel board.

12. Trim all edges to make a smooth fit.

Hunt, Tamara, and Nancy Renfro. *Puppetry in Early Childhood Education.* Austin, TX: Nancy Renfro Studios, 1982.

Foam Rubber Puppets

Foam rubber has been a material of choice for puppets since the advent of the Muppets. It can be sculpted the way many other materials can be, but it has the advantage of bendability, softness, and light weight. Unfortunately, it also deteriorates over time, especially when exposed to the light. The foam breaks down and becomes softer and sticky as well. You may have seen this in a foam rubber pillow at home.

Consider the Muppets and their various shapes. If you think of Bert and Ernie, Miss Piggy, Kermit the Frog, the Great Gonzo, and Animal, all of them have fairly simple head and body shapes. There isn't a great deal of sculpting involved to creating their physical characteristics; most of the interest comes from applied items for eyes, eyebrows, hair, and so on. After the head or body shape has been sculpted, the foam rubber is covered with an outer skin of fabric, and it is this fabric skin which the audience sees.

Foam rubber can be carved into various shapes and turned into puppets. Realistic dragons with very sharp teeth, sweet old grannies, menacing pirates, and many other interesting and wonderful puppets can be sculpted from foam rubber. Just remember that they won't last forever and will need to be replaced after a number of years. Also remember to photograph your work for your records. You can turn to these records if you need to recreate your foam rubber puppets.

Foam rubber can be obtained from upholstery houses or fabric shops. For a comparatively modest investment, you can get *quite* a bit. Also check the catalogues of department stores. They offer foam pillows to replace pillows in older couches and chairs. Try them for a smaller amount of foam rubber to start experimenting with.

I have known of puppeteers who have driven around various neighborhoods looking for cast-off furniture they could raid for foam rubber, but this isn't recommended unless you are really desperate and just starting out. The foam from used furniture is most likely already old and may have begun to deteriorate. On the other hand, if you're desperate, get your truck out and start driving!

Carving or sculpting foam rubber is like carving any other substance in that you need to prepare a sketch and work from that. On the block of foam, draw an outline of what you want your puppet's face to look like. Begin snipping away with scissors to carve the basic shape of your puppet. Start by removing any large portions from the inside of the mouth, the back of the head, and so on. You can refine your carving later. And errors and mistakes can be repaired with contact cement.

Note: Some instructors have written that an electric knife can be used to carve Styrofoam or foam rubber, and I have seen it used in upholstery shops. But I would be cautious. If you have a knife and foam rubber to spare, give it a try. Personally, I enjoy the slower approach of using a bread or ham knife and snipping with scissors. Also, it is easier to avoid major accidents!

As you carve your puppet, keep referring to your sketch as you would when carving any other material. Keep the finished product in mind and work toward it. After you have achieved the rough outline, begin to smooth away the bumps with your scissors. You cannot use another smoothing medium such as sandpaper or a rasp, so fine scissors must do all the finishing work. Once the figure has been carved to your satisfaction, it can be painted with acrylics using a dabbing stroke and applying a bit of paint at a time. After that, the body of the puppet, its wig, and any other finishing touches can be added to complete your puppet.

To make a mouth puppet, make a sketch of the puppet's upper and lower jaw unless the puppet will be like one of the Muppets: a very simple shape. If the mouth puppet is a simple shape, either create a pocket for your hand or cut slits in the foam rubber to accommodate fingers and thumb. (*See* Mouth Puppets.)

Foam rubber is a wonderful contemporary material for making puppets. While these puppets do not last as long as the wood and papier-mâché varieties, foam rubber puppets can be carved in almost as detailed a manner as wood or papier-mâché. (*See* Papier-mâché; Wooden Puppet Heads.) The foam can be more expressive than the rigid medium as it bends, scrunches, and wrinkles as wood or papier-mâché never could. So try it out! Who knows? Foam rubber might be just the puppet-making medium for you!

Allison, Drew & Donald Devet. *The Foam Book: An Easy Guide to Building Polyfoam Puppets.* Charlotte, NC: Grey Seal Puppets, Inc., 1997. Second printing: 2000.
Currell, David. *An Introduction to Puppets & Puppet-Making.* Edison, NJ: Chartwell Books, 1992.

Focus

Focus in puppetry is vitally important and something frequently overlooked by beginners. Focus is the act of pinpointing the attention of the audience on the center of the action, usually aimed at the speaking puppet. It is all too easy to have puppets running around and doing things on the stage. This causes confusion in the audience. Let your puppets slow down and stop the action to hone in on the focus. Don't let your inactive puppets just sit there either. Make sure that all nonspeaking puppets look at the speaker. You can break the focus on purpose by looking away from the speaker to the audience or having another puppet or person begin to speak. But make sure that the focus remains fixed where you want it to be.

Focus in puppetry has to do with who is speaking and who is the center of the action at the moment. The puppet with the focus may not necessarily be the one in the foreground. Additionally, the focus can shift — and in fact needs to shift — as the primary actor shifts on the stage.

Usually, however, the puppet with the focus of the action is the one who is speaking. When that puppet is speaking, all other puppets should stop and look that way. To have other puppets looking around, moving, being restless (unless called for in the script) takes focus away from the speaking puppet. This rule is broken when another puppet is sneaking onto the stage to do something. The focus is then shared between the puppet who has had the focus and the one in the background who is planning to do something.

Practice with two puppets. Have some action going on. When one speaks, the action stops or slows dramatically and the second puppet looks toward the speaking puppet. Then reverse the focus and have the second puppet be the one who is at the center of attention when speaking. The focus of the audience is changed through the act of looking at the speaking puppet.

Use a focus exercise as a group activity for puppet club. (*See* Clubs.) Have each child take a puppet. Begin speaking, and have all puppets look at the speaker. Then, in the middle of your conversation, point to another child and have him or her begin talking. All puppets should look at the speaker. That child can then choose another child as speaker, and so on through the room. Have the children say whether or not people are looking at the speaker. If you like, each child can toss something to choose the next speaker as in the game hot potato.

Another exercise involves a talking stick or some other object which is physically passed from puppet to puppet in a random way. The leader begins with the stick in the puppet's mouth or held by the puppet in some way. The stick can be placed in the free hand or lap of the puppeteer and the improvised conversation begins. The puppet can comment on the taste of the stick or other object or how difficult or easy it is to hold. After a brief statement the puppet decides to carry the stick to someone else. As the puppet moves to the other person, the other puppets track the moving puppet but they do not speak. The talking stick is transferred to the next puppet, who then comments on the stick or the exercise or whatever it likes. Continue until all puppeteers have had a chance to participate.

Focus is critically important if you are using a puppet assistant at story time or choose to use a single puppet in your work. (*See* Assistants.) When, as the leader, you look at the puppet when it is speaking, the audience's focus is transferred to the puppet and away from you. This is good. This is something you want. In the act of moving the audience's focus to the puppet, the puppet becomes more lifelike, and you disappear into the background. In this way, the puppet's character can be developed as an individual performer. You become the second banana, the question asker, and the prompter who keeps the wheel of the conversation moving right along.

Whenever you want to shift the focus, look away from the puppet and talk to the audience. This breaks the focus with the puppet and transfers it back to you. The puppet can look at you or look down if it is embarrassed or thinking about something, but it should not be looking around, shifting restlessly, or talking against you unless it is a part of the script.

With this in mind, you can begin by talking to the audience, then bring in the puppet and talk with it, slowly shifting the focus to the puppet. It can interact with the audience or speak alone, but the puppet is on its own now, acting in its own right. Slowly, you can shift the focus away from the puppet-and-audience to puppet-and-puppeteer, and finally to puppeteer and audience as the puppet goes back into its resting place.

Engler, Larry, and Carol Fijan. *Making Puppets Come Alive: A Method of Learning and Teaching Hand Puppetry*. New York: Taplinger, 1973.

French Puppetry *see* Guignol

Giant Puppets

Giant, larger-than-life-sized puppets are becoming more and more popular in the North American puppetry scene. Beginning as folk puppets, giant puppets now come in many varieties. They draw attention and work very well in street theater, fairs, and other large, public presentations.

Giant figures have been used for centuries in one form or another as part of festivals and parades. Giant wicker men were reported as part of harvest festivals in Briton in the Middle Ages and earlier. The use of these figures survived into modern times. Carnival processions in Europe and giant-sized masks and masked figures in sub-Saharan Africa and India slowly made their way to the Americas and found rebirth in new places.

Street theater, begun in the 1960s to educate as well as entertain, brought a new, more serious spirit to the use of giant puppets. Raising consciousness about racial understanding, poverty, the war in Vietnam, and other compelling social issues were all enhanced by the use of giant puppets. Bread and Puppet Theater, a puppet troupe residing in Vermont, has used giant puppets for years as a signature part of their style of street theater.

Today, giant puppets are found in many places, with some companies focusing solely on the use of giant puppets. Stage presentations, such as *The Lion King*, have used giant puppets to great effect. Commercial enterprises have also begun to use giant puppets in promotional events. The costumed character, like The Chicken and the characters at Disneyland, are spin-offs from the giant puppet concept.

The major element in constructing a giant puppet is weight and durability. The puppet cannot be too heavy or the puppeteer will not be able to manipulate it for long. In addition, any puppet used outdoors as part of a public effort needs to be able to withstand exposure to adverse weather conditions.

Some puppet makers report solving the weight problem with papier-mâché, which is both lightweight and strong. They use molds or armatures on which to build their puppets, then cover the resulting puppet with several coats of varnish. (*See* Armatures; Papier-Mâché.)

Giant Puppet Figures of the Sun, Moon, and Three Attendant Stars

Six-foot poles will go up through the armature, and the puppet will be built on the armature. The armatures are made of chicken wire, which is sold in big, twenty-yard rolls. Each puppet figure will be attached to the pole in at least two places for security. The poles will be placed in a holder worn on a belt around the waist.

Materials

- Chicken wire for the armature: approximately 6 yards for the sun, 3 yards for the moon, and 1½ yards for each star
- Butcher or other wide paper for making patterns for the three giant puppets
- Two 6' poles, 1" square.
- 3 long flexible poles for the stars
- Fabric, ribbon, or crepe paper in complimentary colors for streamers on the star poles
- Newspaper
- Brown paper bags
- White glue
- Water
- Garden sticks for keeping the two sides of the figures apart where necessary to preserve shape
- Pencils
- Ruler or tape measure
- Hot glue gun
- Electric drill and ¼" bit
- Coated wire
- Tempera paints
- Wide paintbrushes
- Clear outdoor varnish
- 5 plastic milk or juice cartons, 1 quart each, with lids
- Belt webbing and closures (buckles) for 5 belts

Assembly

1. Draw a pattern for your puppets. The sun and moon should each be about 3' high. Each star can be from 1 to 2' high and either the same size or three different sizes. From these patterns, check with the estimates of chicken wire given in the materials list and add or subtract wherever necessary.

2. Using the patterns as a guide, form the chicken wire into an armature for the front and back of each puppet figure. Make sure that at least two places for inserting and securing a pole is clearly marked on the armature.

3. Using these points on the armature as a guide, drill holes in the poles for wiring on the puppet figures. (You could attach the poles to the armatures now and build the figures around them, but there will be a great deal of

moisture involved with the papier-mâché, and one wouldn't want the poles to warp.)

4. Tear the brown paper bags and newspaper into 3" by 1" strips.

5. Thin the glue with one part water to two parts glue.

6. Dip the brown paper bag strips into thinned white glue.

7. Apply the strips of brown paper dipped in glue in layers onto the armature. Overlay the strips sufficiently to make a firm surface.

8. Leave open the mounting areas. Poke holes in the wire wherever needed.

9. Follow the layer of brown paper with one of newspaper strips dipped in the thinned glue.

10. If the armatures are not holding their rounded shapes sufficiently well, use the garden sticks, split slightly at the ends, to prop the armatures open while the papier-mâché is being applied and is drying.

11. Let the layer dry after two layers of paper have been applied.

12. Continue to build layers in alternating colors, brown and white, until six layers are built up. Add a seventh and last layer of brown paper as a finishing layer.

13. Let everything dry thoroughly. You may have to prop the puppet figures against a wall or elevate with plastic containers or pails to get a good air flow.

14. Paint with tempera paints and allow to dry thoroughly.

15. Coat with two coats of clear outdoor varnish. Since most varnish gives off toxic vapors, you will have to do this outside. If you are absolutely sure you will not have rain or will only use the puppet figures indoors, you can skip this step.

16. Mount the figures on poles using coated wire.

17. Add the streamers to the stars (and to sun and moon as well if you wish) by cutting or tearing the fabric into strips and tying them the poles.

18. Use hot glue under the knots to secure the streamers to the poles and keep them anchored in place.

19. Make the pole holders that attach to the belts by cutting a hole in the top of a plastic half-gallon milk or juice jug, leaving the handle in place and attached to the jug at both ends of the handle. An alternative is to cut slits as belt guides into the milk jug and thread the belt through that. Make sure that the belt guides are not cut too close to the top of the jug so they won't tear open.

20. Cut the belt webbing to fit the puppeteer with plenty of overlap and finish.

21. Add the belt buckle following the instructions that come with the buckle. Check for fit.

22. Thread the pole carrier onto the belt. Check for fit and comfort.

23. Place the pole into the carrier and adjust for comfort.

24. Now start your parade!

These puppet figures are huge stick puppets and have no hands or feet to move. Life-sized or giant rod puppets can be made using plastic cartons, paper tubes, and other lightweight materials with dowels or garden sticks used to move the hands or feet. Carry the giant rod puppets in a belt cup like the one made for the sun, moon, and stars.

Baird, Bil. *The Art of the Puppet*. New York: Macmillan, 1965.

Bell, John. *Strings, Hands, Shadows: A Modern Puppet History*. Detroit: The Detroit Institute of Arts, 2000.

Flower, Cedric, and Alan Fortney. *Puppets, Methods and Materials*. Worcester, MA: Davis Publ., 1983.

Lade, Roger. *The Most Excellent Book of How to Be a Puppeteer*. Brookfield, CT: Copper Beech Books, 1996.

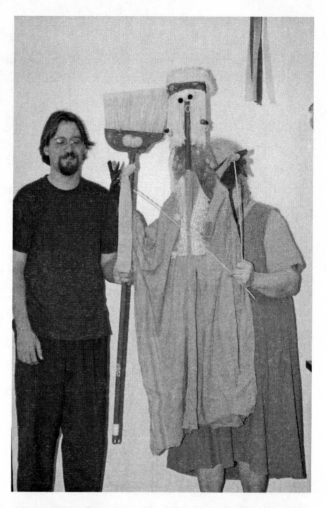

These funky giant puppets are made from a broom and a mop with pom-pom eyes and ponytail-holder mouths. The mop-headed puppet has rod-operated hands, while the broom puppet has no hands at all. In a performance, both puppeteers would be wearing dark-color clothing covering as much of the body as possible.

Glove Puppets

"Glove puppet" is the formal term for a puppet that sits on and is manipulated by your hand. This kind of puppet is called a "fist puppet" in England. (*See* Fist Puppets.) In this book, however, the term "glove puppet" is used strictly for puppets made from gloves. In this case, a glove is either turned into some sort of creature with the fingers forming the legs and the palm forming the body.

For the Cinderella puppet glove, the two mean stepsisters are on the thumb; Cinderella with her broom is on the first finger; and the fairy godmother is on the second finger. The prince and the ball-gowned Cinderella are curled over to signal that they are not "onstage" at this point in the story.

Distinct from a glove puppet is the *puppet glove*, on which Velcro is used to attach small items, characters, or animals to the fingers of the glove and used in storytelling in small groups. This kind of glove has been sold under the brand name "Monkey Mitt" and is often made of hairy, fake fur fabric with the Velcro tabs on the tips of the fingers. (*See* Puppet Gloves.)

Following are directions for making three different kinds of glove puppets.

Glove "Creature" Puppet

Before beginning to assemble your glove "creature," consider the personality you want your creature to have. Will it be silly or serious, debonair or countrified? The material and the color of your glove may give you some ideas. Choose your materials to reflect this personality. If you have a pair of gloves, you can make them the same or you can make one silly, one serious.

MATERIALS

- Glove with individual fingers (not a mitten)
- Decorations such as beads, feathers, ribbon to add personality to the character
- Material for eyes: wiggle eyes, Ping-Pong balls, bowls from plastic spoons, or

buttons (Note: If your puppet will be used by young children, choose eyes that can be sewn on.)

- Glue gun and glue sticks
- Tape (optional)
- Permanent marker
- Acrylic paints (optional)

ASSEMBLY

1. Put the glove on your hand, and arrange all the materials on the glove the way you want them. This may take another person or some tape to hold the items in place while you examine the "creature" for effect.

2. When you have the effect you want, remove the glove and attach the items to the glove with a glue gun.

3. Attach eyes and any trim that need to be sewn on.

4. Put the glove on again and examine your creation. Does it look the way you want? If not, make the changes you need until you have it looking the way you want.

5. Find a play or make up dialogue for your glove "creature" or "creatures."

Puppet with Glove Body and Styrofoam Head

This puppet is a minimalist character — just a body and the head. The head for this puppet can be slightly larger than normal for the size of your hand. Since all puppets are caricatures, exaggeration is expected. Remember to consider the character of your puppet as you gather your materials.

When manipulating this puppet, use the thumb, pointer and center fingers while folding the ring and pinky fingers in toward the palm.

A variation on this puppet may be made by making the hole in the head large enough to accommodate the pointer and center fingers. The arms are then made by the thumb on one side and the ring and pinky fingers working together on the other so that no fingers need to be folded under.

MATERIALS

- Glove or a pair of gloves (not mittens)
- Styrofoam ball (2 if using a pair of gloves)
- Eye material: wiggle eyes, beads, or some other item
- Material for hair, such as feathers, paper strips, doll hair, yarn or some other item (*See* Hair and Wigs.)

- Glue gun and glue sticks
- Plastic knife
- Pencil

ASSEMBLY

1. Use the knife to carve a hole in the Styrofoam ball. Make it large enough to accommodate your pointer finger snugly with the glove on.
2. Test the hole with the glove on until the size of the hole seems satisfactory.
3. Make or arrange eyes and attach them with the glue gun.
4. Make or arrange hair and attach it with the glue gun.
5. Use the glue gun to attach the Styrofoam ball to the glove. The glue will be hot, so use the plastic knife or a pencil inside the finger of the glove to press the material into place.
6. Add any accessories you think will add personality to your puppet or leave it just as it is. Simplicity is best, here.

Glove Puppet Spider

A glove will make a serviceable spider puppet or other generic "creepy crawly creature."

MATERIALS

- Pair of black or other solid color gloves
- 4" × 4" black or other solid color fabric to match or contrast with the glove
- Small amount of fiber fill
- Needle and thread
- Scissors
- Glue gun and glue sticks
- Material for eyes, such as wiggle eyes, beads, or other items

ASSEMBLY

1. Cut two circles from the fabric, 1½" and 2½" in diameter.
2. Sew a gathering thread around the edge of each circle.
3. Gather the circle up just a bit.
4. Stuff one circle with some of the fiber fill. Continue to stuff and to gather up the circle until you have a firmly stuffed ball.

5. Knot your gathering thread and cut it short.

6. Stuff and knot the second circle.

7. Arrange the two circles on the back of the glove to resemble a spider body, small circle in front.

8. Use the hot glue gun to glue the body circles in place.

9. Cut three fingers from the second glove and stuff them lightly with fiberfill. Attach the fingers with the glue gun to the palm and beneath the body so that there are a total of eight legs (including your five fingers).

10. Attach the eyes with the hot glue gun.

Get wiggling!

Henson, Cheryl, and the Muppet Workshop. *The Muppets Make Puppets!* New York: Workman Publishing, 1994.
Hunt, Tamara, and Nancy Renfro. *Puppetry in Early Childhood Education.* Austin, TX: Nancy Renfro Studios, 1982.

Glue Gun Techniques

The glue gun is a small appliance, roughly gun shaped and usually having a trigger. A glue gun holds glue sticks, normally clear rods, but occasionally colored, which are pushed through the gun by means of the trigger. The glue sticks are heated and then become a viscous liquid. This hot, liquid glue can be used to fasten almost anything *to* almost anything. For this reason, it has become the crafter's friend and indispensable companion.

There are a number of safety concerns with the glue gun, and they begin with the gun itself. Even a low-temperature glue gun is hot. It has to be to melt the glue sticks. So the first consideration is protecting people from the hot tip of the glue gun which can cause a burn. When you purchase your glue gun, try to find a high/low temperature gun which will switch between settings with a slide or switch.

Whenever you are working with small children, use the low-temp setting and continually hold the gun in your hand. If you have a staff member who can assist you, by all means ask that person to do so. Otherwise, see if there is a parent in your group who will monitor the children while the craft is going on. All it takes is one burn to turn a happy activity into a miserable one!

The glue, of course, is hot coming out of the glue gun and will remain so for a minute or longer. Finger burns are a hazard with using a glue gun, so if you are sensitive to this aspect, consider other gluing methods or use gloves. Gloves will hamper your movements and flexibility but will protect your fingers. I have never found gloves to be of any use whatsoever, but I don't mind the occasional inconvenience of being burned. I find that the glue gets caught in the fabric of the gloves and is more trouble than it's worth. But if you have sensitivity, practice with gloves. Tight fitting garden gloves might be the best to try.

A necessary attachment for your glue gun is a stand. This will hold your glue gun upright and is a quick, simple solution to any location problems. Place your stand on a sheet of aluminum or place a small aluminum pie plate underneath the glue gun tip. The glue does leak, and the aluminum will not melt as a Styrofoam plate would or stick as a paper plate would. And you can gently wipe the tip of your gun against the aluminum to get rid of annoying strings of glue.

Speaking of "annoying strings of glue," when you are applying hot glue to an object, gently wipe the tip of the glue gun against whatever is receiving the hot glue. Those glue strings are not only messy but they can cause accidental burns as you try to clean up the mess.

When you press one object against another which has hot glue on it, press gently but firmly. Do not squish the pieces together. When you are gluing in place of sewing, remember again that the glue is hot and press gently. You don't want hot glue to ooze out and burn you.

When you are using hot glue instead of sewing, as in creating puppet theater curtains, mark the place where you want the hot glue to go. Press the hem or rod pocket in place with a hot iron. Then lay a small ribbon of glue on the cloth and gently fold over the cloth making the hem or rod pocket. Remember to work in small sections rather than in long strips because the glue will cool and become unusable as a fastening agent if you apply long strips of it. Then another line of glue will have to be applied.

Colored glue can be used to create small designs on an object. Stars, spots, eyes, and other patterns can all be created with colored glue sticks. Use them just as you would any hot glue stick. Draw the design you want first on the cloth you will be using. Provide backing material such as waxed paper or cardboard in case the glue leaks through. As with any unusual material, try out the glue first on a scrap of the material. It may melt, discolor, or harm your main material in some way. Use a steady pressure on the glue gun to create a stream of hot glue. Fill in the design with the glue. Remember that you may need multiple sticks of any given color before your design is finished. Allow it to cool thoroughly. Follow any instructions when washing the material as the glue may peel off.

Finally, remember that this is an electric device. Always use the same caution with a glue gun you would with any other electric appliance, especially when working around children. Consider a surge strip as a protector as well. Glue guns are not very expensive, but you don't want to be replacing them all the time.

Use of the glue gun is almost a given these days. If you haven't used one, do give it a try. Its quick and firm-fastening ability has made it an instant favorite with crafters and hobbyists everywhere. Check in your library for books, especially those on wreath making, that contain other glue gun tips. Check on-line

as well. This handy and versatile member of your tool chest will always be working for you for projects large and small.

Packham, Jo. *Glue Crafts*. New York: Sterling Pubs., 1995.
http://www.about.com/ Subject: Glue gun or glue gun techniques.

Grants and Internships

Grants and internships can assist a puppeteer in furthering his or her education or learning more about one or more features of puppetry. (*See* Courses.)
They can also assist in presenting a performance whose approach is more complex than that normally used by the puppeteer. Grants can help with buying equipment or — possibly — traveling to see and talk with a famous puppeteer.

The possibilities of grants and internships are nearly endless, but they must
be searched out, and that becomes a problem for some folks. I point out a few
here, but to go further you will need to put in some time searching. With the
Internet and your public library at your assistance, this may not be as arduous
as you think.

A first place to look is your state's Endowment for the Humanities or
Humanities/Arts department. It may offer courses in applying for grants as well
as offer grants. It may have an artists-in-residence program or programs built
around special festivals or themes.

Another place to look is on the web pages of the national puppetry organizations. These folks offer small- to medium-sized grants as well as occasional
internships. Grants awarded by Puppeteers of America are minigrants for members, and applications should be sent to the person in charge. (*See* Puppeteers of
America.) Awards are for $100 to $1,000 and are granted every two years. Check
their web site for details.

Scholarships offered by UNIMA–USA (the Union Internationale de la Marionette–United States of America) are for study abroad to increase the knowledge of American puppeteers about other forms of puppetry and to study in
France at the UNIMA school of puppetry. (*See* UNIMA–USA.) This is the twen-
tieth year of UNIMA–USA's scholarship program, which they feel promotes the
organization's "building bridges of international understanding," a primary goal
of UNIMA and UNIMA–USA. See their web site for further details and an application form.

The University of Connecticut offers unpaid internships on a periodic basis.
(*See* University of Connecticut Puppetry Arts Program.) One offered was in the
Ballard Museum of Puppetry and would be a wonderful opportunity for anyone
interested in archival studies or the history of puppetry. If you are in any program which requires an internship of this kind and are able to support yourself
for the summer (car and housing), this would be an ideal internship to apply for.

The Center for Puppetry Arts in Atlanta, Georgia has volunteer opportunities, job opportunities, and sometimes internships for puppeteers. Check with their web site for more information and whom to contact.

Before you apply for a grant, think through your project or request. Why do you want to do this? Why do you need to do it? What will you do with it when you are through? If your request is for a large project, make sure that you have a business plan and a monitoring agency. Ask yourself all the questions you can to ensure that you know your project, resources, and goals inside and out. Seeking a large grant will most likely include an interview with the granting agency, so rehearse with someone who may be able to help you in this matter.

Finally, when you apply for a grant, make sure that you consider the little things. You would be amazed at how many people ignore them! Make sure that the copy of the application you send in is clean and crisp and that everything is spelled correctly. Observe the dates for applications, and make sure that you meet them. These details are important and must be attended to for your application to even make the first cut.

If you want to do something more with your puppeteering or your puppet company, think seriously about applying for a grant. You will need to educate yourself and do some research, but the results will be well worth it!

www.puppet.org The Atlanta Center for Puppetry Arts
http://www.sagecraft.com/ The Puppetry Home Page
www.puppeteers.org/ Puppeteers of America

Greek Puppetry see Karagoz

Greeting Card Theaters

What could be nicer than receiving a miniature puppet theater as a combination gift and card on a holiday? Using card stock or poster board, a holiday scene is created. Several window-like openings or a theater proscenium are incorporated into the design, and finger puppets or very small stick puppets can pop out and put on a little play.

Consider a candelabra such as a Hanukkah menorah or a Kwanza kinara, a string of Christmas lights, or a collection of Diwali lamps. These could be drawn onto an oversized card with openings above each candle holder or lamp. Puppets dressed like candles or people can pop out of the windows and enact a holiday play.

If you don't wish to tie the design of the greeting card theater into a holiday, consider a picture of a garden full of spring flowers with the openings in the center of the flowers. How about a house design, especially if it is personalized to look like the recipient's house, complete with puppets as family members including the family pets? Any scene based on a classroom theme — history, deserts, oceans, geography, cultures — can be incorporated into the greeting card theater format. Even elementary math drills can be involved, with the answers popping out of the windows as puppets beneath the arithmetic problems.

If you cannot find an envelope to accommodate your greeting card theater, you can make one from drawing paper. You may have to pay oversized letter postage, but it will be worth it to surprise and please your friends or relatives. Greeting card theaters are wonderful creations that make excellent gifts, creative instructional tools, and provide lots of fun for those who make or receive them.

Wright, Lyndie. *Toy Theaters*. New York: Franklin Watts, 1991.

Guignol

Pulcinello came to France along with the rest of the *commedia dell'arte* and made his usual raucous impression, becoming Polichinelle. A silk worker from Lyon named Laurent Mourguet changed all that in 1810 with his invention of Guignol. According to anecdotes, a friend saw the puppet's antics and exclaimed, "*C'est guignolant!*" (It's a scream!) And Guignol had his name.

In the early nineteenth century, France was in a recession, and the silk industry was severely depressed. M. Mourguet, a silk worker with ten children to feed, thought he would become a dentist. However, people were so fearful of having their teeth drawn that M. Mourguet began to preface his dentistry with puppet plays. At first, he drew on Polichinelle and the other members of the *commedia dell'arte*. But M. Mourguet's Lyonnaise temperament asserted itself, and a true French character emerged. After the comment of his friend, Guignol had his name at last.

Like Mr. Punch, Guignol has a number of standard plays and a host of supporting characters to assist him in his rambunctiousness. (*See* Punch and Judy.) Of these, the best known are his long-suffering wife, Madelon; his best friend, Gnaffron; Gnaffron's wife; and a policeman. Guignol is a man of the people: shrewd, resisting authority, and eager to depress pomposity. He is goodhearted but also as inclined to violence as Mr. Punch is. He became so popular that he replaced Polichinelle and has become the puppet character of France. Soldiers on the way to the Crimean War insisted on having a puppet troupe accompany them on ships as they made their way to the battlefield.

If you go to Paris, marionette and Guignol theaters are plentiful. Bil Baird reports seeing a Guignol play in the 1950s where the children shouted the responses to the dialogue as it was being spoken! Truly, Guignol is a most beloved character.

Baird, Bil. *The Art of the Puppet*. New York: Macmillan, 1965.
Bell, John. *Strings, Hands, Shadows: A Modern Puppet History*. Detroit: The Detroit Institute of Arts, 2000.

Hair and Wigs

A wig is a covering for the head made to resemble hair. Wigs can be made of a variety of substances: yarn, fur, feathers, or anything that will give the representation of hair to the puppet and to the audience. Wigs need not be realistic, therefore, but they do need to remind the members of the audience of human hair.

Traditionally, a wig is made from some substance and sewn onto a cap or some sort of backing which is then glued to the puppet. This is the usual way a doll's wig is made, and puppetry sometimes follows doll making in technique. Fur can also be used for a man's wig with the leather cut to the shape of the head and glued on.

Since the advent of the Muppets, puppeteers have felt a greater freedom to create puppets more widely and wildly. The use of felt, foam rubber, chenille sticks and feathers has opened a wider world of puppet creation for puppet makers. Whether you are making a wacky puppet, a fantastic puppet, or a realistic

"Miss Lucy," a rod puppet with a head made from a stuffed brown paper bag. The hair is made of curled paper strips.

one, the sky's the limit. You can go wherever your imagination can take you with puppet creation.

First, think about your puppet's character. Is it serious or zany? Is it young or old? What will it be doing in your puppet play, or will it be a general character you can insert into many types of plays? As with eyes, accessories, and clothing, the hair for your puppet should emphasize and build the character your audience sees.

Next, try to find the material you need to complete that character. You may have to try many different kinds of materials before finding just what you want. For that reason, you should have many different types of materials available for making hair, or else plan to make many trips to the hobby stores for materials!

You may need to become a junk shopper, thrift store habitué, and yard sale expert. These are the places you are likely to find the leftovers which will be just right for you: old jewelry and clothing and sometimes even the fake fur you need to complete an outfit.

After finding the right substance for your puppet's hair, you will need to attach it to the puppet's head. You can make a traditional cap and attach that to the puppet's head. The advantage of this sort of wig is that it is removable. If you use a lightweight adhesive or spirit gum, you can switch the wigs from head to head and have many different kinds of puppets for many different roles.

You can also attach the yarn, feathers, or other substance strand by strand using a glue gun. While this may seem to be more time consuming, you can work right on the puppet and achieve a more natural effect. Remember to watch those fingers for burns!

Making a Yarn Wig for a Puppet

MATERIALS

- Yarn sufficient to make the hair (two skeins of yarn in the color you want)
- The toe of a lightweight sock or stocking in a color to match the wig or the skin color of the puppet to use as a base
- Darning egg or form to support the base
- Needle, thread to match the yarn
- Scissors
- Thick craft glue or a glue gun and glue sticks
- Hair accessories

ASSEMBLY

1. Fit the sock or stocking over the head of the puppet, and trim away any unnecessary part.

2. If you want, you can hem the edge of the stocking base cap so it won't fray. Use a darning egg or form to support the cap while you are constructing the wig.

3. Measure the length of the hair for bangs or front hair and the hair which hangs down in the back.

4. Use a cardboard gauge to correctly measure the yarn. Wind about 20 strands for a small head, about 30 strands for a wider head for this portion of the wig.

5. Remove the yarn from the gauge and pin or fasten it roughly into place on the stocking base cap for sewing.

6. Sew the yarn into place on the cap, remembering the hair style you are making for your puppet.

7. Measure the side hair on the puppet.

8. Repeat steps 3–5 for the side hair.

9. Using needle and thread, finish styling the hair for your puppet.

10. Attach any accessories which will help make the hair appropriate for your puppet's character.

11. Attach the wig to the puppet using the appropriate glue or cement. When using spirit gum, remember that the wigs can come off just as with real actors!

Ackley, Edith Flack. *Marionettes: Easy to Make! Fun to Use!* New York: Lippincott, 1929.
Fling, Helen. *Marionettes: How to Make and Work Them.* New York: Dover, 1973.

Hamburger Box Puppets

Hamburger box puppets are big-mouth junk puppets made from those ubiquitous Styrofoam hamburger or take-out boxes. (*See* Mouth Puppets; Junk Puppets.) If you have ever held such a box with the hinge in your hand with your thumb on the bottom and the rest of your fingers on the top, you will have noticed that the box "talks" with no effort whatsoever. All you need is to decorate it, and you have a great junk puppet and a wonderful craft for kids.

One of the problems to overcome in working such puppets is keeping the fingers firmly anchored on the box. If you don't have something to hold the box in place, it will slip out of your hand after one or two "yacks." Try gluing pieces of fine-grade sandpaper on top and bottom to give the fingers some traction, or create straps with strips of plastic or sturdy paper held in place with brads. If you want to use this as a craft for younger children, though, choose the sandpaper; it's safer.

All you need to create this puppet is a bunch of small take-out boxes which you may be able to get free of charge from an obliging restaurateur. In addition, you will need lots of decorations: squares, circles, and triangles cut from colored paper; body parts, such as eyes, noses, and mouths, precut and ready to paste on; scraps of notions; bits of cloth and felt; chenille sticks; and strips of colored paper that can be bent into springy shapes. If you can afford it, have pom-poms, ice cream spoons, the bowls from plastic spoons, Styrofoam packing peanuts, fake fur, colored wire, and anything else which will add to the personality of these puppet creations.

Have some samples made up. You might even have several techniques on a single box. Once the kids see what you are doing, they will run with the ideas and come up with some great creations. If you want younger children to participate, have them come at a separate craft time. Have lots of things premade. Cut out eyes, noses, mouths from colored paper. Have cotton balls or fake fur bits for hair. And remember to put those grip strips on the boxes for easier handling!

To make a body for your Hamburger Box Puppet, fasten a strip of Velcro fastener to the box. Fasten the other half to a sock or long-sleeved glove. Make sure that the glove or sock fastens to both halves of the hamburger box. Decorate the body of your puppet in any way that enhances the character of your puppet. Now put on a play with your great hamburger box puppets!

Renfro, Nancy. *Make Amazing Puppets*. Santa Barbara, CA: Learning Works, 1979.
Renfro, Nancy. *Puppets for Play Production*. New York: Funk & Wagnalls, 1969.

Hand Puppets

The hand puppet generally fits the hand with one to three fingers in the head and remaining fingers and the thumb forming the arms. Puppets can be created from gloves themselves with a head placed on the center finger and the other fingers forming arms. (*See* Glove Puppets.) The hand puppet is visible from the waist up, although it can be equipped with feet. Some interesting variations have taken a glove, added from one to three more fingers, and created insect puppets on top of the glove.

While all puppets are manipulated by hand, only those puppets which sit on the hand should be called "hand puppets." Hand puppets are, technically, glove puppets or they can be called fist puppets in England. (*See* Fist Puppets.)

In fact, the hand itself can become a puppet, developing a character and telling a story. (*See* Hands as Puppets.) All of the actions and characteristics displayed by the conventional hand puppet can and should be displayed by the puppet hand. It is a wonderful way to begin puppetry manipulation, gain ideas, and make the use of a conventional puppet more accurate for the stage.

Portability

The hand puppet has its origins in antiquity, although it is possibly younger than its marionette cousin. The advantage of the hand puppet lies in its portability and the ability of one person to tell an entire tale with only two hands.

Marionettes take space, equipment, and several people to operate the sometimes-complicated string-manipulated puppets. But hand puppets can be folded away along with their stage and carried in a box. One traveling puppeteer can manipulate the puppets and tell tales to the delight of audiences everywhere.

Chinese bag puppet theaters are one type of this ultra-mobile puppet form. (*See* Chinese Bag Puppet Theaters.) A bag is tied around the puppeteer's feet and stretched upward until the theater stage sits on his head. The puppeteer leans back against a wall for stability and then manipulates the tiny puppets above his head as the show goes on. The whole theater can fit into a box, be carried easily by one person traveling from place to place, and be performed in marketplaces and village centers.

Punch and Judy shows are another form of compact puppetry. A few characters tell a wide variety of tales, and the performer can stay in one place or travel around the countryside. The whole theater can be set up in minutes.

History

Hand puppets were known in Rome, India, and China in antiquity. Competing with the grander marionette theaters, hand puppets were relegated to the masses: to marketplaces and fairs, to religious holidays and special occasions when people would come together to celebrate in an informal atmosphere.

Hand puppeteers were also of the people and were quick to pick up on local scandal and gossip, learn which officials could be safely satirized and which should be left alone. Since all villages had similar daily dramas, the puppeteers could easily poke fun at village stereotypes with the certainty that their audience would know someone like the character they were using and laugh uproariously.

Hand puppets were not only ephemeral but vulgar, so they escaped the notice that their grander marionette cousins attracted. It was easy enough for the puppeteer to pack up and leave town when things got tough; everything one needed to perform a puppet play could be packed into a box and loaded onto a wagon or even a hand cart.

After the fall of Rome, all forms of theater disappeared, including the puppet theater. Without the patronage of the wealthy, marionette theaters could not survive. Furthermore, the newly formed Christian church did not look with favor on theater of any sort since it smacked of idolatry. However, hand puppeteers survived as traveling performers. They disappeared from written chronicles after the fall of Rome, but reappear in the background of illuminated manuscripts from the fourteenth century. They form such a natural and expected part of the background in the illustration that they must have been well-known forms of entertainment at fairs and during religious holidays.

Gradually, the marionette theater made its reappearance, first in the churches, then in the marketplace, and finally in their own theaters. The first known picture of Russian hand puppets dates from 1636 and shows a puppeteer like the Chinese bag puppeteer at a country fair. There is a dancing bear in the background, and several urchins in the foreground are watching the show. As usual, the hand puppet is in its element among the people at some lively gathering.

As time went on, various countries began to develop distinct styles of hand puppetry, usually derived from the commedia dell'arte of Italy. The favorite character was Pulchinello who became Punch in England, Polichinelle and then Guignol in France, and Kasperle in Germany. So popular were these figures that theaters were either sent along with the military or were created for military units as they went off to war. (*See* Guignol; Punch and Judy.)

With the rise of the modern era, the hand puppet came into its own. Because a hand puppet could be made of many found objects, giving rise to the term "junk puppet," it allowed or encouraged artists to create puppets of new and intriguing form.

Hand puppets, by their mobility and simplicity, create an atmosphere of intimacy that marionettes cannot. This makes them perfect for television. A whole range of puppets and puppet shows blossomed—first on radio with Edgar Bergen and Charlie McCarthy recreating some of their vaudeville routines. Later on, television hosted *Kukla, Fran, and Ollie*; *Beany and Cecil*; and the *Howdy Doody Show*.

It was the hand puppet, and its extension the ventriloquist's dummy, that gained the hearts of the viewers through the ability to create endearing characters and the feeling of intimacy. The Kuklapolitans and Beany and Cecil caught the fancy of television audiences, and individual performers like Shari Lewis, Senior Wencis, Topo Gigio, and Waylon Flowers and Madame drew viewers into the private worlds they created. People got to know and love these characters which furthered an interest in adult puppet theater.

The Muppets, creations of Jim Henson and his crew of talented puppeteers and puppet makers, bridged the gap between puppets as theater for children and puppets as cabaret theater for adults by being cute and satirical at the same time. Their snappy patter, coupled with wild colors and often zany appearance, created puppet theater which could be appreciated by both children and adults. "The Muppet Show" exemplified this, being a weekly variety show with a continuing storyline and a continuing cast of characters laboring mightily to put on a show each week in an old theater.

Today the most popular use for hand puppets is as a teaching aid. In libraries, schools and religious institutions everywhere, hand puppets are being used to connect children and books, teach religious stories, show young children how to brush their teeth, and bring the delight of creative theater to a wide range of children and adults.

Construction

Hand puppets construction can be simple and basic, with an almost minimalist puppet consisting of the hand and a head placed upon the index finger. They also can be complex, with elaborate costuming which conforms to the story and helps set its mood.

Hand puppets can begin at the minimalist stage and work up to puppets of great beauty and complexity. A step up from the head-and-hand puppet is the head with a simple drape of cloth for the body. That is the hand puppet at its most basic: a head presenting the character of the puppet plus a body. The body need not be decorated in any way that supports the character, although it should not detract from it.

I have two wooden-headed, hand-carved hand puppets from Portugal — a fisherman and a clown — which illustrate this example. Each is filled with character which resides in the face of the puppet. Neither body is dressed in a costume representing the occupation of the puppet. Instead, the selection of the materials making the body reinforces the sturdy practicality of the fisherman and the vibrancy of the clown. The mit-shaped hands of the puppets are part of the body and fit over the finger and thumb easily.

The eye is drawn to the faces of these puppets because the simplicity of the body allows the eye to rest on the face rather than be distracted from it. So when you make an all-purpose hand puppet, take great care with the face. Make sure that it expresses what you want of the puppet's character and that the body of the puppet does not detract or distract from that.

The hand puppet's body is necessary but secondary to the face and head. If you can find a general sort of material which will provide a great background for your puppet's face, as the Portuguese puppet makers did, then use it for the body of your puppet. You will be able to dress the puppet up or down as you wish. If the basic body material reflects the character of the puppet in a general way, all will be well.

In making the body, remember to provide plenty of room to put the puppet on without a struggle. Don't follow the contour of the hand and arm too closely or the body of the puppet may be too tight to put on quickly and easily. A baggy body is better than a close-fitting one.

Hands can be attached to the body, but your puppet need not have hands. The imagination of the audience will supply the hands. So don't feel badly if you can't find just the right hands for your basic puppet. Make the entire body of the same fabric, and don't worry about the hands. (*See* Hands for some further suggestions.)

Traditionally, hand puppets in Europe rarely have feet, but those in Asia frequently do. This creates a question: Should you put feet on the hand puppets you make?

It may not make any difference to you. After all, a hand puppet is seen chiefly from the waist up, so why have feet? In that case, the choice is easy: When you make your puppets, they will not have feet.

On the other hand, you may feel that the design of a puppet requires feet because of its character or the design of the puppet's costume. In this case, remember that the feet will be attached in front of the puppet glove and will not be manipulated by anything. Manipulation of the feet begins to take your puppet into bunraku territory and may require a rethinking of your puppet's design. (*See* Bunraku.)

You will also have to hold the puppet higher to let the feet be seen. Either that or the feet will flop or dangle in front as Mr. Punch's do.

Two excellent pictures of puppets with feet are on the cover of *Puppeteer* by Kathryn Lasky and on page 37 of David Currell's *An Introduction to Puppets and Puppet-Making*. A Chinese-style puppet with feet is seen on pages 8–9 of Meryl Doney's *Puppets* from the World Crafts series. A picture from a bunraku performance is shown on page 20 of Doney's book.

One final word about the basic puppet. Professional puppeteers hang their puppets upside down from a ring on the playboard shelf inside the puppet theater and slip the puppets on like gloves. The ring is attached at the bottom of the puppet costume and is not seen by the audience. When the puppet is removed, it is hung back in its place on the playboard. This allows easy putting on and taking off of the puppets, although practice is needed to make the actions smooth. Hanging them in the same place each time helps to find them in the reduced light of backstage.

If you make the body of the puppet flare out at a given circumference, you can find a metal ring in a craft store which will fit the bottom of the puppet body and facilitate putting the puppet on and taking it off. The ring will hold the bottom of the puppet body in place at a given flare so you won't have to struggle getting the puppet off and on.

You know, now, that a hand puppet consists of a head and a body, but what about costumes? With puppets, less is more, and caricature is the word. You must decide: Is this puppet to be a generic one or a puppet dedicated to a specific play? If it is to be generic — that is, if it is a general character to be used in many plays — consider making the body of the puppet as nonspecific as possible. A young girl puppet can be dressed up to be a princess by adding a crown and perhaps a single piece of glittery jewelry. A young boy puppet can become a business man by adding a tie, a prince by adding a crown and a cape, and a farmer by adding a straw hat.

Think about making the generic outer body over a muslin underbody. Although you would do so for a more-complex hand puppet, there are several advantages to having a muslin underbody for your generic puppet. First, the underbody gets the wear and tear of abrasion against your hand and the stress of being pulled on and off. Second, the ring mentioned previously is attached to the underbody; if you like, the outer body can float free, although it would be far better to have it attached to the underbody to prevent accidents in the placement of the costume. Third, if you want to change costumes or outer bodies, it will be easier to remove and replace them if you have a fixed underbody. The outer bodies become like costumes and can be changed at will.

Making a more complex puppet, dedicated to a specific puppet play, requires some planning. After you have decided on how to tell your story and how many puppets you will need, you can construct your puppets to specific drawings. Make sketches of each puppet. The sketches need not be elaborate, and you may find yourself deviating from the sketch, but it gives you a point of focus and a place to start.

The heads should be made first, especially if you want to have a uniform appearance to them. Make underbodies for each with rings attached. Make sure that the underbodies slip on and off easily. Then construct the costumes and sew them in place, attaching them to the underbody ring to prevent accidents in placing the costumes. Since you will not have to worry about undressing these puppets or changing their costumes, you can sew the costumes directly onto the underbody. Make sure that the costumes move easily and fit well without impeding the movement of the hand and fingers. Finally, add the wigs and hats, if any. Again, check to make sure that the accessories don't inhibit the puppet's movements in any way.

Getting the costumes just right may take some time. If you want a quick overview of getting a puppet play up and ready for presentation, read Lasky's *Puppeteer.* It is most illuminating and will give you an idea of the time involved for getting a play together.

After you make your puppets, make loose muslin bags for them. The puppets will hang upside down by their rings with the bags around them and be kept clean and free of dust and dirt. On a tag affixed to the bag, write the name of the puppet as well as a photograph of it, its play, and, if necessary, the act of the play when the puppet appears. That way, you can have all the puppets for one play grouped together in order and ready to go.

Making a hand puppet can be as simple or as complex as you choose to make it. Whatever you choose to do with your puppet planning, remember to use and enjoy them! Your hand puppets will give you and your audiences hours, perhaps years, of pleasure.

Manipulation

Manipulation of hand puppets is the method by which the hand puppet is made to imitate the actions of living people and, through those actions, tell a story. These movements are more akin to mime than to acting, and the use of gestures is more important than speech. In fact, it should be possible to tell a simple story with puppets without using words at all.

Practice performing simple actions with your hands or your puppets as a part of your regular rehearsal routine. If possible, do this practice on a daily basis, just as if you were practicing an instrument. Your instruments are your hands, and they will make your puppets come alive. By practicing with them regularly, you will improve your puppetry technique and discover what your hand puppets are capable of doing or not doing.

Movement of hands and puppets should be kept simple and restrained. Although there are times when a puppet will make broad, exclamatory gestures, overstatement is the hallmark of the beginning puppeteer. Very little movement is needed for the puppet to tell its story. In addition to simplifying the movements of your hand puppets, you need to know how your puppet's actions are perceived by the audience. How does a puppet that has no visible legs walk or run across the stage? How does it show emotion? How do you show a puppet asleep, eating, or performing any one of the normal, everyday actions of normal life? Begin by observing people as they walk, sit, stand, run, look around. Your task will be to simplify the movements of people and transpose those movements to your puppets.

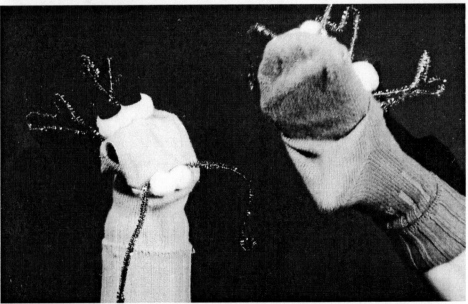

Opposite and Above: Hand puppets. Morris the Dragon approaches his friend Boris the Dragon with a suggestion, but Boris is not impressed. Morris pleads, then loses patience.

Start with your bare hands and a large mirror in which you can watch their movements. Decide on a task: showing your hand asleep, waking up to the alarm, yawning and going off to wash and dress. With your hand drooping slightly, pantomime breathing deeply and perhaps snoring. The alarm sounds! Your hand shows shock and surprise at being awakened, then turns off the alarm with a sharp motion. Have your hand yawn, start to fall back asleep, wake back up by shaking itself, then walk off stage toward the bathroom. You can add any other small events such as scratching yourself, sneezing — anything that will complete the picture of waking up.

Now think of other activities which are a part of your daily routine: taking a bath or a shower, cooking a meal, working in the garden, walking the dog. Keep it short and simple at first, then work up to longer scenes. The idea here is to sharpen your pantomime skills, to discover how a hand might tell a story with these basic actions. It will also give you a chance to discover how to do something. How does a handless puppet like a hand scratch itself? How does it dry off after a bath? Do you need to have a prop, or can you accomplish the movement on your own with just your hand?

Another thing to watch out for is hand-arm position. Watch your hand and arm in the mirror. Which position shows your hand to be most awake? To have the best eye contact with the audience? What happens when your hand-arm begins to droop or the arm to curve? As you walk your arm across the stage, how does your body need to move in order to keep your hand's posture established? How does your hand-arm need to turn in order to continue walking straight across the stage?

As you work with your hands or your puppets, be gentle with yourself. Try just a few things: walking across a stage from one side to the other; entering the stage area, looking around, then walking off the other side; walking to center stage, being surprised by something, then turning around to hurry off the way you came in. Learning how to turn around on the stage and head back the way you came is an important move and you alone can decide how you can do it best. Switch back and forth so that both hands receive an equal workout.

As you get to feel comfortable with your one hand on stage, transfer what you have learned to a single puppet on stage. Is there any difference between your hand alone and your hand with a puppet on it? What do you do differently? What is uncomfortable and needs to be changed? What do you do well?

After you become comfortable with a single hand, add the other hand. Have your two hands meet, pass one another on the stage, and walk off stage. Can you do this without strangling yourself? Can you actually *get* to the other side of the stage? Or do you need to make some modification in your actions, perhaps let one hand go down a set of stairs while the other hand goes off stage?

Try out some simple skits with your "hand" puppets. Have your two hands meet, and have one hand something to the other. Have your hands act as if they are meeting one another after a long absence. Have one hand cry on the shoulder of the other. Is the other hand comfortable with this or not? How about an argument? Your hands could come on stage with one carrying something the other wants. They greet each other, argue over the object, then either make up or go off in a huff (or a hurry, depending on how you write your skit). After you are satisfied that your hands can do the acting, try the actions with puppets. Again, note any changes which occur when switching from hands to puppets. These little improv skits are just like ones actors use to hone their skills.

Create your own set of improv skits for your puppets, and keep them on cards where you can record comments if you wish. Check with a puppetry book such as Engler and Fijan's *Making Puppets Come Alive* for additional skits and pointers. And remember that regular practice will steadily improve your puppetry skills.

Baird, Bil. *The Art of the Puppet.* New York: Macmillan, 1965.
Bell, John. *Strings, Hands, Shadows: A Modern Puppet History.* Detroit: The Detroit Institute of Arts, 2000.
Currell, David. *An Introduction to Puppets & Puppet-Making.* Edison, NJ: Chartwell Books, 1992, p. 37.
Doney, Meryl. *Puppets.* New York: Franklin Watts, 1995.
Engler, Larry, and Carol Fijan. *Making Puppets Come Alive.* New York: Taplinger, 1973.
Hunt, Tamara, and Nancy Renfro. *Puppetry in Early Childhood Education.* Austin, TX: Nancy Renfro Studios, 1982.
Lade, Roger. *The Most Excellent Book of How to Be a Puppeteer.* Brookfield, CT: Copper Beech Books, 1996.
Lasky, Kathryn. *Puppeteer.* New York: Macmillan, 1985.
Watson, Nancy Cameron. *The Little Pigs' Puppet Book.* Boston: Little, Brown, 1990.

Hands

Puppet hands are present to augment the character of a puppet, not to carry things. They gesture, point, perhaps even wave, considering the action of the play or the character of the puppet, but they need not be realistic. They can add to the character of the puppet by extension, adding refined hands to a princess, huge hands to a giant, or thin, twisted hands to an evil villain. No matter how they are constructed, though, the hands are of secondary interest to the face and clothing of a puppet. It is more important to notice the face and dress; hands and feet will be sketched in by the imagination of the audience.

Hands for puppets may be the most challenging element of puppet construction. Beginners feel that puppet hands must be realistic, but making truly realistic hands is quite a challenge requiring excellent sculpting skills. Puppet hands need not be realistic. Remember, caricature and exaggeration are the hallmarks of puppet design.

Many traditional or ethnic puppets do not even have hands. The arm ends in a stump even on highly decorated puppets. This is especially true of the puppets of India.

Mitten Hands

The next step up in sophistication is the mitten hand. At its most basic, the hand is shaped like a mitten with the thumb protruding and all fingers together in a unit. It is usually made of felt or perhaps cardboard or some stiff material and sewn into the body of the puppet.

A variant on the mitten hand would be a simple object like a bead attached to the end of the arm. This would be good on a junk puppet, a puppet that represents a child's toy, or an experimental puppet where everything is stylized. (*See* Junk Puppets.)

Another stylized hand good for a junk puppet can be made from a plastic fork. The tines become the fingers; one outer tine can be trimmed short to represent the thumb. The handle of the fork becomes the rod which manipulates the hand and arm.

There are many variations on the mitten hand which suggest fingers but are not truly articulated or sculpted and are, therefore, still suggestive rather than realistic. For a cloth puppet, a soft sculptured hand is a next step up in reality. Begin with a mitten hand, sewn in two layers and lightly stuffed. Then carefully stitch in marks to indicate the location of thumb and fingers. The hand is sewn into the body of the puppet but does not have the fingers reaching up into the hand.

Sculpted Hands

Hands can also be made of polymer clay or wood and sculpted in a basic sort of way. For the clay, mold it into a general hand shape with the fingers either extended or clinched. The "fingers" can even be formed to hold something, such as a wizard's wand, a soldier's spear, or a farmer's hoe. Use modeling tools to etch in the outlines of fingers and thumb. Remember to score a ridge at the end of the arm to facilitate attachment of the arm to the puppet.

Wooden hands are a bit more complicated. Choose some easy-to-work wood such as balsa of ½" thickness, and saw the hand shape from the wood. Then use a rasp or file to complete the indication of fingers and thumb. Again, the fingers are not detailed but suggested. The marks used to suggest the fingers need not even break through the wood if it is thick enough, but can just be "Vs" in the wood. The hand basically stays a mitten. If the hand is broad and flat enough, the shape of the hand can be painted on top of the outlined shape.

Molded Hands

Hands made of tissue-mâché have a greater possibility for articulation. (*See* Papier-Mâché.) The tissue is primed with glue and folded to make fingers and thumb. More tissue is covered with glue and folded around the fingers to make the palm of the hand. The fingers can be formed into a curved shape over a tube and allowed to dry. Remember to trim the fingers and thumb to the proper size before allowing them to dry. When they dry, it will take a saw to cut through the fingers! So plan in advance.

Hands can be molded over an armature made of wire and covered with Sculpy or papier-mâché mash. The armature can be a simple one made of single strands of wire bundled together or a more complex form for greater articulation and detail. (*See* Armatures; Papier-Mâché.)

For a more elaborate form, create the outline of a hand. Place your hand on the block and trace around it; then hammer nails into the wood along the traced outline. Wind fine wire gently around the nails, leaving a twist at the wrist area for attaching the hand to the puppet body. Remove the resulting armature carefully from the wood block. Create a reinforcing twist of wire at the upper knuckle area and middle of the palm. Apply the Sculpy or papier-mâché mash over this framework, gently covering everything. Leave as is or finish by incising the fingernails and a few wrinkle lines in the Sculpy or papier-mâché mash with a modeling tool or an orange stick. Cure by allowing the papier-mâché to air dry, or follow the directions on the Sculpy package. (Feet can be molded in the same way.)

Remember that whatever material you use, the hands must not be too heavy or they will drag down the cloth of the puppet body and be extremely hard to manipulate. The best thing you can do for the hands of your puppet is to learn to use them expressively in mimetic gesture.

Currell, David. *An Introduction to Puppets & Puppet-Making*. Edison, NJ: Chartwell Books, 1992.

Fling, Helen. *Marionettes: How to Make and Work Them*. New York: Dover, 1973.

Flower, Cedric, and Alan Fortney. *Puppets, Methods and Materials*. Worcester, MA: Davis Publ., 1983.

Hands as Puppets

The simplest puppet to make is the hand itself with no adornment. (*See also* Fist Puppet.) If you want to make it fancy, add a pair of Peepers or other eyes. Gloves can be worn if you wish. Garden gloves in colors or patterns may add character to your hand as a puppet. If you enjoy this idea, longer white cotton gloves can be dyed in colors which will emphasize the character of the puppet hand. As with the fist puppet, you can add wigs, hats, or any other accessory which will enhance the puppet's character. But your hand/glove puppet is best left fairly unadorned with details filled in by the audience's imagination.

Practice with your hand as a puppet. This will enhance all your work in puppetry. All alone, have your hand walk, sing, dance, sit, stand, and do any of the many ordinary acts of daily life. Have your puppet hand enter a stage, walk across the stage, bow, and exit; have it enter, look around, "find" a chair, sit down in it, stand up, and exit. Add your other hand and have the two interact. You will find that hands as puppets can do one thing ordinary hand puppets have difficulty with: picking up things. This adds many possibilities to your work. By practic-

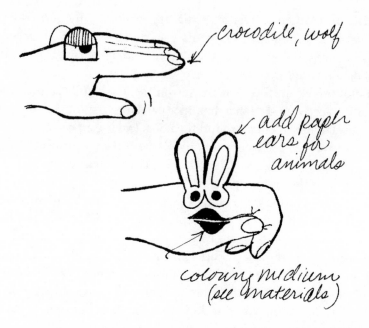

crocodile, wolf

add paper ears for animals

coloring medium (see materials)

The hand as a puppet from Nancy Renfro. Facial features either drawn right on the hand or made from simple paper cut outs and attached to the hand. Wigs, scarves, hats, jewelry, and other props can also be added to a "hand" puppet, but they need to be securely attached.

ing these simple but important exercises, the puppeteer can make the puppet hand come alive.

http://hobeyford.freeservers.com/peepers/ This is the site of Hobey Ford's invention: Peepers. These great puppets are a pair of eyes on a connecting "U" which can turn any hand into a puppet.

Hanging Stages

Hanging stages can be made of cloth, paper, or corrugated bulletin board paper. They can be hung from ceiling tile supports and rolled up out of the way when not in use. If you have access to an old window shade that's wide enough, you might even press it into service!

The following instructions presume the presence of a ceiling tile support grid which will allow you to hang lightweight materials. If you don't have those supports, try another style of theater or ask your maintenance personnel about methods of anchoring the upper rod to the ceiling. You need not attach the stage permanently. It can be put up and taken down for each performance and rolled up for storage.

The great thing about a hanging stage is that it can be just about whatever you would like as a two-dimensional screen design for your puppetry. You can have a castle, Jack's beanstalk, a magic tree, a giant flower, a gypsy caravan, or a traditional theater. You can have a single opening or you can have several so that puppets can pop up unexpectedly in surprising places.

When constructing a hanging stage, minimal tools and simple construction methods are used. Use materials that do not require hemming or finishing off. Apply decorative effects with a glue gun or some other simple method. Use scraps, cast-offs, leftovers, and recyclables wherever possible. This will be a great example for the kids!

The worst thing about the hanging stage is that it is just a screen. Children can run behind the stage and see what you are doing. If the parents or care givers will not supervise them, this can be a real drawback. However, if your audiences are pretty well behaved and you are short on space and money, a hanging stage can be a great way to get started in puppetry.

CONSIDERATIONS

The first step in creating your stage is to choose a design and draw it on grid paper, if necessary, so that you know exactly how big the stage will be and where all the openings (if you have more than one) will lie. Ideally, the stage will be a large rectangle of paper or cloth. Anything in the design which sticks out — the turrets of a castle or a nest on the branch of a tree — will fit within that rectangle. If you decide to let those projections stick out beyond the rectangle, you will have to be concerned with support and reinforcement. The second question will be: will it roll up easily and safely without tearing or damaging those projections? If you are using a window shade, does the mechanism work? How thick can the decorations be? Consider all these things when designing your hanging stage.

MATERIALS

- Two 1" dowels, at least 36" in length (If you plan on a wider stage, check with a lumber yard to see what is available to make the supports for your stage.)
- Cord for hanging your stage to the ceiling and securing the stage when it is rolled up
- Any hanging hardware necessary to attach the stage to the ceiling
- Paper or material, at least 36" wide and 8' long
- Fusible Pellon interfacing material to reinforce fabric and prevent fraying
- Scissors
- Pencil
- Yardstick or measuring tape
- Staple gun and staples

- Glue gun and glue sticks
- Paint, if necessary
- Other additional materials needed according to your design

ASSEMBLY

1. Draw your design on the paper or fabric. Locate the position of all openings in your design. Do not cut anything yet.

2. With assistance if necessary, loosely fasten the material to the upper rod or support and hang the material from the ceiling to make sure that all the holes are correct and that they can be reached easily by you. *Note*: You should not have to use a step stool to reach any of the openings when you are performing! That's just asking for trouble.

3. Roll up the material and mark the location of ties to secure the stage when it is not in use.

4. Unroll the material and cut out the openings. (If you are using fabric for the background material, first reinforce the openings with fusable Pellon. Then cut out the openings.)

5. Decorate your background to match your drawing. Remember to use simple materials and basic fastening methods. Paint and the glue gun should star here.

6. Let any wet materials dry thoroughly.

7. Turn under any raw edges, and firmly attach the material to the rods using the staple gun.

8. Hang the stage and make any adjustments necessary. Then get ready to enjoy your stage!

Hanging Toy Theaters

A toy theater is a small box — anything from a shoe box to a small kitchen appliance box will do — which contains all the elements for a puppet play: curtain, scenery, and actors. This is theater in miniature, and traditionally, toy theaters replicated a real stage show. Used in Victorian parlors and nurseries, toy theater was a way to introduce children and adults to the joys of theater while still at home. Originally an entertainment for adults, plays and pantomimes were soon being written for children to present. This theater form remained widely popular in England until World War II when most of the original engraving plates were destroyed by the bombing of England. A hanging toy theater is one that hangs around the puppeteer's neck.

The idea for a hanging toy theater came from Edie O'Dor of the Playful Otter Puppet Company (North Carolina). A hanging toy theater presents the advantage of mobility while operating the theater at the same time. Puppeteers who like to work Renaissance fairs and other public events could use the hanging toy theater to wander around the fair and bring entertainment to greater numbers of people. It might be a real selling point to the organizers of the event as well.

The hanging toy theater also provides freedom for the hands and a fairly stable working area while using a toy theater since balancing a toy theater on one's lap while operating the puppets and scenery is not desirable. If you are working with a circle of children and do not have easy access to a table, hanging the theater around your neck presents a good alternative.

CONSIDERATIONS

To make a toy theater that will hang around the neck, you will have to consider containing all elements of the theater—including scene changes and so on—within the box of the theater so it can be easily switched around without too much trouble. Here are some questions to ask yourself:

Are you going to present a single play, then wander about to another location? Or will you be in one place for a couple of shows before you move on?

Is the hanging toy theater to be used in a school or library situation?

Will it be used by you and then available to others to experiment and play with?

Where will the theater hang on your body? Where will the puppets be operated: from above or below the theater?

Will this performance be for a seated audience or a standing one?

Here are some additional things to consider. If you are planning to present more than one play as you wander, you will need to plan a storage area in the back of the theater. This may also require a thicker box and a simplification of the stage settings which you use. You will have to experiment to see.

Using a single curtain will reduce the need for storage space in your theater. If you plan to announce the coming play with a sign on the curtain, you can produce two plays and have an announcement for each on either side of the stage curtain. However, you will need to be careful to have the correct play announcement showing when inserting the curtain card!

Usually, a traditional toy theater has an open top to make scenery changes. The puppets are inserted from the side or from the top. With a hanging toy theater, you may want to change the scenery from the top and insert the puppets from the bottom. It depends on what you are physically comfortable with. The following directions are for a traveling hanging toy theater with room for storage in the back.

Materials

- 1 small- to medium-sized sturdy box deep enough to store scenery changes and large enough to have a good viewing area (If the box is too large, it will be clumsy; if the box is too small, it will not have enough storage space.)
- Pencils
- Ruler
- Craft knife
- Scissors
- White glue or hot glue gun
- Staples and staple gun
- Rope, ribbon, or cord (to hang the box around your neck)
- ½" electrical tape to bind off the cord
- Paints and paint brushes or markers
- Poster board or foam core board
- Skewers for each puppet and at least 7 dowels that are ⅛" in diameter and 3" longer than the width of the box to support the scenery and act as controls for the puppets (If your box is greater than a 12" skewer, use all dowels.)

Assembly

1. Remove the top from your box if it has one. Mark a rough square or rectangle at least 1" to 1½" wide on the front part of the box. This will become your proscenium arch area.
2. Design the front of your stage on the front of the box and remove the unnecessary center portion.
3. Decorate the front of the stage and the back of the box and allow any paint to dry.
4. Measure the side of the box and divide this measurement into fourths. Then measure and divide the back fourth into fifths with one mark at the very back of the box. (See step 5 and adjust marks throughout the side of the box if you feel there will not be enough room in the back quarter to comfortably hold everything. If there just isn't enough room, find a bigger box or eliminate one of the two scenery units. Storage is more important than elaborate scenery!)
5. Cut a notch at each quarter point, plus one at the very front for the curtain.

This will give you a place to hang two scenery units plus the backdrop at the third notch, assuming that you have room. (See step 4.)

6. Behind the third, or backdrop, notch, cut four more closely spaced notches with one at the very back of the box. This will hold the scenery for the second play, plus an envelope for the second play's puppets and a resting place for the curtain while the play is going on.

7. Using the poster board and paints or markers, design, draw, and color in the front curtain with play announcements (One on each side.).

8. Make the backdrop and scenery for two plays. Like the curtain, the backdrop will have designs on both sides and be reversed when the plays change.

9. Allow the theater and scenery to dry.

10. Make your puppets from poster board. Paint and cut them out.

11. Paint the puppet rods (either skewers or dowels) black.

12. When your puppets are dry, mount them on the black skewer or dowel rods.

13. Make the Pellon envelope

14. Cut 7 dowels so that they are 3" longer than the width of your box.

15. Mount the scenery, curtain, backdrop, and puppet envelope by stapling or gluing them to the dowels.

16. Hang the scenery, curtain, backdrop, and envelope to test the accuracy of the mountings.

17. If you want to make a facade which will rise above the top of the theater and hide the movement of your hands a bit, design the facade, make it from poster board or foam core board, and attach it now.

18. Find the halfway point on the sides of your theater. Measure 3" down and slightly in front of the middle point, and make a hole slightly larger than the diameter of your holding cord.

19. Paint and decorate the sides of your theater. Allow the theater to dry completely.

20. Measure from the hole on one side of the theater and around your neck to the hole on the other side of the theater. You will need help for this step. Add 6". This will be the rough length for the rope or cord which will hang the box around your neck.

21. Bind one end of the rope or cord with ½" electrical tape to prevent it from fraying.

22. Insert the rope into one hole from the outside. Tie a secure knot in the rope end and, holding the theater in its proper place, insert the rope into the opposite hole. Adjust the rope or cord for length (remember to stand up straight), mark the place with a pen line or bit of thread, and tie a knot in the rope or cord.

23. Cut the cord by its knot, leaving enough room to bind off this end of the cord with electrical tape.

24. Assemble your audience, hang and adjust your theater, and put on both of your plays!

A good addition to the hanging toy theater is a pocket for storing puppets. This pocket can be made from Pellon as follows:

1. Use the back of the toy theater as a pattern to cut two sheets of heavy Pellon or other heavy material. Trim the two pieces so they are slightly smaller than the back of the theater and won't show from the front.

2. Sew the two pieces of Pellon together around three sides, leaving one side open at the top to form the opening of the pocket.

3. To keep the pocket closed, glue Velcro buttons to the inside of the pocket with hot glue.

4. Glue the bottom piece of Pellon to the theater back using hot glue around all four sides of the pocket.

Wright, Lyndie. *Toy Theaters.* New York: Franklin Watts, 1991.

Hinges

Hinges are a fact of life in puppet making. Unless you have a stick puppet, you will need to make hinges to allow the puppet to move freely and expressively. These hinges need not be complicated, but you, as the puppet maker, should be aware of the kind of hinges that are needed in each particular situation and that are available for you to use.

Brad or Thread Hinges

The brad or thread hinge is usually used to join the upper and lower parts of limbs on a shadow puppet or jumping jack. For this hinge, there is usually no reinforcement, unless the puppet will get a great deal of use. In that case, a piece of strapping tape on the back of the limb portion would serve to reinforce the joint.

For a brad hinge, a hole is made in the two portions of the limb, the holes are lined up and the brad inserted and gently folded back. The tines of the brad are usually folded back again to make the tines fit within the confines of the puppet limb. The tines must be loose enough to permit easy moving of the limb portions.

This type of hinge can also be used to make a joint in the mouths of masks and puppets. The hinge in this case should be reinforced with clear strapping tape and perhaps even washers because the weight of the parts will add to the wear the hinge receives in use.

If the puppet is small or the use of a brass brad seems to be too obvious and out of harmony with the puppet's character, a thread hinge can be made. This is a loose loop of thread through two holes made in the puppets joint. While the joint will not be quite as flexible as the brad joint, it will be quite flexible as long as the joint is made loosely enough. Make a spacer of cardboard to hold the two parts of the limb apart and sew with a loose tension on your thread for no more than two rounds. Tie off and clip the threads close to the knot. Test for flexibility.

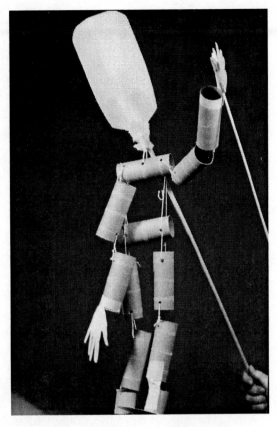

String hinges on a rod puppet control the height of the puppet while adding almost no weight. Paper tape hinges on the hand and neck allow movement.

Flexible Hinges

The flexible hinge is used not only for attaching rods to shadow puppets and some rod puppets but also for joints in some paper or light cardboard puppets. The flexible hinge is made with masking tape, paper tape, or paper and glue. Here's how: Take a 3" to 4" strip of masking tape which is 2" wide. Make a 1½" × 1" cut in one end of the tape. Press the two halves of the tape against the hand or foot to be manipulated. Make a "pinch" about a half inch long above the hand or foot. Wrap the other end of the tape around the end of the rod which will be doing the manipulating. This will leave a small, flexible hinge attaching the rod to the hand or foot and will make movement smooth and more natural.

A flexible hinge for a puppet can be used to hinge two pieces of paper or poster board together, or it can join two cardboard tubes to make a joint. In either case, the joint is made of a strip which forms the hinge and a piece which reinforces it. The hinge piece is cut to size, put in place, and tested. Does the joint move easily enough, or has it become bound in some way? When the joint has been adjusted and moves easily, it is reinforced with another strip. Remember that any kind of tape or paper and glue can be used as long as it is sturdy enough to stand up to the wear and tear it will receive.

A cloth puppet can have hinges sewn right into the material or body of the puppet. A cloth marionette needs to have an unstuffed strip of fabric joining the upper and lower half of the limb. This can either be a strip of fabric tape, or it can be an unstuffed portion of the body of the puppet. As you stuff the limb and come to the joint, stop and sew the material closed. Leave a small portion (usually about ½") of empty fabric, then sew the material on the other side of the joint. Proceed with stuffing the limb as before. This type of hinge can also be used at the waist if you want the marionette to bow or bend.

Double Eye Hinges

Another kind of hinge is used to join heavier materials together yet still have them move. It is a variant on the familiar hook-and-eye closure except that there are two eyes in use at right angles to one another. When forming the limbs of a marionette, an eye-shaped screw is inserted into plastic wood or screwed into the wood of the limb. The two eyes are joined together by opening one and closing it around the other eye or — if you are making the eye from heavy wire — by inserting the wire of the second joint into the first while forming that eye. This joint should not only support the heavier material used in the limbs but also allow for flexibility and mobility of the limb.

These are some of the hinges which you will use every day in building basic puppets. More-complicated hinges can be found in books on woodworking, doll making, and advanced puppetry. Remember that no matter what hinge you use, it should be both strong and flexible and assist you and your puppet in creating easy movement on the stage.

Flower, Cedric, and Alan Fortney. *Puppets, Methods and Materials.* Worcester, MA: Davis Publ., 1983.
Lade, Roger. *The Most Excellent Book of How to Be a Puppeteer.* Brookfield, CT: Copper Beech Books, 1996.

History of Puppetry

The history of puppetry is ancient, beginning when human beings wanted to make more of their masks or of their dolls than they had been doing. Bil Baird feels that the puppet is an extension of the mask, so let us begin there.

Humans began using masks—according to what we have found through archaeology — during the Ice Age when priestesses and priests donned animal or bird skins to recreate the movements of the animals in worship and in preparation for the hunt. The mask was the head of the animal, preserved along with the pelt or feathers, worn entire by the priest, priestess, or medicine person. When the humans put on the mask, they *became* the animal or bird and imitated its movements and calls.

How did we move from the human portraying or being possessed by the divinity to a substitute — a figurine — with movable limbs? Probably both existed together, but the movable figure carried great power since it appeared to move on its own.

An audience may endow puppets with special features the puppets do not possess. Puppeteers will talk about audience members who admire the mouth parts on a puppet which has none or people who are sure that puppets hanging on the wall are moving. These people are not psychotic; they have simply come under the special spell of the puppet. If people today can feel so surely that puppets are alive, it is no wonder that in earlier ages puppets conveyed the majesty and mystery of religious experience.

Most cultures have had puppetry in one form or another, and many times this began with depictions of divine happenings and mythical events. Something so powerful as a puppet play could not involve itself with the ordinary activities of ordinary men. Like the Greek drama, these plays concerned the lives of goddesses and gods, queens and kings, because only these exalted figures could live life on a grand enough scale to warrant the attention of drama and puppetry.

The traditional shadow puppet drama of Indonesia is one such puppet drama where only the actions of divinities and royalty are involved. (*See* Wayang.) The plays are extensive, last sometimes for days, and are performed at religious festivals and at the great stages of life: birth, marriage, and death. The plays are presented at night, and the shadow puppet screen is lit only by an oil lamp.

Other traditional puppet dramas reach back into antiquity (that useful time invoked when we just don't know the origins of an institution). Because of the ephemeral nature of puppets and puppet theaters and the low status of puppeteers and actors in general, the likelihood of early puppets and equipment surviving over the ages is unlikely. It is left up to the written comments of travelers and observers, the murals of houses and tombs, and the illustrations in books to provide the evidence about the presence of puppets in a society. This anecdotal evidence may appear only by accident, as when an illustrator decides to include a pair of jousting puppets as the background in an illuminated letter in a book from the Middle Ages, for instance.

The fortunes of puppeteers rose and fell with the success and failure of politics. When all went well, theatrical performances of all kinds were welcome. When things turned bad, the theaters were closed, and the puppeteers had to put their equipment away and perhaps go into hiding. Governments often looked with disfavor on puppeteers, actors, and others who entertained for money. Such entertainers usually had no fixed address and traveled all around, so they could spy and spread unpopular ideas and rumors.

Frequently, persecution of the theater went hand in hand with religious restrictions on dress, housing, and public appearance. This is happening right now, in the twenty-first century, in countries where extremely conservative, theocratic governments liken puppetry to idolatry and have banished theater presentations.

In spite of such concerns, puppeteers were always welcome at fairs and other public gatherings. They enlivened an otherwise dull routine with a bit of color and a chance to hear old stories. They could lampoon local officials, for these were often generic figures, and people could interpret things as they chose. If a puppeteer could pick up a bit of local gossip and put it into the play, well so much the better. People could steal a laugh in an otherwise inflexible, irremediable situation.

In China, India, or Europe, the life of a wandering puppeteer was fairly the same. It was that of the entertainer or the person with a little theater on the street which could move easily from one place to the next with few transportation problems. They made their own puppets, wrote their own plays, and provided whatever music a puppet play might have.

In addition to the folk tradition, China, Japan, and the Ottoman Empire also had playwrights and musicians writing specifically for the puppet theater, which caused parts of the total puppet theater to be elevated to high art. This influence then fed back into the "legitimate" or live-actor theater and to the enrichment of the whole.

Europe still held puppets in low esteem, however, and kept the puppeteer to the streets and fairs. In Europe, puppetry was a humble profession, used for entertaining children and the lower classes. The characters and plays of European puppetry grew out of the commedia dell'arte. Even England's Mr. Punch is Polichinelle in disguise. It was a rowdy theater of the common people and much loved by them.

In the seventeenth century, puppetry began to change in Europe. Marionette opera grew up with the live-action counterpart and was soon just as popular. One of the first operas to be written for marionettes ran for twelve years, beginning in Florence in 1670. The great distinction between these productions and the puppets commonly seen in the streets and at fairs was that of location. The elegant marionettes of M. Acciajuoli played in theaters with seats and played to a cultured audience.

Theater in Europe was going through a great change at the time, and the marionette theater was in the thick of it. In France, Jean Baptiste Lully and the comic playwright Molière had cornered the opera and spoken theater world through the generosity and intervention of King Louis XIV. Marionette theater and opera was a guerilla operation, being closed down in one place and opening up in another. Marionette theaters would steal the most popular operas and plays and put them on with marionettes, not live actors. This sniping and rivalry went

on for over fifty years. The legitimate theater wanted to limit the number of marionettes and force them to use the swazzle, a squeaky whistle-like noise maker
which is still used by Punch and Judy professors today.

Gluck, the great German composer of the day, wrote for the marionette
opera as well as the legitimate opera. Haydn, too, composed for the marionette
opera with one of his finest works, *Philemon and Baucis*, written for marionettes.
Mozart wrote no marionette operas, although the Salzburg Marionettes presents
an elegant and compelling *Magic Flute*. Apparently, Mozart was also enamored
of Kasperle, the German-Austrian version of Polichinelle, and went to masked
balls dressed as the impudent puppet character.

Not only marionettes but *ombres Chinoises* or Chinese shadow puppet plays
were presented as well. Hand puppets thrived, too, and there is a painting of the
eighteenth century which shows a troupe of hand puppets entertaining nuns and
their friends at a convent. Theaters for puppets could be small or large, but
engravings of the time suggest that they were as spacious and attractive as any
legitimate theater.

Puppet theater in Europe continued to develop into more flash and greater
spectacle. Puppets were expected not only to walk and talk but to do acrobatics;
to explode from one puppet into several different, smaller versions; to play various musical instruments; and to do everything but breathe, talk, and dance on
their own. This was puppet vaudeville, with many dazzling acts combined into
a spectacular whole. By the end of the nineteenth century, these spectacular
mechanical marvels captured the "wow factor" solidly but left theater far behind.

Slowly, puppeteers struggled to find their way back to acting and presenting a story rather than producing gasps of acclaim from the audience. Puppeteers
attached themselves to artists and artistic movements such as Dadaism to find a
new way of being and presenting themselves. Writers such as Georges Sand and
her son created hand puppets and presented salon productions for small audiences. At the same time, puppeteers continued to emphasize technical excellence
in the creation of puppets. As a result, hundreds of theaters sometimes holding
thousands of spectators came into being and influenced people, cultures, and
other puppeteers as a result.

Also at this time, the first organization for puppeteers—UNIMA or Union
Internationale de la Marionettes—appears. (*See* UNIMA and UNIMA–USA.)
This is a startling event; for before this, puppeteers would try to shut one another
out to protect their professional secrets, going so far as to wall in the back stage
and post guards.

Before World War II a real effort to create a puppet theater of lasting import,
rather than temporary spectacle, was made by the puppeteers of Europe. Unfortunately, the rise of the Nazis and the beginning of World War II put a stop to
that. So puppeteers turned to stealth to keep up the morale of their fellow coun-
trymen. They went underground, creating puppet plays to encourage resistance

to the Nazis, and were tortured or even put to death as a result. In some of the prison camps, people made puppets from scraps and put on plays.

European puppeteers who fled to Britain and the United States before and during World War II influenced the creation of a more vigorous puppet theater, centered chiefly in New York. They were ready, too, when television came along, to create puppetry fit for a new medium.

Still, in the United States, puppets were considered to be entertainment for children. Adults were left out of the mix until the 1960s. Then, with the rise in street theater and the introduction of the Muppets, puppet theater once again began to take on an adult appearance. Street theater, with Bread and Puppet Theater being perhaps the best known of this group, sought to educate people on the problems and topics of the day through a playful seriousness. They frequently used giant puppets so that all could see, and they teamed music and action for a lively presentation.

Jim Henson's Muppets began as a more-adult approach to puppets, marrying comedy with a wry sensibility to unusual puppet forms to create something new. *The Muppet Show* followed in this tradition, marrying sly, adult-oriented humor with warm and familiar puppet creations to make a recurring show which would appeal to all ages.

Adults are still left out of the puppet experience in the United States, but puppeteers' education continues through organizations, professional training programs, and festivals. (*See* Atlanta Center for Puppetry Arts; Festivals; Internet Links; National Day of Puppetry; Puppeteers of America; UNIMA and UNIMA–USA; and University of Connecticut Puppetry Arts Program.) In fact, there is now even greater involvement with a more sophisticated children's puppetry in schools, libraries, health centers, and religious organizations.

This is an exciting time for puppetry and a great time to join in the flow of puppetry history. No matter how you decide to get involved, do so! Puppetry can use all of the fans it can get. Where else can you become part of history as well as having so much fun? Puppets can help, entertain, and teach. They can do anything you want or need. Try one on today, and see where it will take you!

Baird, Bil. *The Art of the Puppet*. New York: Macmillan, 1965.
Bell, John. *Strings, Hands, Shadows: A Modern Puppet History*. Detroit: The Detroit Institute of Arts, 2000.
Doney, Meryl. *Puppets*. New York: Franklin Watts, 1995

India and Puppetry

Puppetry is an ancient institution in India, with a mention of marionettes appearing in the *Mahabharata* which dates them to at least 200 B.C. Puppets are seen as divine beings in miniature, sent to earth by the gods to entertain and educate. Shiva, the Destroyer, and Parvati, his wife, or Brahma, the Creator, are all responsible for the creation of puppets.

In one story, Shiva and Parvati saw a group of dolls in a dollmaker's shop and briefly brought them to life. When the pair finished with them, the dolls became lifeless again and dropped to the floor. The toymaker cried out and objected, but Parvati said, "You made them. It should be up to you to give them life." The gods went on their way, and the toymaker, in response to the divine command, added strings to his dolls and so made the first marionettes. In another story, the mouth or breath of Brahma, the Creator, made the first puppeteer, Adi Nat.

As in many other countries, India felt that live actors should not portray divine characters, that it was death to do so. Puppets became the substitutes for divinities in India, Southeast Asia, and China.

India, which has all the puppetry forms—marionettes, hand puppets, and shadow puppets—influenced puppetry in all the places where Indians traveled or migrated. The shadow puppetry of Southeast Asia can trace its origins to Hindu immigrants who brought puppetry with them as they moved into Bali and Java. (*See* Shadow Puppets; Wayang.)

The chief subjects of Indian puppet drama are the *Mahabharata* and the *Ramayana*. Both plays are equally old and concern themselves with the philosophy and religion of India. They are filled not only with religious devotion, but also have action and drama, ogres, demons, monkey kings, and all manner of excitement.

Religious education was not the only reason for creating puppet plays, however. Rulers in ancient India recognized the importance of puppetry and encouraged and supported the puppeteers in creating plays which exalted the ruler's valor and good deeds. One of those plays, about Amar Sing Rathore of Nagpur in central India, is still performed today. It is possible to find vestiges of plays about him in India and as far away as Tunisia, where puppets in his image can be found.

Generally, though, the puppet plays were meant to educate the illiterate in an entertaining manner. The puppet plays could last for days, sometimes even weeks, depending on the purpose of the play. Puppet plays were offered as part of festivals and as part of the celebrations marking transitions in life. The puppeteers set up in a courtyard of a home or temple and presented their play. The plays were well known to the audience and enjoyed by all who attended.

Modern India is striving to preserve its vast puppetry history, train new puppeteers, and move puppetry into the classroom where it can again be used as an educational tool. With such a treasure trove of ancient and modern possibilities, India has rich resources indeed in the world of puppetry.

Baird, Bil. *The Art of the Puppet*. New York: Macmillan, 1965.
Bell, John. *Strings, Hands, Shadows: A Modern Puppet History*. Detroit: The Detroit Institute of Arts, 2000.
Doney, Meryl. *Puppets*. New York: Franklin Watts, 1995.
http://www.kamat.com/kalranga/art/puppets.htm This wonderful site created by Dr. K. L.

Kamat not only has pictures of Indian leather puppets, it also has information on the presentation of puppet plays.

Indonesian Puppetry *see* Wayang

Internet Links

Anyone who works with the Internet knows that lists of links can be notoriously unreliable. Sites appear and disappear and cannot always be trusted. That said, this list of links to puppetry sites has been chosen with hopeful longevity in mind. They are organizations, societies, and web sites which have shown themselves to have some staying power. Please enjoy these sites as an open door to the worldwide stage of puppetry. If the web address is no longer available, put the organization's name in your favorite search engine.

ASSOCIATION QUÉBÉCOISE DES MARIONNETTISTES

http://www.aei.ca/~aqm/
This is the site of UNIMA–Quebec and is written in French. It has tour dates, member companies, and events going on in Quebec and in other places involving their members.

ATLANTA CENTER FOR PUPPETRY ARTS

http://www.puppet.org/
The Atlanta Center for Puppetry Arts is the premier center in the United States for informing and educating the public about puppetry. Through the center's programs, more than 100,000 children and adults are entertained and taught about puppetry and what it means to be a puppeteer. Through its volunteer and internship programs, the center educates puppeteers for the future.
The center's "links" page is a metasite which will connect you with all the major puppetry organizations and many wonderful puppet troupes worldwide.

FELLOWSHIP OF CHRISTIAN PUPPETEERS

http://www.fcpfellowship.org/
The Fellowship of Christian Puppeteers was established in 1974 by puppeteers who wanted to use their talents within ministry and as a witness to their faith. The membership form can be printed out from the site and mailed in.

ONTARIO PUPPETRY ASSOCIATION

http://www.onpuppet.org/
This site covers puppetry activities in Ontario, Canada. It has a link to the Canadian Museum of Civilization with much information on puppetry. It also has a link to the Association Québécoise des Marionnettistes.

PUPPETEERS OF AMERICA, INC.

http://www.puppeteers.org/
Puppeteers of America is another important organization promoting the education of puppeteers and the public about the wonders of puppetry. It has a metasite with links to much important information for puppeteers, including articles from *Puppetry Journal.*

THE PUPPETRY HOME PAGE BY ROSE SAGE

http://www.sagecraft.com/puppetry/
The Puppetry Home Page is a glorious metasite of information about puppets, puppeteers, and puppetry. If you want information on puppetry festivals, puppetry troupes in your area, or puppet styles from around the world, you can find the information here. It also has information on internships, scholarships, and educational opportunities. If you have a question about puppets, you can probably find the answer here.

UNIMA

www.unima.org/
UNIMA, Union Internationale de la Marionette, is the major organization for puppeteers worldwide and should go on your list of must-joins if you are going to be a pro. According to the web site for the Atlanta Center for Puppetry Arts, "This global organization was founded in 1929 and is the oldest international theater association. There are chapters in forty-three countries, and UNIMA was adopted as a member of the International Theatre Institute in 1959, UNIMA is a member of the United Nations Educational, Scientific and Cultural Organization (UNESCO)."
UNIMA's purpose is to promote friendship and worldwide understanding through the use of puppets and puppetry. It also offers workshops and training for puppeteers. Information about membership in UNIMA is available through its web site.

UNIMA–USA, INC.

http://www.unima-usa.org/
UNIMA–USA was started by Jim Henson and is the American branch of UNIMA. Its web site is another metasite with links to schools, festivals, internships, and the like. The address of UNIMA–USA is 1404 Spring Street NW, Atlanta, GA 30309-2820, U.S.A.

UNIVERSITY OF CONNECTICUT PUPPET ARTS PROGRAM

http://www.sfa.uconn.edu/Drama/Puppetry/HOMEPAGE.HTML
The University of Connecticut offers BFA, MA, and MFA programs in all aspects of puppetry. Founded by Dr. Frank Ballard, the program seeks to train puppeteers and produce experienced professionals who have a firm start on their careers. The department hosts a museum of puppetry which opened April 1996.

Islamic Puppetry

Islam forbids the making of idols and graven images, and so I was surprised to see a report on the Fourth International Puppetry Festival held in Lahore, Pakistan, in 1998 where there were Islamic puppets from Tajikistan. I had seen Sesame Street-like puppets used in Islamic religious educational videos, but that was in the United States. Of course there are the traditional Wayang Golek rod puppets of Java, commissioned in the sixteenth century and used to spread Islam in Java with the Menak Cycle of puppet plays. (*See* Wayang.) However, with changing times come different needs. How would Tajikistan use puppetry in an Islamic way to present a puppet play?

This report was titled "The Fourth International Puppet Festival Pakistan October 1998," by Rose Beauchamp, who had attended the festival and gave a complete report about it. I quote from her entry on the troupe from Tajikistan at the URL http://www.pinz.org.nz/pakistan_99.html

> The most distinctive and unique for me was the troupe from Tajikistan (formerly part of the Soviet Union) with "Reflections about War and Peace." The Tajik group comprise ten performers who include Islamic style puppets—with no features on the puppets—mask, dance and stilt work as well as traditional songs, poems and music on Tajik instruments. The performance is like the original circus. I was amazed when a boa constrictor joined in the act. I took it to be the best puppet I'd ever seen for the first five seconds!
>
> "Reflections about War and Peace" includes the literature, customs and techniques of the theatre of Tajikistan, as well as a story created out of their own sense of personal responsibility for conflict and in creating peaceful life.

It would seem, then, that the Tajikistanian performance is part of a festival scenario similar to that found in Africa or in other traditional societies. (*See* African Puppetry.) There, the puppetry takes place within and as an element of a festival.

More importantly, though, is the use of faceless puppets to comply with the Islamic edict against idol making. Having seen pictures of faceless puppets in a modernistic play, the lack of features does not detract from the effectiveness of the puppets. In fact, it gives the imagination freer reign to complete the puppet by imagining features.

Because of the increase in adherents to Islam in the United States and Canada, it is important to know of these puppetry possibilities. Schools or libraries in areas where there are a great many Muslims may want to know the feeling of the community on this issue of puppetry. The faceless puppet may offer an alternate way to satisfy almost everyone in the area.

Japanese Puppetry *see* Bunraku

Jumping Jacks

A jumping jack is a dancing puppet of limited range and movement. A string in the back of the jumping jack allows the arms and legs to fling up into the air when the string is pulled. Jumping jack engravings in Europe date from the eighteenth century, but the history of the puppet may go back much farther.

The jumping jack puppet is made in five parts: the body (containing both head and torso), two arms, and two legs. Each limb has two holes near the joint, one beside the other. One is for joining the limb to the body; the other is for joining the limbs to one another. When the limbs are joined to the body, the joint needs to be loose and flexible, permitting easy movement. A loosely folded brad or a string joint should do the trick. (*See* Hinges.)

After attaching the limbs to the body, join the arms to each other and the legs to each other with a piece of string which crosses the back and links the limbs. Make sure that the string joining the limbs is slack, permitting easy movement and allowing the arms and legs to come to rest beside the body.

To make the jumping jack move in its traditional way, attach a long string first to the upper string joining the arms, then to the lower string joining the legs. The thread should dangle down behind the jumping jack. When this string is pulled, the arms and legs should fly up. A plastic bone ring can be attached to the string to facilitate movement.

The jumping jack may be mounted on a rod or it can have a second string attached to the head which becomes the holding string. Provide this holding string with a ring as you did the lower string. Hold on to the upper string and pull the lower one. Your jumping jack should fling its arms and legs wide.

The drawback to the head string for puppeteers is that it takes both hands to operate the jumping jack. Also, the puppet tends to turn on the string. Try mounting your jumping jack on a rod instead. Use a lightweight rod of bamboo or a garden stick. Split the stick and mount the jumping jack in the split. Tape or glue the jumping jack into place. Cover up the split with paper, foil, or anything which will add to the costume design. To disguise the mechanism, a piece of paper cut to the pattern of the torso can be pasted onto the head and allowed to fall down loosely in the back.

An alternative idea, which will allow the jumping jack a greater range of character and participation, is to draw a second character on the back of the jumping jack. When the puppet is turned around, it becomes the second character. In this way, two jumping jacks could become four characters. The mechanism will show, so use a color of string which will blend in with the costume's colors and be less noticeable. Using braces, stands, or holders in which to mount the puppets will permit use of both hands and greater manipulation of the characters.

Some plays with four characters that you might consider are: *Goldilocks and the Three Bears; Little Red Riding Hood* (Little Red Riding Hood, the Wolf, Grandmother, and the Woodsman); *Hansel and Gretel* (Hansel, Gretel, the Witch, and the Father); *The Three Billy Goats Gruff* (the three Billy Goats Gruff and the Troll); *Three Strong Women* (the Three Strong Women plus the Wrestler).

Cinderella can be told with three jumping jacks: Cinderella, The Fairy Godmother, The Two Stepsisters, and The Prince. Draw Cinderella on a single jumping jack with one side being raggedy Cinderella and the other side in her ball gown.

Use focus and minimal movement to move from one character to the next. By slightly jiggling the control thread, that jumping jack becomes the center of attention when its arms and legs move. Remember to plan in several events where the characters can fling their arms wide for emphasis or in surprise. If your character will not be using its legs, leave them off and have only the arms move.

Now assemble your puppets, gather your audience, and put on a play!

Baird, Bil. *The Art of the Puppet*. New York: Macmillan, 1965.
Doney, Meryl. *Puppets*. New York: Franklin Watts, 1995.

Junk Puppets

A junk puppet is one that is made from found materials. It can involve giving voice and personality to an ordinary object such as a coffee pot, pair of shoes, rock, or some other item, or it can be the act of taking an ordinary object — such as a lunch bag, bottle brush, pair of scissors, or dust mop — adding facial features (eyes are a bare minimum) and any other thing which would help create the puppet's character, and using the result as a puppet.

Nancy Renfro as well as Cheryl Henson and the Muppet Workshop are two authors who exemplify the junk puppet ideal. They can take just about anything and turn it into a puppet because the central idea of *puppet* is making an inanimate object come to life in order to play to an audience. Nancy Frazier, Nancy Renfro and Lori Sears discuss this in their excellent book on the essence of puppetry called *Imagination: At Play with Puppets and Creative Drama*. The exercises in this book take ordinary objects and have future puppeteers work singly or in groups to create puppet characters and improvise situations. For instance: choose a kitchen object and give it a voice and a personality. Select a swatch of material from a group of materials and give that swatch a voice and a personality. Put the cloth "character" in an improvised situation and see how it would function.

Junk puppets are also a child's puppet. Kitchen spoons, paper bags, and the hand itself become the simple puppets of childhood. (*See* Hands as Puppets.) Dolls and stuffed toys can become puppets, too, but they must be playing *for* and not *with* others. So when a child talks with a doll or stuffed toy or miniature soldiers or action figures this is play, not puppetry. When children gather together with their dolls, action figures or other toys and talk with them, they are still playing. However, when one, two, or a few children use those same dolls, action figures, or toys to act out a scene for other children, it becomes puppetry — even though puppets are not involved.

Try junk puppetry yourself. Look about your house, library, or classroom and gather together an assortment of everyday objects. Work with the objects and see if you can give them character and voice. Have fun with the produce section of your refrigerator! How would celery or tomatoes or potatoes sound anyway?

Gather up paper tubes, plastic cartons of various sorts and sizes, cereal boxes, and any other recyclables you can find. Connect the recyclables into human figures and see what you get. Remember that you need not always have legs and feet for a puppet. Even a marionette need only move from the waist up. With planning of the actions needed, legs can be ignored or concealed.

Make your own puppet-construction area with supplies of tubes, cartons, eyes, wig material, and cloth to drape for clothing. Remember that you will need a glue gun and glue sticks plus all the basics of crafting: pencil, scissors and craft knife, measuring tape, ruler, and butcher paper if you need paper for patterns.

Once you have a group of junk puppets, assemble them and put on a play!

Frazier, Nancy, Nancy Renfro, and Lori Sears. *Imagination: At Play with Puppets and Creative Drama*. Austin, TX: Nancy Renfro Studios, 1987.
Henson, Cheryl, and the Muppet Workshop. *The Muppets Make Puppets!* New York: Workman Publishing, 1994.
Renfro, Nancy. *Make Amazing Puppets*. Santa Barbara, CA: Learning Works, 1979.
Renfro, Nancy. *Puppets for Play Production*. New York: Funk & Wagnalls, 1969.

Karagoz

Of all the characters in the puppet repertoire, Karagoz and Punch must stand alone as both the representatives of a culture and a puppetry type. Interestingly, each draws on the same slapstick style which is both vulgar and satirical.

Briefly, Karagoz in the shadow-theater puppet of Turkey and Greece that performs as a treat during religious holidays. Karagoz, best friend Hacivat, and his many other friends and accomplices on the stage allow the venting of pent-up emotions during the fast of Ramadan, permit the criticizing of governments and officials who would otherwise be untouchable, and provide humor and comic relief for the human condition.

The puppets are made of pierced and painted camel hide or water buffalo hide which has been worked with oil to make the pieces semitransparent. Head and torso are joined with the far hand and arm reduced to a half a hand peeking out from the torso. The torso is jointed, linking it to the bottom half of the body.

Hacivat is Karagoz's primary opponent, even though Hacivat is Karagoz's best friend and good neighbor. Both of Hacivat's arms are rigid, placing him at the mercy of Karagoz, whose left arm is jointed and free to move. The legs are a unit and are joined to the lower torso, allowing movement in the legs.

Rods are attached to the center of the upper part of the puppet's body, allowing for rough-and-tumble, acrobatic movement. Karagoz plays are vigorous, and the puppet is created for action! Karagoz, whose name means "Dark Eye," has a tie to the phallic deities of old as well as to the Three Stooges and the Marx Brothers. His life is full of violence, sexuality, humor and confusion.

One place to see a Karagoz performance in the pre–World War II days was a coffeehouse. Normally off limits to women and children, the coffeehouse would become open to all and a place of village entertainment during the fast of Ramadan. Then, in the evening, the coffeehouse would open its doors, and the performing troupe would begin to tell a tale of Karagoz and his friends.

According to Ersin Alok (*http://www.armory.com/ssahin/articles/ article8.html*), the story goes that in the Turkish capital of Bursa there were once two laborers working with a crew building a mosque. This was during the reign of Orhan Bey (1324–1360). These two laborers were called Karagoz and Hacivat, and they were quite a couple of comedians. They kept the other laborers in stitches with their jokes and antics. Unfortunately, this caused a delay in the work schedule. When the sultan heard of their activities and the delays they caused, he had Karagoz and Hacivat executed. The people missed the comedians, and the sultan was filled with remorse that he had acted in such a hasty manner. A man named Seyh Kusteri made leather cutouts of the two and recounted their antics to amuse the sultan and relieve his grief. This was the beginning of the Karagoz plays. On his web site, Alok goes on to say:

> Karagoz came to represent the ordinary man in the street, forthright and trustworthy. He is virtually illiterate, usually unemployed, and embarks on many money-making ventures that never work. He is nosy, tactless, often deceitful and inclined to lewd talk. Like his European counterpart Punch, he frequently resorts to violence, beating Hacivat and the other characters.

Alok comments that a Karagoz-style shadow stage is set up in the coffeehouse or other venue with an oil lamp lighting the muslin from behind. This muslin shadow screen is called "ayna" or mirror. Bil Baird (*The Art of the Puppet*, chapter 5) states that this shadow puppet stage echoes the Indonesian and Hindu feeling in that the shadow stage is a point at which divine messages can be transmitted and truths about humanity revealed.

There are a number of stock characters in the Karagoz repertoire. Like Punch and Judy, characters have been reduced to stereotype. Beside Karagoz and Hacivat, Alok continues,

> [There are] dancers, djins, witches, and monsters as well as nameless characters such as The Arab (a sweet seller who knows no Turkish), a black servant woman, a Circassian servant girl, an Albanian watchman (who is noisy and insolent), a Greek (usually a doctor), an Armenian (a footman or money changer), a Jew (a goldsmith or scrap dealer), a Laz (a boatman), and a Persian (who recited poetry with an Azeri accent).
> In addition to these nameless stereotypical characters, there are several that make regular appearances. There are the drunkard Tuzsuz Deli Bekir who carries a wine bottle, Uzun Efe with his long neck, Kanbur Tiryaki the opium addict with his pipe, Alti Karis Beberuhi the eccentric dwarf, the half-witted Denyo, the spendthrift Civan, and Nigar, who spends her time chasing men.

According to Alok, the chief puppeteer is called a "Karagozcu, Hayali, or Hayalbaz" who is assisted by an apprentice. There is also a "sandikkar" who places the puppets in a chest or "sandik." The songs are sung by the "yardak," and the tambourine played by the "dairezen."

Before the coming of cinema and television, Karagoz was the most important entertainment in Turkey and Greece. After falling into disfavor, Karagoz is now making a comeback with annual festivals in Bursa, Turkey.

According to Baird, the placement of the rods in the body of Karagoz and the other shadow puppets of this type enable them to turn somersaults, do back flips, and generally act in a more acrobatic and vigorous manner than other shadow puppets.

Karagoz is not meant to be refined. Instead, he is vigorous and often bawdy. Possessed of a gigantic phallus in the classic plays (which links him to ancient Roman phallic deities, clowns, and Greek new comedy), Karagoz proclaims himself to be an innocent victim of his own physiognomy. In other plays, he uses his native wit to get himself and his friend Hacivat both into and out of complex and humorous situations.

A wonderful site created by Mr. Diker not only has brief plot outlines of both classic and modern Karagoz scripts, but also has patterns for the puppets. Holes show where the rods have been attached.

Baird, Bil. Chapter 5: "Karaghioz: A Turkish Delight." *The Art of the Puppet.* New York: Macmillan, 1965.

Bell, John. *Strings, Hands, Shadows: A Modern Puppet History.* Detroit: The Detroit Institute of Arts, 2000.

Doney, Meryl. *Puppets.* New York: Franklin Watts, 1995.

http://www.armory.com/ssahin/articles/article8.html Alok, Ersin. "Karagoz-Hacivad."

This site is frequently difficult to enter. As an alternative route, try http://www.Turkey-web.com/arts_and_humanities/index.htm and choose "Turkish Shadow Play."

http://ieiris.cc.boun.edu.tr/assist/diker/kksce Diker. Classic and Modern Karagoz Puppets and Plays.

http://bornova.ege.edu.tr/ncyprus/kahve.html North Cyprus Home Page. "Cyprus Village Coffee Houses (Kahve)."

Life-Sized Puppets

Because of our greater knowledge of international puppetry conventions and styles, life-sized puppets from Europe, the Caribbean, and South America present themselves as possibilities for expressive puppetry. We see Bunraku puppets from Japan, for instance, and realize that more could be done with our own puppetry styles. (*See* Bunraku.) The life-sized puppet is coming into its own.

A life-sized puppet gives the opportunity to surprise the audience with the dramatic size of the puppets. Their size focuses attention. If you have something important to say, a life-sized puppet might be the attention-getting gimmick you need.

Life-sized puppets can also present details in sculpting or costume which would be lost on a conventional-sized hand puppet or marionette. If you want to present key elements of a culture, for instance, life-sized puppets would permit you to do that without taking the shortcuts costumers and sculptors must when working with smaller, standard-sized puppets.

Manipulating a life-sized puppet means that you are working more in the area of mime. Gestures, gait, head manipulation must be slow, graceful, and fluid. Tiny, jerky movements will not easily be seen the way they would, for instance, in a hand or rod puppet. In addition, practice to coordinate the efforts of several puppeteers becomes crucial.

The life-sized puppets I have used are large paper marionettes used to tell folk tales at story times. Sometimes, I use only one: the Story Teller. At other times, I use more than one puppet but pose them on a stand. Using this kind of puppet requires careful planning of the story to coordinate movement of the puppeteer with the story.

Other possible puppets are life-sized Bunraku-style puppets manipulated by two or more puppeteers, large rod puppets with more than one puppeteer; and giant puppets where the puppet may be whole or in parts as in the parts of a face. (*See* Bunraku; Giant Puppets; Rod Puppets.)

Working with a life-sized puppet requires that the puppeteer rehearse in a different way than he or she normally might. Instead of getting small motor movements just right, you will be working with the whole body. The puppet's actions will mirror your own, so you become like a dancer as you work to portray the story through movement. I find myself making the gestures I would want the puppet to make as the story unfolds. At the same time, I am moving the control strings and enabling the puppet to do what it needs to in order to advance the story. I'm dancing with my puppet.

When working with more than one life-sized puppet, I have a couple of laundry stands where I can "park" the puppets while they are silent. These are fold-up stands meant to hold hangers filled with dry laundry. Instead, they are holding puppets in place until their next scene. The puppets become part of the scenery and backdrop as well. I dress in dark colors and manage to fade into the background this way.

Stands could just as easily be made of wood and painted black, brown, or navy blue to fade into the background. They are nothing more than an inverted, L-shaped rack on a stand, or you might find something else just as good. The point is to persist until you find just the right thing that works for you.

If you are going to work with a group manipulating your life-sized puppets, you must plan enough rehearsal time to make sure that everyone knows what they are supposed to do. The movements should be assured and flow smoothly, one into the other. If you can work with a mirror so that everyone can see what they are doing, so much the better. Practice as dancers do to assure graceful, coordinated movements and success.

Life-sized puppets can be made from any material, but keep the controls fairly simple. A life-sized puppet can have facial features manipulated by hand controls. Arms and legs can be manipulated separately. Instead of elaborate hand controls for hands, the puppeteer's own hands might be used.

In the paper puppets I use, there are three control strands: one strand goes to the head and one to each arm. If it were needed, I could manipulate the legs as well, but gesture and voice are more important to me than leg movements.

Life-sized puppets can also be worn by the puppeteer. Big Bird of Sesame Street is a prime example. This is not a costume but a puppet with movable beak and eyes. In fact, almost all the Sesame Street Muppets are about the size of the toddlers who appear on the show. The Muppets are manipulated by the pup-

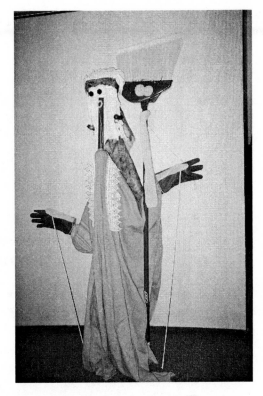

Mops and brooms are standard household items that can be used for life-sized puppets. They are large but not unwieldy.

peteers who carry them above their heads with more than one puppeteer being used to create some puppets.

Life-sized puppets offer wonderful possibilities to puppeteers. Their size draws the audience's attention, giving weight to what they are saying, and cultural or historical detail can also be conveyed through more-detailed sculpture and costuming. Try out a life-sized puppet! It will give you a chance to act in a dramatic manner, make a statement, and really capture people's imaginations. The puppets need not be complicated, just large. You will enjoy the new freedom to move about with your puppets! Try it!

Lade, Roger. *The Most Excellent Book of How to Be a Puppeteer*. Brookfield, CT: Copper Beech Books, 1996.

Lighting

Lighting for most puppet stages is very simple: one or at the most three overhead light sources give the stage a complete source of light without creating many shadows. Good lighting permits the puppets to be seen easily by the audience without throwing the stage into shadow. This can be accomplished easily with simple materials you can find in any hardware store. You needn't be a lighting expert to light a basic puppet stage effectively.

The basic lighting set-up for a small hand puppet or marionette stage would place one light in a clamp-on aluminum reflector at the top of both sides of the stage, focused onto center stage, the most important area of the stage and where all the action takes place. A third light source would shine down directly onto the stage to wash the whole stage in light. Spotlights would not be used since most puppet productions are not that complicated. Of course, there is no lighting back stage.

Use reflector lights you can buy in any hardware store and a plain, frosted bulb. Try a pink bulb (the kind that is supposed to cast "flattering" light) if you want a softer, rosier light; but a plain bulb should be sufficient. You can also alternate the pink and white bulbs to soften the white light but refrain from too rosy a color on the stage. Try the pink lights above and the white lights on either side of the stage. Remember that you want a balanced effect without too many shadows.

You can experiment with colored clear glass bulbs if you want a special effect which will last for an entire scene of your play. This would be easier than using the special acetate filters for theatrical lighting. If you have the lights clamped in place, you can change them between scenes for effect. Have your alternate lights ready to go, and switch them out during the scene change.

Lighting for the basic puppet stage can be operated from a home appliance surge protector power strip you can now buy in hardware or even grocery stores. Plug all your lights into the strip and turn them on at the power strip. Fasten the power strip in place so that it will be secure and out of the way. Turn the lights on just before you open the curtain or have the puppets come on stage to remove the announcement placard.

If you have access to a person who doesn't mind installing a dimmer switch and creating a miniature lighting board, you can use the dimmer to turn on all your lights. It gives a gentler introduction to the lights and does not seem quite so mechanical or harsh. On the other hand, if someone hits the dimmer switch, you could find yourself on a dimly lit stage. Also, if someone hits the power switch, everything will go dark, so remember to place the lighting panel in a place that is available but not in the way.

Lighting for the basic puppet stage need not present a problem to you, but it does need to be attended to. Having inadequate light for your stage will make the puppet experience less than optimum; the puppet's features will be hard to see, and their actions may be obscured by shadows. Basic lighting is easy to acquire, install, and operate and will make your puppetry experience that much more enjoyable.

Currell, David. *The Complete Book of Puppetry*. Boston: Plays, Inc., 1975.
Currell, David. *Puppets and Puppet Theatre*. Wiltshire, England: Crowood Press, 1999.
Lasky, Kathryn. *Puppeteer*. New York: Macmillan, 1985.

Limberjacks

The limberjack is a combination toy, musical instrument, and puppet which originated in the "hills and hollers" of the Appalachian Mountains of the American Southeast. The limberjack consists of a thin wooden paddle with a long handle and "Jack," a puppet with a rod in his back.

The special thing about "Jack" is that he is jointed at every possible point except the head and neck. The joining pins are not inserted tightly but are loose so that Jack can move easily. The arms and legs swing about wildly. Jack can kneel as well as whirl about, but his movements are not predetermined. Instead, Jack moves to the rhythms of the song being sung or the tune being played.

Whoever is performing with Jack sits on the handle of the paddle and holds Jack's rod in their hand. Jack's feet rest lightly on the paddle at the paddle's outer end, and the limberjack performer taps a steady rhythm on the paddle. The paddle bounces, causing Jack's feet to bounce as well. The arms swing in time to the rhythm while Jack tap dances on the paddle, creating a rhythm for others to sing or dance to.

The limberjack is a wonderful folk creation and shows great ingenuity by combining a rhythm instrument, a doll, and a dancing man puppet. It is a portable percussion instrument which can be taken anywhere. The rod can be made to be removed so that the whole can fold flat and be carried anywhere in a basket or knapsack. Best of all, it takes almost no skill to play. If you can tap out a rhythm, you can play a limberjack.

If you have an opportunity to purchase a limberjack, do so. Very little rehearsal will reward you with wonderful returns as a very special addition to your story hour or puppet performance.

Management *see* Business of Puppetry: Management

Marionettes

A marionette is a puppet which is manipulated by strings. The strings may be few, as in the Kathputli puppets of India or the Orlando rod puppets of Sicily, or they may be many. The operator stands behind or above the puppets, sometimes on the ground and sometimes on a raised platform behind the stage. Sometimes the operator is traditionally visible or may choose to be so in more-modern puppetry. Usually, though, the operator is behind the scenes, working the puppets from behind a curtain.

History

The history of the marionette is a complicated one. It would appear that marionettes may have been known to the ancient Egyptians who used them in their religious rites. Marionettes appear to have been known to the ancient Greeks and Romans, for we hear of them through the disparaging comments of others. After the fall of Rome, the marionette disappears, only to reappear by the late Middle Ages in churches as they perform special dramas as part of the church calendar. In fact, the early church fathers seem to have preferred puppets to live actors, feeling that the latter were corrupting. The first Nativities were performed by puppets which became known as "little Marys" or marionettes.

By the end of the nineteenth century, marionettes had become wonders of mechanical invention. Their inventors and master puppeteers surrounded their backstage performance area with curtains so that rival puppeteers could not see what went on behind the curtain or how the marvels were performed. A bit later, in a reaction to all the gadgetry, puppetry became simplified and more serious, involved in producing a rival to the legitimate theater. In Europe, puppetry was still for children, but adults were being drawn in to special performances of their own.

Today, marionettes span the range from performances strictly for children to elegant performances of opera and legitimate theater. The mechanical wonders of the past are gone, and in their place is a more mature, more adventuresome theater willing to try for beauty or for the unusual. A puppet, as the Japanese playwright Chikamatsu realized, presents a more pure, a more refined essence of human emotion. Puppets don't get in the way of the written word, trying to interpret it through their own personality as a human actor might. The puppet is there to reflect our own perception of the play, of the emotions being presented. The marionette is a part of this new puppetry world as it has been for centuries and will continue to amaze and enthrall its audience for ages to come.

Simple Marionette Controls

Marionettes are usually thought of as extremely complicated puppets whose intricate controls absorb the total attention of at least one person. While this can be true, it need not be so for every marionette, especially for beginning puppeteers who may be just trying out the form to see if it suits them.

Very interesting, effective marionettes can be made to operate with very simple controls. Depending on the skill of the puppeteer, these can be as complete and as effective as the more complicated marionettes.

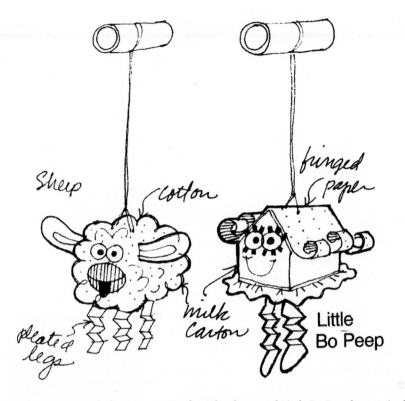

Simple marionette controls from Nancy Renfro. The sheep and Little Bo Peep have a single con-rol made from a paper tube to move the marionettes back and forth. Spring legs from pleated paper add the suggestion of leg movement. This control is simple enough for older children to operate.

In India, the traditional Kathputli marionettes of Rajasthan, in northern India, have almost no controls at all. There is a string attached to the head and back and one attached to each of the arms and no other controls. Even the dancing animals have only simple string loops attached to the front and back of the animal. Although the controls are simple, their manipulation is not, and the puppets are able to achieve wonderful, magical effects with these simple mechanisms.

The life-sized spring-legged puppets also have minimal string loops for manipulation of the puppets. (*See* Spring-Legged Puppets.) The springy quality of the legs lets them move on their own. The chief movement is in the arms and hands with gesture and voice being the basis of expression for the puppet. There is a long thread loop for the head and a longer one for each hand. As the puppeteer moves across the stage with the puppet, the control loops are shifted from hand to hand with the head control loop always in the middle. The purpose is to free up the arms of the puppet for gesture which conveys the emotion of the story.

Another simple control is the one-rod control made of a dowel or paper towel tube. The control has three strings: one for the head and one each for the arms. The legs of the marionettes are either left to move on their own or are not worried about. This simple control is a step up from the Kathputli marionettes in complexity and may be easier for a one-person puppeteer to operate.

My first foray into using marionettes employed just such simple controls. I made marionettes for *Jack and the Beanstalk* out of tubes, paper, and poster board and used only these simple controls mentioned above. The children were suitably frightened of the giant and pleased when he got his comeuppance. It gave me a chance to use marionettes and see whether or not I enjoyed using them. Later puppets, used for the puppet club, continued to use the simple controls to good effect. For the one-person puppeteer, it would seem that the use of marionettes is out of the question. However, I have seen one puppeteer, Jim Gamble, who appears on the stage along with his marionettes. He wears black or dark, conventional clothes. When using more than one marionette in a scene, he sometimes uses stands to rest and pose one marionette while using another. While this is not a simple control, it is an approach to using marionettes for the one-person puppet company.

Because of Jim Gamble's reliance on the assumption that the marionette's presence will draw the eye away from him, he boldly steps right onto the stage in the middle of all the props and scenery. He even talks with the puppets and the audience. We in the audience willingly ignore the puppeteer as we follow along with the story. While this approach is not for everyone, it is one way for the lone puppeteer to work with marionettes. The ability to proceed as if the puppeteer being on stage is the most natural thing in the world is the trick that carries the day.

Marionettes can become as complicated as you want them to be. On the other hand, effective puppetry can be achieved with simple marionettes using simple controls. Don't refuse to work with marionettes or limit yourself because you are by yourself or have only limited experience. Take a chance with simple marionettes and see what you can accomplish. You may surprise yourself and delight your audience!

Intermediate Marionette Controls

Although marionettes can be operated with simple controls and given a great deal of personality, for greater amount of movement and expressive content, a more complex control is needed. The standard Euro-American marionette control is the "airplane" control, so called because its long central rod and short crossbars remind puppeteers of the outline of an airplane. There are other complex controls in other countries: a paddle control in China and Japan, a circular head control in India, but the "airplane" is the control Europeans and North, Central, and South Americans know best.

The basic airplane control actually comes in two parts: the airplane which controls the head, shoulders, lower torso, and the arms, and a second detachable arm which controls the legs and feet and is usually held slightly in front of the marionette. In manipulating the more complex control, your second hand which controls the feet will also frequently assist with the arms and hands to help raise one or the other.

Helen Fling, in *Marionettes: How to Make and Work Them*, page 95, shows a control which can be manipulated with one hand. The one-person puppet company who wants to work with marionettes might want to consider this control.

I have some children's marionettes made in Mexico which have a very simple, one-person airplane — bi-plane, I should say!—control. The strings are shortened so that the legs and arms are already part way up. By rotating the control from side to side with the fingers, the marionette moves satisfactorily if not subtly. I have an elephant built on a variant of that control and it, too, moves along rather well. These are not subtle controls and, for the one-person puppet theater I might suggest the simpler Indian Kathputli control. (*See* India and Puppetry.)

To string your marionette, you will need your control, a stand to hold the

Intermediate marionette controls from Nancy Renfro. Raggedy Ann has a central control to move her entire body back and forth and an additional control to move her arms.

control and the marionette, and some heavy cotton thread or fishing line. If you can find silk fishing line, carpet thread, or buttonhole thread, that would be the best. These threads are strong and thick with a matte (not shiny) twist. Otherwise, try crochet thread or #5 Perle cotton.

Your puppet should be finished and dressed. Hang your control at the height you will be holding it while at work which is normally waist height. Using a square knot, string the shoulders first, then the head, then the back. Check from time to time to ensure that the controls are level and at the working height you want. Then string the hands and finally the feet. Continue to test the controls to ensure that all the elements of the puppet hang easily and at the right level and that the tension on the head and shoulders is just right.

Practice with your marionettes to become comfortable with them. If you are a one-person puppet company, consider building holding places on your stage with hooks or rods so that more than two puppets may stay on stage at a time or so that puppets may be posed in place while curtains are being opened and closed. Most of all, enjoy your marionettes and the joy they will bring your audience!

Manipulation

Marionettes can take years to learn to manipulate expertly. Everyone needs a place to start, so let's begin here. You will need a marionette (perhaps more than one) and the type of control it will be using. Begin with something simple, perhaps a single-rod, paper-towel-roll control.

The first thing to do is find the floor in relation to your hand. You need to hold the puppet erect yet keep it in touch with the floor. If your puppet "flies," that is, loses contact with the floor, it will not seem realistic at all and will cause shouts of laughter from the audience. If your puppet sags—if your hand sinks too low—your puppet will not look realistic either.

You may want to use a mirror and a practice surface to see what you are doing. By checking up on yourself in this way, you can correct whatever is amiss in your technique. Take one part of the marionette's body at a time. You will not learn how to control everything at once, so work on the body a bit at a time.

When I was a child watching Howdy Doody on television, I noticed that he walked with "the puppet walk," a knees-high, tap-tap-tapping of the feet across the floor. It looked something like marching, something like running, and it wasn't "natural" at all. On the other hand, these were "puppets made for children." Was it assumed that this kind of puppet could not walk in a "natural" way?

Helen Fling, in *Marionettes: How to Make and Work Them*, suggests using the "marionette swing." This requires the two-part airplane marionette control. Instead of the knees coming up as in the Howdy Doody puppet walk, Ms. Fling has the puppet rising slightly and the legs swinging forward, guided by the bar of the two-part control. Practice with your marionettes until you find a rhythm and a walk which pleases you.

Remember in your work with marionettes that the fingers can lift strings as well as the controls can. In fact, to have your puppet wave or do the can-can, you will need the assistance of your fingers in manipulating your puppets. Learn to hold the rod or the bar of the airplane with the two middle fingers, leaving the first and little fingers free to manipulate strings as needed.

This is a good time to mention practice marionettes. I have mentioned stand-in puppets to be used during early rehearsals for puppet shows. Consider using them for manipulation practice as well. If you have a general method of constructing your puppets, make a blank figure which you can use to practice working with the various parts of the marionette. Just as with the hand puppet, you can have practice routines for marionettes as well.

The first routine you must master, of course, is having the marionette enter and walk across the stage. After that, try entering, turning to the audience, waving to it, and exiting. Then enter, bow to the audience, and exit. You can also have the marionette sit in a chair then get up, or lie down and get up from a bed. Also try various types of walking and moving: marching, running, skipping, skating, and hopping.

Gestures are another important technique for marionette manipulation. How do you express worry, laughter, looking far off in the distance, or looking out a window or door? What about the gestures in giving a speech or declaring one's love or having an argument? Remember: the hands are not the only part of the body which can gesture; the head is active as well. Practice with the head of your marionette as well as the hands.

Posture is another refinement you will want to practice so that you can distinguish between the attitude of a prince, a poet, or a peasant. Body language tells us a great deal about the character of a person. If they stand erect and look straight out at us, we feel that person is comfortable and self-confident. If they slouch, they could portray fatigue or servility or a beaten-down personality. In your exercises, portray a person who is cheerful, one who has had a bad night of sleep, one who has just had great news, and one who has had awful news. Think of various characters in stories you know. How would they carry themselves?

Practice is the key to making your marionettes work smoothly and properly, doing just what you want them to do. Take some time regularly to practice with your puppets so you to have their operation set in your muscles. That way, you will be able to do more and more with your marionettes. Together, you can do wonderful things!

Ackley, Edith Flack. *Marionettes: Easy to Make! Fun to Use!* New York: Lippincott, 1929.
Baird, Bil. *The Art of the Puppet.* New York: Macmillan, 1965.
Bell, John. *Strings, Hands, Shadows: A Modern Puppet History.* Detroit: The Detroit Institute of Arts, 2000.
Currell, David. *Puppets and Puppet Theatre.* Wiltshire, England: Crowood Press, 1999.
Fling, Helen. *Marionettes: How to Make and Work Them.* New York: Dover, 1973.
Hunt, Tamara, and Nancy Renfro. *Puppetry in Early Childhood Education.* Austin, TX: Nancy Renfro Studios, 1982.
Lade, Roger. *The Most Excellent Book of How to Be a Puppeteer.* Brookfield, CT: Copper Beech Books, 1996.

Marketing *see* **Business of Puppetry: Advertising and Marketing**

Mask Puppets with Movable Mouths

A mask puppet is not worn but, instead, is a puppet in its own right. The mask puppet can be made from paper, foam rubber, or whatever material suits your character and the design you have in mind. Two rods are used: one to hold and turn the entire mask and one to move the mouth. The mouth need not move much, just enough to suggest talking. While the modern mask puppet will not have legs or a body, in ancient times, small bodies were attached to the mask, forming a transitional element. This is seen in Canadian Northwest Coast tribal masks. (*See* American Indian Puppetry.)

Mask puppets can discuss cultures or illustrate how the masks themselves might be used within a culture. Mask puppets can also be made of the sun, moon, stars, wind and other natural phenomena. Other puppets, such as those of fish or other kinds of sea life, can be made to look like masks and manipulated with rods and made to talk.

When making a movable jaw, it is good to remember that the lower part of the jaw moves in normal speech. Also remember that a great deal of movement is not necessary to convince your audience that the puppet is talking. In fact, puppets without mouths have elicited comments about how clever their mouth parts were. Just remember not to exaggerate or overdo the action of the character.

CONSIDERATIONS

Remember to hinge the puppet's jaw for easier movement. This can be done with tape, cardboard washers, or anything that will reinforce and strengthen the jaw hinge and provide ease of movement. (*See* Hinges.) The only jaw that doesn't need this treatment is the ponytail holder mouth. (*See* Ponytail Holder Movable Mouth.)

For ease of construction, try to use a mask with a contour or with a seam down the middle. A mask built on the corner of a box or plastic milk carton will work just fine. If you are using a bottle or other rounded surface, remember that the mouth portion must be slightly wider than the bottle in order to move well.

MATERIALS

• Box, soda bottle, plastic milk jug, or whatever you plan to use to make your puppet
• Pencil
• Markers
• Eraser
• Craft knife or scissors
• Brads
• String
• Masking or plastic tape or cardboard for washers
• 2 dowels for the puppet's rods
• Any materials you will need to complete the design of your mask puppet

ASSEMBLY

1. Locate the eyes on your puppet mask and mark them.
2. Locate the position of nose and upper mouth and mark them.
3. Measure the length of the upper mouth.
4. Make the lower mouth ½" to 1" longer to create leeway between the upper and lower mouth and allow for a circular hinge portion which you will attach to the upper mouth.
5. Cut out all mask parts: eyes, nose, upper mouth, and the lower mouth portion.
6. Reinforce the hinge position where the mouth will move. Use either tape or cardboard washers.
7. Join the upper and lower mouth parts with brads or loosely tied string.
8. Check the flexibility and the smoothness of the joint.
9. Decorate the mask.
10. Attach the rods to the mask and the mouth so that they are firmly in place.
11. Check the mouth again for smoothness of operation.
12. Give your mask a character and put on your play!

Feller, Ron, and Marsha Feller. *Paper Masks and Puppets for Stories, Songs, and Plays.* Seattle, WA: The Arts Factory, 1985.
Mills, Winifred H., and Louise M. Dunn. *Marionettes, Masks and Shadows.* Garden City, NY: Doubleday, 1928.
Wright, Lyndie. *Masks.* New York: Franklin Watts, 1989.

Masks

A mask is a representational object which is worn over the face or the head and face. It can be a religious or secular object and can represent concrete, imaginary, or fantastic persons, animals, or beings.

A mask is a partial disguise usually worn to conceal the identity of the wearer and often to reveal the character represented by the mask. Although masks usually cover just the face, they can also cover the entire head and even become a part of the costume below.

In some cultures, the mask retains its old power to connect with forces larger than the wearer: to represent gods, demons, heroes, and villains. The person wearing the mask may become temporarily infused with the power of the mask and act, speak, or move in ways characteristic of the mask and not of the person.

European and American society of the last two hundred years has seen the mask as both simple disguise and metaphor for the human being within society.

People going to a masked ball may have felt able to act with greater freedom and carelessness since they were disguised. However, the mask worn within society becomes a metaphor for the psychological masks we all wear — parent, teacher, student, boss, employee — during various phases of our lives. Sometimes all may be worn in a single day. Removing the mask and showing our authentic selves requires trust and faith and is rarely done.

Within the last few decades, the use of masks has become a way to present theatrical characters in a new and more interesting way. *Cats, The Phantom of the Opera,* and most especially *The Lion King* have shown an imaginative use of masks and puppetlike forms.

Of course, the movies have been using masks and prosthetic devices for ages. Where would Mr. Spock, the Star Wars Cantina scene, Borgs, and Klingons have been without the special use of masks or masklike appliances?

In the world of puppetry, the mask can become a puppet itself. If you have ever walked through a museum, gone to a carnival or Mardi Gras parade, or just seen an artfully made mask, you may have wondered what those masks might have had to say for themselves. Masks as puppets can tell stories, discuss culture (and why individual masks are important), and become the central focus of a puppet presentation. The talking mask is not only a chance to create a character; it is a gateway into another dimension — a new way of looking at things.

Both Japanese Bunraku and Canadian Northwest Coast tribal people have a tradition of movable masks whose faces can reveal another dimension of personality. (*See* Bunraku; American Indian Puppetry.) I have seen at least one Bunraku puppet whose face transforms from serenity to jealousy or fury with a flip of internal controls. The masks of the Northwest Coast peoples frequently have moving parts which open to reveal another face. The ability to reveal a second face, to give an indication of an inner conflict or a hidden character trait, makes the mask useful in more-complex puppet plays.

Masking a puppet character could happen for several different reasons. The first would be transformation, as in the prince regaining his human form in *Beauty and the Beast.* Another would be the emergence of true character, as when the beautiful but evil queen reveals her true self as an ugly enchantress in *Snow White.* Yet a third reason would be as part of a story during a masquerade sequence.

Using a mask requires hands, and, if you are using just your own two hands, you might prefer using a transforming puppet rather than a mask. Check *Puppeteer* by Kathryn Lasky to see the description of the dwarf-into-wizard transformation in *Aladdin and the Magic Lamp.*

Masks are not common to puppetry. However, with their use in theater and their value as cultural objects, masks have great potential. As an element of more-intricate puppet theater, the mask can be used to reveal an alternative face and thereby create a story of greater complexity than usual.

Feller, Ron, and Marsha Feller. *Paper Masks and Puppets for Stories, Songs, and Plays.* Seattle, WA: The Arts Factory, 1985.
Lasky, Kathryn. *Puppeteer.* New York: Macmillan, 1985.
Mills, Winifred H., and Louise M. Dunn. *Marionettes, Masks and Shadows.* Garden City, NY: Doubleday, 1928.
Wright, Lyndie. *Masks.* New York: Franklin Watts, 1989.

Mime

Mime is the ability to tell a story without using words, only with gestures. The ability to make an audience believe that a wind is blowing when there is none, that stairs are there to be climbed when none exist, is the power of mime. Short sketches are interpreted through movement, and the skill of the mime is judged by how believable the story becomes to the audience.

Puppetry is basically a mimetic activity. The puppet should be able to tell a short story through movement alone. Words in puppetry are an embellishment; emphasis should be on gesture alone. If you cannot tell your story in gesture, you need to reconsider and reblock your story.

By learning mime, you learn how to move your body through space and tell a story. By transferring what mime teaches you to the workings of your puppets, you will have another dimension for telling a story. The use of life-sized puppets, Bunraku puppets, and giant puppets can all be enhanced through the use of mime and movement. (*See* Bunraku; Giant Puppets; Life-Sized Puppets.) If nothing else, knowing how *your* body works can help you move the bodies of large puppets.

Furthermore, the use of the body plus movement plus props can lead to new forms of puppetry. New methods of expression may present themselves, and new stories emerge. If you have the opportunity to study mime, even for a bit, do so. It can only add to your repertoire of skills and deepen your understanding of the power of gesture. You will have a better understanding of how your puppets can move expressively, and you may find new avenues of puppetry opening themselves up to you as a result of your study.

Mouth Puppets

A mouth puppet is one in which the head opens to reveal a movable mouth and which appears to talk. There are several kinds of mouth puppets: a wide-mouth puppet which appears to have a circle for a mouth; a box mouth; and a foam-rubber shaped head. There are other kinds of movable mouths which have been mentioned in this book, but they do not make mouth puppets. (*See:* Mouths; Sock Puppets.) The mouth puppet has a wide mouth which opens the entire face.

Mouth puppets can be made of felt with a round mouth that can open wide. In operation, the hand must be held in an inverted "U" position to allow the face to be seen.

Barbara Aiello's troupe, Kids on the Block, uses this kind of puppet. Bert and Ernie of *Sesame Street* are also mouth puppets.

Following are instructions for making a box mouth puppet, but there are many more kinds to try.

Oatmeal Box Mouth Puppet

MATERIALS

- One large, sturdy box, such as an oatmeal box
- One yard of stretchy material such as jersey or some other knit in a color you want for the face (Old tights or stirrup pants can be used for this as well.)
- #5 Perle cotton (thick embroidery thread) in a color to match the face cloth
- Felt for the mouth
- Pellon or fusible interfacing for the mouth
- Optional bandanna, collar, or ruffie
- Optional wig
- Eyes
- Body for your mouth puppet (This can be a doll's body without its head or a

pair of children's footed rompers stuffed with fiberfill. The body must be dressed and ready to go.)

- Craft knife
- Scissors
- Pencil
- White glue
- Thread
- Ribbon
- Strapping tape
- Poster board
- Eyes
- Newspaper or freezer paper
- Straight pins
- Sewing machine or needle and thread

ASSEMBLY

1. Using the craft knife, cut the box almost in two leaving at least 2" or more as a hinge for the head.

A mouth puppet can be made with a cardboard mouth. Mouths for this type of puppet are characteristically wide and face-splitting.

2. Reinforce the hinge with strapping tape.

3. With the craft knife, carefully cut a space for your fingers and thumb in the box without cutting through the hinge.

4. Open the cut box and carefully lay it on some freezer paper or newspaper. Draw an outline of this shape for the mouth covering, and cut it out to make pattern A.

5. Use pattern A to make a second paper pattern B, but add a 1" margin around pattern B's edge for overlap.

6. Cut out pattern B.

7. Divide pattern A in half and use this pattern to cut two pieces of felt from A to be used as a pocket for your fingers.

8. Use the pattern A halves to cut two pieces of fusible interfacing to reinforce the mouth. Fuse the interfacing to the felt mouth pocket pieces using an iron.

9. Cut one piece out of felt using paper pattern B (with the added margin).

10. Pin the smaller pieces of felt to the larger single piece, matching the felt at the outside edges of the mouth. This should leave a margin between the upper and lower pieces of felt and an opening at the mouth hinge for your fingers.

11. Using a sewing machine or needle and thread, sew the pieces of felt together close to the edge of the smaller pieces of felt. Do not sew over the opening for your fingers!

12. Firmly fasten the mouth to the puppet with glue. If you think that won't be strong enough with all the handling it will get, reinforce it with strapping tape. The outside edges of the mouth will be covered by the face material, so strength, not beauty, is your goal.

13. Test the mouth pockets when everything is dry.

14. Sew the stretchy material into a tube if it is not in a tube shape already.

15. Fit the tube over the box leaving extra material above and below the head. Use thread to gather the material together at the back of the mouth. There will be wrinkles in the cloth which must be smoothed out as much as possible.

16. Carefully cut a slit in the stretchy material above and below the head hinge which will allow access to the mouth manipulating slits. You won't be able to move the mouth a great deal, but that's fine. Small is better with mouth movements.

17. Tie off the material below the head, and sew it to the body of the puppet.

18. Disguise the lack of neck, if you want, with a ruffle, bandanna, collar, or other neck covering item of clothing.

19. Tie off the material on the top of the head. A wig can be placed over this, or the tied-off material can be left like a little kid's top-knot and a ribbon tied around it.

Attach eyes, insert your hand, and you're ready to go with your mouth puppet!

Henson, Cheryl, and the Muppet Workshop. *The Muppets Make Puppets!* New York: Workman Publishing, 1994.
Hunt, Tamara, and Nancy Renfro. *Puppetry in Early Childhood Education.* Austin, TX: Nancy Renfro Studios, 1982.
Wallace, Mary. *I Can Make Puppets.* Toronto: Greey de Pencier Books, 1994.

Mouths

Having a mouth on your puppet often is not necessary. Like the characters of Joan Walsh Anglund, people looking at the "mouthless" puppet will provide one in their imagination. They may even compliment you on the great mouth mechanism you have for your puppet without a mouth. The absence of a mouth combined with a round face adds innocence and wisdom to a character as in the Anglund drawings.

You may feel, however, that your puppet's character must have a mouth that moves. At the same time, you may not want a puppet with a gaping mouth. (*See* Mouth Puppets.) In addition, you don't want it to be too complex, either, or take too much time to make. Whew! What a list.

The first criterion for consideration is to use an item that moves on its own: a trash can with a lid on a spring; hinged set of salad tongs, tea strainer, meatball maker, or any other object which moves on its own in a mouthlike manner. The object is then dressed to create the character you want.

The second criterion is to use an item which can be caused to move like a mouth. This could be the sleeve of a shirt or the opening in an oven mitt. First, see if the opening needs to be reinforced to hold its shape with lightweight wire, interfacing, or some other stiffening agent. Then decide whether you want your hand in the puppet or a rod doing the mouth manipulation. Your hand is usually easier, as it can move the mouth properly. In this way, you can not only have talking laundry, you can also make a book, stack of papers, ham and cheese sandwich, or any other stack of linear objects acquire the ability to talk and comment on the situation at hand.

Other than objects which move with a mouthlike motion or can be turned into a mouth, there are three kinds of simple mouths for puppets that are not of the wide-mouth variety: the ponytail holder movable mouth, where you make a mouth for a rod or stick puppet, the puppet for which this mouth works best;

the cardboard tube sliding mouth and a hinged jaw which can be moved by means of a rod. (*See* Cardboard Tube Sliding Mouths; Hinges; Ponytail Holder Movable Mouths.) The latter may make your puppet more complicated than you want, but it does answer that laundry list of demands!

Hinged Jaw

The hinged jaw is made as if it were a bandage covering the lower part of the face. It is hinged at the point where the upper and lower jaws connect and is moved up and down by means of a rod. The mouth can be made in two ways: with a crease or bend in the middle or with a smooth appearance. The smooth mouth will make your puppet look as if it had a "bulldog jaw;" that is, the lower jaw juts forward and over the upper teeth the way a bulldog's jaw does. It gives the puppet a great deal of character, although it probably wouldn't be used on a heroic figure because we expect our heroes to have been to the dentist and gotten their teeth straightened and capped so they twinkle! Right?

The lower part of the face will be cut away on your puppet and end at the upper lip and nose so that the movable jaw completes the face. The jaw itself is cut slightly larger than the face so that the mouth will move more easily and fit well.

A hinge is made at the point where the upper and lower jaws attach. The hinges can be drawn as part of the jaw pattern and reinforced with clear strapping tape. The two sections of the mouth are joined with brads or with string depending on the design of your character and how readily you want the jaw hinges to show. Don't join the sections too tightly. Leave quite a bit of room so that the jaw will move easily. Attach a rod to the lower part of the mouth, and start talking!

Sponge Mouths

Another simple mouth can be made in a foam or sponge head and consists of a slit or opening in the face where the mouth is plus an interior slit below the mouth on the underside of the puppet to accommodate the fingers. The fingers are inserted in the interior slit and move slightly, creating mouth movement. (*See also* Sponge Puppets.) Don't think that you must have a huge mouth movement; a little bit is better than a lot in puppetry, especially where mouths are concerned.

Henson, Cheryl, and the Muppet Workshop. *The Muppets Make Puppets!* New York: Workman Publishing, 1994.

Hunt, Tamara, and Nancy Renfro. *Puppetry in Early Childhood Education.* Austin, TX: Nancy Renfro Studios, 1982.

Wallace, Mary. *I Can Make Puppets.* Toronto: Greey de Pencier Books, 1994.

Music

Music adds a new dimension to a puppet presentation. Even if it is a little clip which introduces a short play for toddlers, music draws the attention of the audience and can set the mood. This is the reason movies and television shows have theme music. When you hear the orchestra begin to play that familiar tune, you know your favorite TV show is about to begin. In addition, music can provide focus, especially when you have decided not to use a curtain. While the music is playing, your puppets can enter and remove the playbill which announces the show. The choice of music is up to you, but the decision to have music at least to introduce your play is an excellent idea.

In a longer production, music helps carry the action along, signals when there will be a scene change, and provides closure when the play is over. When you are planning your puppet play, keep the presence of music in mind. Go to your local library and check out some CDs to listen to. Make notes about the music, including the name of the composer and of the recording. In fact, you can do this for any piece you hear. Make an index of music you have listened to so that at a future time, when you need a particular sort of music, you can go to your music index and find what you want.

Remember that you want your music to support the scene which is playing. You don't want to mismatch the music and the story, either. Don't have classical music playing for a story which takes place in the Appalachian Mountains. For that setting you'd want to make sure you have some banjo and fiddle tunes, some hammered dulcimers, and perhaps some country singing. You can mix and match music and theater styles, but that takes quite a good ear and lots of experience. When you pick out your music, try to stick with the basics.

If you have never listened to theater music before, go back to your library and check out some recordings of Gilbert and Sullivan or Rogers and Hammerstein music. See how the overture introduces all the music that is to come and builds excitement for what will follow. Unless you hire some musicians to compose music for your play, what you find will not be as tight a fit as music composed for an entire play, but you can do rather well if you keep the mood of the play in mind. Work at the music scene by scene. Focus on the opening and closing of each act of your play plus an overture (music to play before the curtain goes up and when the play is over). This should give you enough music to add interest and appeal to your play.

How to introduce your music into the play is usually the second biggest music problem confronting puppeteers. If you have someone who is willing to be your music assistant, you will need to rehearse with that person and let him or her know the cues to bring up the music. That is why so many puppeteers like to prerecord their performance. That way, they have a single tape with everything on it and needn't worry about another person not being able to make it on performance night.

If you decide to have some music play as an introduction to a brief skit, you can play your CD or tape on a portable player. Make sure that the player is in an easily reached location. Load the music and cue it to the point when you want the music to begin playing. When you enter the backstage of your theater, you can hit the play button and bring up the music. At the point where you begin your skit, bring the music volume down, hit pause, and begin your skit. When the skit is over, hit the pause button again to remove the pause feature, and then bring up the music. If the music is soft enough, it can just play through the end of your program.

As you can see, even this little bit of added music will take some rehearsal. You will need to position the tape or CD player in a good location and practice bringing the music up as well as turning it off in the dark. Glow-in-the-dark paint on the "pause" or "play" button may be of use here.

If a particular section of music is needed for your skit, you may want to pre-record it so that it is cued up correctly and you have only what you want. That way, when you hit "play" you will have only what you want to hear.

You may also want to see what your area's theatrical, music, or electronics shop has to offer in the way of specialized equipment for turning your player off and on. A remote control which you can work with your feet or more effectively and quietly than the "off" button of your CD player would be a real boon. Check with them, explain your needs, and see what they have to offer. Spending a bit of money now may help prevent gray hairs and heartburn later on.

Like all the other elements of puppetry, adding music to your play will take some getting used to. You will have to learn to listen to music and make note of things you feel will be an asset to your play. You will have to match the music to the mood of your play. And you will have to find equipment which will add to the ease of playing your music behind stage. Finally, you will have to rehearse in order to integrate your music into the puppet play. When you do, however, you will have added another wonderful element to your puppetry which will make it that much more exciting to watch and enjoy.

Currell, David. *The Complete Book of Puppetry*. Boston: Plays, Inc., 1975.
Currell, David. *Puppets and Puppet Theatre*. Wiltshire, England: Crowood Press, 1999.
Lasky, Kathryn. *Puppeteer*. New York: Macmillan, 1985.

National Day of Puppetry

The National Day of Puppetry falls on the Saturday of the last full weekend in April and is sponsored by the Puppeteers of America, Inc. It was first held in April 1999 and is a whole day to celebrate puppets and puppetry. It is a local initiative, with state guilds, schools, and libraries organizing their own activities.

On this wonderful day, floats, parades, workshops, and shows all celebrate the wonder that is puppetry. Contact the Puppeteers of America through their web site, www.puppeteers.org, to find out more about it, or go to your library and check the index of *Chase's Annual Events* or *The Teacher's Calendar*. You will find out much more about this nifty celebration: the precise date of the event, local guilds in your area which might be participating, as well as ideas and contact people to help celebrate the day. (*See also* Festivals.)

National Puppetry Conference

The mission of the National Puppetry Conference is to be a catalyst for the professional puppet artist's growth and development through both the exploration of performance styles and skills, and the production of new works-in-progress for the puppet theatre. The conference focuses on empowering puppet artists to create through the visual imagery and kinetic form of the puppet and enhancing their work through a collaborative dramaturgical process.

In 1964, the renowned puppetry team of Rufus and Margo Rose helped George C. White, the founding director, establish the Eugene O'Neill Theater Center. This center for the theater arts, which encourages the puppetry arts, continued through the efforts of puppet artist, Bart Roccobertson, Jr. Finally, Jane Henson established the Rose Endowment for Puppetry which supports the annual puppetry conference.

The conference staff consists of professionals from all areas of puppetry arts. While there are performances from artists-in-residence and visiting troupes, the conference participants are encouraged to participate in hands-on theater and puppetry experiences. The participants not only get to observe other puppetry styles but also to work on their own material and strive to develop an insight into their own style. The week ends with performances by the participants and staff.

An application to attend the conference must be sent in early. In 2001, the deadline for the conference was April 1, 2001, for the conference to be held on June 9–21, 2001. Check the National Puppetry Conference web site at for further information. As with so many other conferences and festivals, this is an exceptional opportunity for learning and for meeting other puppeteers.

National Puppetry Festival

The National Puppetry Festival is sponsored by Puppeteers of America (*www.puppeteers.org*) and is more like a convention than a festival, with talks, workshops, and special presentations over several days. It is given on odd-numbered years and is always held in July at a college or university.

This festival is a chance for puppeteers to get together, to trade ideas, and to learn from one another. There are workshops, demonstrations, performances, and open mike nights. While there is a general, overarching theme each year, the focus is upon teaching, learning, and the exchange of ideas about puppetry.

Continuing education credits are offered for up to fifteen contact hours. In the 2001 national festival, workshops were offered in writing, music, visual arts, history, drama, movement, recreation, and early childhood education. The Puppeteers of America urge teachers and librarians to contact their state boards or licensing agencies to check on these credits.

Registration and housing costs are kept as low as possible. Puppeteers are usually not rolling in money! On the other hand, check with your accountant. You may be able to deduct all or part of the cost of the national festival as a professional expense.

Conventions, festivals, and other workshops are great places to gather information, learn new things, and exchange ideas with other like-minded professionals. They can also be great places to network and make contacts. Consider putting these gatherings on your schedule. The information gained and the contacts made will more than compensate you for the time and expense involved.

Noses

Noses are a part of a puppet's character-creating facial elements. Think of a pig with a teeny-tiny snout, a cow with a human nose instead of a muzzle, a cute little girl with a great big nose, or wicked sorceress with a cute little button of a nose. It could happen, but we wouldn't believe it. In the case of the animals, we know what they look like. A pig with a teeny-tiny snout wouldn't be believable. The puppet play would have to explain it, so the nose becomes an important element of puppet design.

As for the humans with different noses, these play into our beliefs about people and what their characters say they should look like. A wonderful story by Jane Yolen called *Sleeping Ugly* plays into these very assumptions with a beautiful but mean-spirited princess, an ugly but kind-hearted young girl living in the forest, and an elderly woman who is a fairy or witch. After an accident sends all three into an enchanted sleep, a young prince must figure out what to do about the situation. Jane is ugly and her nose takes an "L" turn at the bottom. It adds to her plainness and underscores the realization that anyone choosing her as a wife would have to be looking beyond surface beauty to the reality of the situation beneath. Jane's nose helps to set her character.

If you are serious about making puppets, you should begin a collection of noses: egg carton snouts for pigs, fingers from gloves that can be stuffed and sewn on, hoses and Slinkies for elephant trunks as well as strange, fantastic creatures, and our old friends packing peanuts, buttons, pom-poms, and so on. Anything that looks as if it might serve as a nose should go into your nose box. Then, when you are looking around for the right nose to put on your character, you will have a set of things to choose from.

When you are thinking about noses, consider how the nose contributes to a character, and don't be afraid to play with the idea. Consider Jane in *Sleeping Ugly*. Who says that a princess *must* conform to our ideas of beauty — or a prince, for that matter? Try reading some of these alternative stories about princes and princesses, for example, *Shrek* by William Steig. (If you've seen the movie, you will *not* be prepared for the book! It turns fairy tale conventions on their head.) Also read *The Paper Bag Princess* by Robert Munsch and *Tarzanna* by Babbette Cole.

One playlet in an old *Sesame Street* concerns Bert and Ernie switching noses. Ernie is in a playful mood and detaches Bert's nose and puts it on his own face. Bert, the tall thin puppet, has a tall, thin nose. Short, round Ernie has a short, round nose. To see the noses in the wrong place jars us out of our ordinary perceptions of these characters. First of all, we are not normally able to switch noses with other people. Secondly, we have become used to seeing Ernie and Bert looking a certain way. When these things are changed around, it gives our brains a tweak, and they wake up a bit and look at things a little differently. Like an animal who thinks it will be happier if it only has the attributes of other animals, nose switching could partake of this fairy tale convention and make for an interesting puppet play.

Another brief nose-switching episode occurs in Raymond Briggs's *The Snowman*. The boy has seen his snowman creation come to life and invites the snowman into his home. In the kitchen, the snowman finds a bowl of fruit and for a lark switches his oval, squatty apple nose for a number of other things: orange, cherry, pineapple. He tickles the boy with the pineapple leaves, then puts his own nose back in its proper place. It's just a moment in the story, but it establishes the character of the snowman as playful, creative, and generous.

Consider all these things when you are choosing the nose for your puppet character. The nose, like the beak on a bird, is the most prominent element of the face and the first thing people may notice about your puppet. Keep everything supporting the character of your developing puppet. And remember that Gonzo of the Muppets wouldn't be the same without his nose! Your puppet should be the same: a character with a memorable and appropriate nose.

Henson, Cheryl, and the Muppet Workshop. *The Muppets Make Puppets!* New York: Workman Publishing, 1994.

Object Theater

Object theater takes junk puppetry to a new height and could be called *found-object theater*. (*See* Junk Puppets.) Junk puppets take ordinary materials and turn them into puppets by adding eyes, facial features, perhaps even costumes. Just about anything can be turned into a puppet if you use your imagination. These recycled puppets then perform as puppets do, playing their part to entertain, amuse, and inform.

In object theater, however, there is a greater purpose than simple amusement. By using real-world materials, object theater calls attention to, say, the condition of the environment and the need to conserve and recycle. By manipulating found objects, the puppeteer can show that without conserving and recycling, we will all be buried under our own waste.

The puppets used in object theater are not changed into puppets, they are used as they are. They become animated without altering their appearance and are used in their real-world or found state to enact the puppet play. You may not even need a puppet theater in the traditional sense.

Paul Zaloom is probably the best known of the object theater puppeteers. Although he began with Bread and Puppet Theater, he is now better known as Professor Beakman of television's *Beakman's World*. He continues to create puppet shows for adults and for children separate from his television show. The basic concept of taking real-world materials and animating them in some way to make a point or teach a lesson — in this case, science — is a foundation of the *Beakman's World* concept. The object theater concept is extended through traveling *Beakman's World* shows sent to museums throughout the country.

Mr. Zaloom began his work, which became object theater, by animating and playing with everyday objects and seeing what they had to say. You might do the same by gathering and playing around with various objects. How do they relate to one another? Is there a connection between them which you cannot immediately see but which may emerge in the course of the conversation? It is an advanced form of child's play with the informed mind of an adult.

Give object theater a try and see if you like it. Your focus may be more mundane: good nutrition, the joy of reading, or cleanliness and good health, but you may find that getting everyday things to talk may put across a lesson you've been trying to teach.

Paper Bag Theaters

Just about anything can become a puppet stage, and the possibilities for portable stages are nearly limitless. The paper bag theater is just such a stage, originally designed by Nancy Renfro. An ordinary brown paper bag can become a small stage for one or two puppets who hide in the bag and pop up to sing a song or recite a poem. Since the bag and puppet are a unit, holiday themes are frequent choices. You need only one or two characters to create a play, and the decorations on the bag set the mood.

Rudolph's House   Duck Pond   Tree

Paper bag theaters from Nancy Renfro. A paper bag can be decorated inexpensively. The puppet enters from the bottom of the bag.

The idea is to take a bag and decorate it in the desired theme, then have a puppet or two pop out of the top of the bag and sing a song, recite a poem, or tell a story appropriate to the theme. The puppets are simple stick puppets; some possibilities are

a girl or boy and a Diwali lamp

Santa and a Christmas tree

a Hanukkah and a shammes candle

a leprechaun and a rainbow or a pot of gold

a tree and some birds or animals for Earth Day or Arbor Day.

In some cases, more than one puppet must be mounted on a single stick.

Materials

- Brown paper grocery bag for a large theater or small lunch bag for a miniature theater
- Scissors
- Pencil
- Ruler
- White glue
- Paints and paint brushes or markers
- Poster board

- Craft sticks, straws, or skewers a little longer than the paper bag is deep for the puppets

ASSEMBLY

1. Draw a design on your paper bag in keeping with the theme your puppets will represent.
2. Paint or color in the design.
3. Cut a slot or holes in the bottom of your paper bag for the sticks of your puppets to extend through.
4. Check the length of your sticks, straws, or skewers to make sure they are long enough.
5. Make your puppets out of poster board, or draw the figures on plain paper, color them in, and paste them on poster board.
6. Mount your puppets on the rods you have measured in step 4. The puppets will sit inside the bag and will pop out of the top of the bag, bouncing up and down by means of the sticks extending through the bottom of the bag.
7. Gather your puppets, get your audience, and put on a play!

Hunt, Tamara, and Nancy Renfro. *Celebrate! Holidays, Puppets and Creative Drama.* Austin, TX: Nancy Renfro Studios, 1987.
Hunt, Tamara, and Nancy Renfro. *Puppetry in Early Childhood Education.* Austin, TX: Nancy Renfro Studios, 1982.

Papier-Mâché

Papier-mâché is surely the puppet maker's very good, if not best, friend. It is lightweight and inexpensive, and it makes durable (some would say, indestructible) puppet parts, especially heads for hand puppets. The following information in no way implies a complete work on all the things you can do with papier-mâché or all the techniques involved in working with it, but it will get you started.

Papier-mâché is paper and glue used either with a mold or as sculptured pulp (mash) to create things. You can make puppet heads, of course, or dishes, lawn sculpture (if heavily varnished), boxes—all sorts of things with just paper and glue. In the eighteenth century, Europeans fell in love with papier-mâché luxury items, first from Asia and then from European artisans. George Washington even thought to use it on the ceilings at Mount Vernon.

Laminated Papier-Mâché

Traditionally, papier-mâché has been made from torn paper mixed with a flour paste. Now, however, with the advent of white glues of all sorts, papier-mâché can be reliably made with thinned white glue which does not require drying between layers as flour paste does.

The most basic method of using papier-mâché is to tear paper into strips about an inch square, dip them in glue, and laminate these strips over whatever mold, armature, or item you wish to duplicate. The papier-mâché is manipulated, not sculpted into shape. A minimum of four layers of papier-mâché is needed to make an item thick enough to stand on its own. When dry, the item can be gently sanded, given one to five coats of gesso, sanded in between each application of gesso, and painted in whatever manner you like.

Papier-mâché can also be molded over a core of paper, aluminum foil, or Styrofoam which can remain intact or be cut away as with traditional clay molds. Not only can the usual paper-and-glue laminate be used but also a sort of molding compound of soaked paper can be made to sculpt anything going over the core. Tissue-mâché is done like this, with the tissue paper becoming soaked with glue so that it can be molded into shapes for noses, ears, eyebrows, and the like. (*See* Tissue-Mâché Puppet Heads.) Paper towel or plain toilet tissue can also be used in this way.

When you are using newsprint, try to obtain the unprinted kind which is frequently used by moving companies to wrap things in. Newspaper ink may be toxic, and it grays and weakens the entire paper mass. Unprinted newsprint is still being recycled into paper, which is a good thing.

Papier-Mâché Mash

Laminated papier-mâché is not to be confused with papier-mâché mash which is boiled and softened paper that can be sculpted. Papier-mâché mash can be wrung out and frozen, then thawed for further use. This helps preserve your hard-made paper blends and prevents souring.

Ronnie Burkett has a wonderful, on-line essay about his trials and tribulations with papier-mâché mash. I heartily recommend that you read it. Papier-mâché is, as he points out, nontoxic. You can recycle all sorts of consumer-end paper materials into papier-mâché. It can be shaped into molds or sculpted directly. Finally, he points out that two to five coats of gesso, alternating with sanding, can produce a fine, smooth surface with no bumps or texture. Mix skin tones into the gesso to save on time.

The recipe I enjoyed the most was the one Burkett got for paper egg carton mash. Simply soak the ripped up cartons in water. When soggy, place them in a blender or Cuisineart and whirl until everything is smooth. Wring out the water. The mash can be used as is or a bit of white glue added as a further binder. Add some oil of wintergreen or cloves to prevent the mash from souring.

Remember that papier-mâché mash takes a great deal of time to dry. (One layer of the laminate form will dry overnight, but that's four days and nights of applying the strips, then letting them dry!) Papier-mâché mash pressed into a mold needs to be a thin enough layer to dry in a week, yet thick enough to stand up to the sanding and general wear that your puppets will probably get. One recommendation from Burkett is to use a rubber mold, press in the layer of mash, then place in the freezer for six hours or so. When sufficiently frozen, remove it from the freezer and peel away the rubber mold, and dry the unmolded papier-mâché form in a low-temperature oven. Do not use the oven if you have molded over a Styrofoam base. The Styrofoam will melt, releasing toxic fumes!

If you try either laminated papier-mâché or papier-mâché mash techniques and find that you enjoy it for all the reasons given above, do read up some more on the technique. Not only should you read books on papier-mâché technique but on paper making in general. Paper is frequently pressed into molds to create artworks, and this may further your knowledge of creating puppets. As Mr. Burkett says, when you've tired of the expensive — and toxic — modern molding materials, come back to papier-mâché!

Making Papier-Mâché Puppet Heads

Puppet heads made of papier-mâché are strong, light, and will last a very long time. They are easy to make and can form the basis for a flexible, creative troupe of puppets. Because they are so inexpensive to make, puppets with papier-mâché heads are the friends of the cash-strapped librarian, teacher, or child worker.

MATERIALS

The materials for making papier-mâché puppet heads are quite inexpensive: newspaper, tissue paper, or brown paper; white glue and water; nonhardening, oil-based clay for molding the head, and gesso and acrylic paint. Jigs for holding the heads while molding can be made from scrap wood and dowels or from empty soda bottles filled with sand, pebbles, or clean dirt. A coping saw will be needed to saw the papier-mâché head apart when it is dry.

ASSEMBLY

Using the nonhardening, oil-based clay, sculpt the face you would like on the jig, making sure that there is a neck with a slightly outward turning ridge at the bottom. The ridge will be used later on to fasten the body of the puppet to the head.

Next, tear the newspaper into one inch squares. If you have access to a paper shredder with a ½" width, try shredding the newspaper that way to cut down on your time. After shredding, tear the newspaper strips into 1" lengths. Do the same with the brown paper and the tissue paper so that you have a supply of several kinds of paper prepared for working.

Using the tissue paper dipped in water, cover the clay with a layer of tissue paper. Do not let the tissue paper dry out as it will fall off the clay. This layer will assist in releasing the papier-mâché from the clay mold.

Thin some white glue with water to a milky consistency in a small dish. Dip square after square of the newspaper in the thinned glue mixture and cover the mold completely with a layer of newspaper. It is not necessary to let the white glue dry as you would if you used flour-and-water paste, but you can wait for the layer of paper to dry if you wish. In this way, you can work on several puppet heads at a time.

Alternate layers of newspaper with layers of brown paper until you have built up four layers in addition to the tissue paper layer. When all the layers are dry, saw the papier-mâché puppet head apart from ear to ear. Dig out the clay and smooth the sawn edges of the puppet head. Glue the puppet head back together and allow it to dry thoroughly.

When the glue is dry, paint the puppet head with a coat of gesso, and then paint features in with acrylic paints. Affix hair to the head (*see* Hair and Wigs) and make and attach the body. If you wish to vary your puppet's roles, make the body of the puppet one which can be dressed and undressed. This will require a wardrobe of clothes for the puppet. A better idea might be interchangeable bodies which can be attached at the neck rim. (*See* Hand Puppets; Hand Puppet Construction.)

Currell, David. *An Introduction to Puppets & Puppet-Making*. Edison, NJ: Chartwell Books, 1992.

Flower, Cedric, and Alan Fortney. *Puppets, Methods and Materials*. Worcester, MA: Davis Publ., 1983.

Lade, Roger. *The Most Excellent Book of How to Be a Puppeteer*. Brookfield, CT: Copper Beech Books, 1996.

Peep Shows

A peep show is a tableau enclosed within a container which has only one small window and perhaps a way to let light into the container. When I was a child, you could get Easter egg peep shows made of large sugar eggs which contained a springtime scene. Nothing moved. The idea was to view a miniature world in this small enclosure which could only be seen by looking through a small opening in one end of the sugar egg. Otherwise, all was invisible, only the outside of the decorated egg was seen.

A similar scene can be made today by purchasing a very large 6" Styrofoam egg. Cut about 1" off the small end of the egg. This will become the viewing port. Cut the egg in half, and hollow it out to a thickness of ½". Remember to use a dust mask while working with the Styrofoam dust.

Flatten one side of the egg so that it will lie on a surface without rocking. Fit the two halves together and look through the viewing port on the small end of the egg. Make sure that your view of the opposite end is unobstructed and that the light is filtering through the Styrofoam to light the scene.

On the far end of the bottom half of the egg, create a springtime or Easter scene by gluing colorful figures of poster board or heavy paper onto the egg. Remember that depth can be created by using several rows of figures in your scene. Glue the egg back together. You can decorate the egg, but do not affect its transparency. The sugar eggs I remember were decorated with icing at the opening and around the middle where the two halves came together.

A similar container can be made of papier-mâché over a 6" or larger Styrofoam egg. (*See* Papier-Mâché.) To make a form to mold the egg, cut one inch off the short end of the Styrofoam egg. Also cut between ½" and ¾" off the large end of the egg. This will become the light source at the back of the egg. Flatten a section on the side of the egg. Mark a ¼" band around the egg that will divide the top half from the bottom half. This will not be covered by any paper.

Cover the egg, except the band, with tissue paper dipped in water. This will create a release layer, making it easier to remove the Styrofoam from the papier-mâché when the glue is dry.

Dip newspaper cut in 1" × 2" pieces into white glue thinned with a little water. Cover the egg with the glue-soaked paper, making sure not to cross the band. Leave a little space around the band in the middle to make removing the papier-mâché easier.

Apply four layers of papier-mâché. If you like, alternate colors of the paper in order to tell what layer has been made. For instance, you can begin with newspaper, then make a brown paper bag layer. Follow up with a newspaper layer and finish with a brown paper bag layer. When the glue and paper are dry, gently pry the upper and lower layers from the egg form.

Paint the inside of the egg if you want to. Make the little spring scene at the back, gluing the figures into place. Remember to use several rows of figures to create depth in your scene. Glue the two halves of the egg together. Then fasten white tissue paper over the back of the egg to close the egg but leave the light source available. Decorate the egg if you wish with paints, cut-out pictures, or colored tissue paper.

Shoe Box Peep Show

A peep show can be made from a shoe box or any other small box about the same size. (*See* Cardboard Boxes.)

MATERIALS

- Small box the size of a shoe box
- Poster board
- Markers or paints and paint brush
- Tissue paper
- Pencils
- Ruler
- White glue
- Craft knife
- Scissors

ASSEMBLY

1. Make a box with four sides if you do not have one available. Score the folds of the box and the tabs which will eventually fasten the box. Do not glue the box together just yet.

2. Cut a quarter-sized hole in one short end of the shoe box. This will be the viewing or peeping hole.

3. Cut a rectangular opening in the other short end of the shoe box, leaving a margin of 1½" on all sides of that end.

4. Draw your miniature scenes on poster board, color them, and cut them out.

5. Glue the tissue paper over the large open area in the short end of the box. This will let the light in.

6. Position the layers of scenery in the box. Use several layers to create a feeling of depth.

7. Fold the box together loosely and view the scene, checking to see if the scene looks the way you want it to and that enough light is getting through. Remember to have the box pointed toward a strong light source such as a window in daylight.

8. Glue the scenery in place.

9. Glue the box together.

10. Invite your audience to view your clever work!

Baird, Bil. *The Art of the Puppet*. New York: Macmillan, 1965.
Wright, Lyndie. *Toy Theaters*. New York: Franklin Watts, 1991.

Philosophy of Puppetry

Every puppeteer's philosophy of puppetry is different, and that's as it should be, for puppetry is at heart a way to express the self. The puppeteer is the human agency for bringing an inanimate object to life. Whether that object is a finely hand-crafted work of art or a junk puppet made from recycled materials or a found object animated on the spot, the puppet and its actions expresses the self of the puppeteer.

Sometimes the desire of the puppeteer is to create the most beautiful and intricate presentation to which a puppet could possibly aspire. At other times it may be to educate and provoke thought while entertaining. It may be to spread understanding of the world's cultures through the presentation of a world of stories, or it may be to depict the world's suffering, whether the suffering is ecological, political, or societal.

To create your own philosophy of puppetry, you need to be acquainted with yourself and with what your own goals happen to be. You also need to realize that those goals will change over time; the framework may stay the same, but the expression may change. You also need to know what puppets and puppetry can do. You may need to educate yourself about the different kinds of puppets and puppetry: how these forms look, what they can do, and what they have done over time. If it is possible, you may want to apprentice yourself to or work for various puppeteers to experience working with different kinds of puppetry on a professional level. You may also want to visit museums, attend performances, and get to know puppeteers first hand.

There is quite a movement to have an adult, thought-provoking sort of puppetry removed from the realm of the nursery and into the world arena. This puppetry wants to make its audience think about the world and what is going on in it, what effect the actions of individuals and groups are having on world health, ecology, or peace. While children need to consider these issues as much as adults do, the aim is to provide theater for mature audiences.

We are also beginning to see puppetry as spectacle in America. While Europe has enjoyed these sorts of puppets and giant figures for centuries, America is beginning to enjoy the possibilities of the grand gesture of a giant puppet. Whole communities can become involved in such displays. They concentrate effort on a communal level and make a statement about a problem or about just having fun. Under the direction of an experienced puppeteer, communities or groups can express themselves in this new and creative way.

Most of all, you need to experiment and take chances as a puppeteer. Explore yourself, your world, and the world of puppetry and see how they all intersect. At the same time, you need to experiment with materials and see which of these you enjoy working with. Finally, after you have explored all these avenues—which are never-ending, by the way—you will come back to the beginning and, as T. S. Elliot says, know it for the first time. You will have given yourself a chance to experiment many avenues of puppetry. Now you can know who you are, know what you want to do with your puppetry, and begin!

Boylan, Eleanor. *How to Be a Puppeteer.* New York: McCall, 1970.
Currell, David. *The Complete Book of Puppetry.* Boston: Plays, Inc., 1975.
Finch, Christopher. *Jim Henson: The Works: The Art, the Magic, the Imagination.* New York: Random House, 1993.

Polymer and Air-Hardening Clays

Polymer clay is a new clay, capable of being molded, rolled, cut, and stacked into the most remarkable combinations of colors and shapes. Beads, buttons, and other jewelry items have been made with polymer clay as well as faces, hands, and feet for dolls and figurines. After the polymer clay has been molded, it can be hardened in the oven and painted or glazed when finished.

Polymer clay is not for everyone. It is somewhat expensive, heavy, and takes some work to learn how to use. The baking process releases toxic fumes, so the work must be done in a well-ventilated area. On the other hand, polymer clays can be blended to produce better or more interesting flesh tones than craft clays produce, and the sculpting is more rapid and direct. (*See also* Craft Clays.)

Air-hardening clay has been on the market slightly longer than have polymer clays. It is not a dough but is a clay which hardens in air. It is non-toxic, but it should not be used for eating utensils. The color range of most air-hardening clays is limited to terracotta, gray, and white, although Crayola has a line of brightly colored air-hardening clays to use in schools. I place Celluclay, a premade papier-mâché mash reconstituted with water, in this class as well as PaperClay, a new product on the market. These products can be sculpted and produce excellent results while speeding up the production time on puppets.

Because of its weight and expense, it might be thought that these clays would not be appropriate for inexpensive puppets. However, the clay can be pressed into molds and can be sculpted like any other clay. When sculpted over a form, it makes an excellent puppet head, even rivaling porcelain if handled right. Air-hardening clay is breakable; but with careful handling, it can be used for quite some time, and it is repairable. If you enjoy sculpting but dislike the stages one must go through to produce a papier-mâché head, consider using polymer or air-hardening clay. It doesn't cost much for a block or two as an experiment. Who knows? It may be just what you've been looking for!

Ponytail Holder Movable Mouths

Having a mouth on a puppet can be a neat thing. It's not really necessary because people in the audience will imagine one for you. However, having a movable mouth can add to the character of your puppet. If you are interested, try the ponytail holder movable mouth. It's about as simple a mouth as you can make for your puppet. It's cute and funny. It's also cheap as well as easy to do. What a deal!

The ponytail holder movable mouth is detailed in *The Muppets Make Puppets*. They use it for rod or stick puppets, and I think these are the best puppets for this simple mouth. Take a plain ponytail holder, not the scrunchy kind, a

bone ring, some string, and some hot glue. Glue the top of the ponytail holder to your puppet. When the glue is dry, tie one end of a string to the middle of the bottom of the ponytail holder and the other end to the bone ring.

To use your ponytail holder movable mouth, hold the rod of the puppet and put your finger in the bone ring and wiggle it up and down. The mouth will move and look as if it is talking. The mouth can open wide to scream, sing a long note, or laugh uproariously.

That's all there is to it! What a great puppet accessory: a mouth that moves, adds character, yet doesn't take a lot of time or money and is still fairly easy to use.

Henson, Cheryl, and the Muppet Workshop. *The Muppets Make Puppets!* New York: Workman Publishing, 1994.

These mop and broom puppets have mouths made of elastic ponytail holders. The springy, always-open mouths add to the puppets' goofy appearance. Such a mouth is operated by means of a thread (just visible on the mop puppet in this picture) attached to a bone ring.

Pop-Up Puppets

Pop-up puppets are a variety of toy theater where the puppet is contained within a small theater structure and pops up to perform by means of the rod upon which it is mounted. Pop-up puppets are portable and can be useful for informal puppetry situations, but this doesn't mean that the pop-up puppet is small. In fact, it can be quite large and long, depending on the design of the puppet. (*See also* Paper Bag Theaters.)

A pop-up puppet consists of a container, a puppet, and the rod on which the puppet is mounted. As such, it becomes a wonderful first puppet for young children. You can take a drinking cup with a seasonal motif printed on it, a drinking straw, and the cut-out of an appropriate seasonal character, perhaps a cut-out from a second, identical cup. Color in the character if necessary, and cut it out; then paste it on a scrap of poster board to make it stiff, and tape the

Browser, a pop-up puppet, is hiding in the cone, just peeking out.

character to the drinking straw. Use a pencil, pair of scissors, or other pointed tool to poke a hole in the bottom of the cup. Insert the straw into the hole from inside the cup. Trim the straw if necessary so that it is not too long. And there you have it: a puppet theater in a cup!

Any number of small containers can be used: sand pails for a summer or seashore theme; a winter mitten or cap for a snow-time theme. Try all sorts of containers. See what your imagination can come up with.

All pop-up puppets are created on the same principle as the drinking cup mentioned previously, but the theater can become more elaborate. A shoe box can become a puppet theater by having several pop-up puppets, their rods worked from above, and scenery in the box. Nursery rhymes, Aesop's fables, as well as seasonal themes are good for this sort of theater since few characters are needed to present a show. They do well for young audiences at Toddler Story Times since they are familiar and not too imposing.

Shoe Box Pop-up Theater

MATERIALS

- 1 shoe box, with or without a lid
- Poster board

Bowser is part-way out of the cone, the normal operating position for this type of puppet.

- Paints and paint brushes or markers
- Craft sticks
- Pencils
- Ruler
- Craft knife
- Scissors
- White glue
- Optional wrapping paper or other paper to cover the shoe box

ASSEMBLY

1. If you wish, cover or paint the inside and outside of the shoe box and let the paint and glue dry.
2. Cut a ½"-wide slot in one long side of the shoe box. This will become the top of the theater and the place where you operate the puppet rods. If you are concerned that pressure placed on the thin wall of the shoe box while cutting will deform it too much, cut from the inside of the box on a firm, protected surface.
3. Create puppets for the theater using poster board, paper and paints or markers.
4. Mount the puppets on craft sticks with glue or tape.
5. Add any other touches you think will create a better theater. The lid, if you have it, may be cut down and used to add any touches (fences, border, foot lights, etc.) you think will add to the character of the theater performance. Or the lid can be placed back on the box to make a self-contained story box theater.
6. Put on your play for an appreciative audience!

Bowser is fully extended in "surprise" mode.

Hunt, Tamara, and Nancy Renfro. *Celebrate! Holidays, Puppets and Creative Drama*. Austin, TX: Nancy Renfro Studios, 1987.

Hunt, Tamara, and Nancy Renfro. *Puppetry in Early Childhood Education*. Austin, TX: Nancy Renfro Studios, 1982.

Practice

Practice is not rehearsal; practice in puppetry means working to perfect the puppet type you prefer — hand, marionette, rod, shadow, etc.— or to establish a technique new to you. Regular practice is important with puppetry, just as it is with music. A lot of time is not necessary; a few minutes spent in a focused way is better than an hour or more of scattered effort. Fifteen minutes five days a week is better than an hour here and a half hour there. Steady work builds up skill and muscle memory. Your hands learn what they need to do, and you discover areas where you may need more work.

You will want to plan how you will organize your practice. Because this is a physical activity, you may want to take some time to warm up and perform a routine of hand and finger stretches. On the other hand, you may be pressed for time and can do only a couple of hand limbering exercises. Try to warm up, though. It will focus your mind and make all your work easier.

Next, you may want to perform some simple, basic activities to warm your puppets up and get both of you in the mood to work. After these introductory exercises, proceed to a simple skit or improv for your puppets. (*See* Hand Puppets, Manipulation; Marionettes, Manipulation.)

You may discover that fifteen minutes will not cover everything you would like to do. Whatever time you allot for yourself, do not wear yourself out. You will lose focus, and practice will be less effective.

You may discover that you want to cover basics on certain days and improvs on other days. Whatever you do, make sure that everything is covered in a week's worth of practice. Allow yourself time to try new things as well. You may want to allot one day to this exploration. How will you discover whether or not you enjoy a new technique or can incorporate it into your plays if you don't try it out first?

Your regular practice should include any portion of a puppet play you do not feel comfortable with. You will know from your rehearsal time whether you are having difficulties or not. (*See* Rehearsal.) Whether it is making a puppet move in a certain way to achieve a specific effect or a basic move you feel you just don't perform very well, practice should include time for focusing on troublesome areas in an upcoming performance.

Practice is a most important part of your work in becoming a puppeteer. Even if you have only fifteen or twenty minutes a day to offer to this work, you should use it as it will improve your abilities as a puppeteer. You may even discover new ideas for puppet plays springing into mind from exercises or skits performed in practice. Relationships you did not realize before may emerge and new possibilities for plays and skits offer themselves to you. Even if they don't, you will have the confidence which comes from working steadily with your puppets. Practice is a wonderful gift you can give to yourself (and your audience and puppets) every single day!

Engler, Larry, and Carol Fijan. *Making Puppets Come Alive: A Method of Learning and Teaching Hand Puppetry.* New York: Taplinger, 1973.

Frazier, Nancy, and Nancy Renfro. *Imagination: At Play with Puppets and Creative Drama.* Austin, TX: Nancy Renfro Studios, 1987.

Preschoolers' Puppets

Whether it's acting out a favorite nursery rhyme or fairy tale or cartoon, children enjoy using puppets. Unfortunately, not all puppets are best for all ages. Simply giving a child a toy theater or a hand puppet, even one made up in the likeness of a favorite character, will not guarantee a child's knowing what to do with the puppet. (*See* Hand Puppets; Toy Theaters.) It's best to match children with the kinds of toys they can use.

Puppetry may be lost on babies and young toddlers. They are only beginning to understand how stories are put together and how books are used. To leap from the printed page to a toy that seems to be alive is a big step for them. Their comprehension skills aren't developed enough to make the jump.

Toddlers and young children also lack the fine motor coordination which puppets require. To give a child a puppet requiring coordinated finger motion when their fingers are still so small is, again, to ask more of them than they can provide. So what do you do if you want to introduce small children ages 2½ to 4 years old to puppets?

The types of puppet I would consider for this young age are the stick puppet, with its variant the pop-up puppet, finger puppets, and wrist puppets. (*See* Finger Puppets, Pop-Up Puppets, Stick Puppets, and Wrist Puppets.) Although bag puppets are also a possibility, they are actually fairly difficult to manipulate for children with small hands. (*See* Bag Puppets.)

Finger puppets are great because the band or ring which holds the puppet can be sized big enough to encompass two or more fingers, giving a tiny hand more control over the puppet. Fine-motor control is just developing for these little ones, so a band that can be enlarged is just great. Make a couple of these many-fingered puppets, and your little one can have them talk to each other. This may not be puppetry as this book has defined it, but it is a chance for the young child to make up a little story concerning its two little characters, and that's the beginning of story creation. (*See* Puppets Defined.)

The finger puppet is also easy because almost any sort of picture can be attached to a band to make a puppet. Photographs of family members, pictures cut from magazines, even paper dolls can be mounted on a band to become puppets.

The same is true for the wrist puppet, although a three year old may think it is more a bracelet than a puppet. Like the finger puppet, almost any small figure can be mounted on a band of soft elastic or a Velcro-closure strap to become a puppet. You can combine finger and wrist puppets like this: make a flower wrist puppet and a butterfly or bee finger puppet, a seashell or starfish wrist puppet and a fish finger puppet, or a house wrist puppet and a boy or girl finger puppet. With these combinations, a child can create and act out a simple story with the two puppets, one of which is stationary and the other which moves.

Stick puppets also offer the options of simple puppetry to young children. To introduce a new look you might copy figures from it and mount the figures on straws with tape for the makings of a skit about the book. The child can color the copy adding to the fun.

This becomes a reading readiness activity when the parent works with the child to recreate a story with puppets made from the illustrations from the story. First, the parent reads a favorite story the child knows and enjoys. Then the parent makes the stick puppets and offers them to the child. The parent should prompt the child to recreate the story by asking leading questions and encouraging the child to talk. Remind parents not to be critical; the idea is to encourage story construction and (perhaps) check reading comprehension. If it becomes a chore or a test, the child will be turned off. Keeping it casual is the best approach here.

Stick puppets can also be used as the finger and wrist puppets were. Cut figures from magazines, photographs, or children's drawings and tape them to straws, pipe cleaners, or craft sticks. Encourage the children to tell stories with the puppets they have made. Stick puppets also can be substituted for the finger puppets in the wrist puppet/finger puppet pairs.

Pop-up puppets are more-elaborate puppets which contain puppet and theater in one unit. (*See* Pop-Up Puppets.) Start with a stick puppet. Take a paper cup big enough to hold the puppet, and poke a hole in the bottom of the cup. Insert the stick puppet, and move it up and down. Now you have a puppet that can sing and dance or pop up to tell a story. Holidays are excellent times to make pop-up puppets since so many cups and other items are decorated in holiday or seasonal themes. Cutting out figures to mount on straws and put in cups is an easy task, and seasonal items can be very rewarding. A flower, bird, or butterfly popping out of a flower-decorated cup or a squirrel or pumpkin out of a cup with an autumn theme is an easy-to-make puppet a young child can enjoy.

Just about any learning activity can be puppetized. Number matching, color naming, and letter-sound recognition can all be turned into puppet games. Make stick puppet pairs with a number on one stick and a number of items on the other stick. Or make a stick puppet with a letter and a puppet with an item which begins with the sound of that letter. Puppets for color naming are easy to make if you mount colored items on sticks to be identified by a child. For instance, a picture of a bird can be copied in several different colors of paper or colored in with markers or crayons. Mount them on sticks, and use them to identify colors.

First puppets can have many uses for children, but they must be matched to the capabilities of the child. Young children have poorly developed fine-motor skills and are just beginning to appreciate stories. Puppets should be simple, requiring little manipulation and allowing children's imaginations free play. By using finger, stick, pop-up, and wrist puppets, you can introduce young children to their first puppets and the fun of story creation. They will need some instruction and encouragement, but that's fine. Their puppet skills will grow as they do.

Hunt, Tamara, and Nancy Renfro. *Puppetry in Early Childhood Education.* Austin, TX: Nancy Renfro Studios, 1982.
Wallace, Mary. *I Can Make Puppets.* Toronto: Greey de Pencier Books, 1994.
Watson, Nancy Cameron. *The Little Pig's Puppet Book.* Boston: Little, Brown, 1990.

Props

A prop is any item or article which is not attached to a person. Clothes are, quite obviously, not props, but a shield for a knight, a shepherd's crook, or a basket of flowers could be. Human actors spend much time training to use props naturally and subtly so that their use will not detract from the natural flow of movement on the stage unless required by the action. Even props on the scenery walls should be attended to; for, as the playwright Checkov is reputed to have said, "Do not show a gun on the wall in the first act if you do not intend to use it in the third." That is a little strict, perhaps, but props such as guns and other weapons are intended to be used and draw attention to themselves. The general run of props should not do so.

Puppets have difficulty with props because their hands usually are not flexible. A hand puppet will often pick up an item and clutch it to its breast since the hands cannot flex as human hands would. The exception, of course, is always present; and in this case, it is the Bunraku puppet with articulated fingers. (*See* Bunraku.) The Bunraku samurai can grasp his sword or the lady her fan, but this ability in puppets is rare.

Props should, in my opinion, be kept to a minimum. Must the elves in *The Shoemaker and the Elves* carry the shoes or pick up their hammers? Can they not be shown already using their tools and have them attached to their hands? What about the glass slipper in *Cinderella*, or the poisoned apple in *Snow White and the Seven Dwarves*? Mime could fill in, here, with the eating of the apple. Some stage business could be used to disguise fastening the pillow with the glass slipper onto the page's hands.

On the other hand, it is not impossible for puppets to use a prop. In *Anansi and His Six Sons*, one of the sons must throw a rock at a hawk who has attacked his father. A wad of paper on a string made a serviceable attempt to duplicate that action. In *The Thirsty Crow*, pebbles must be dropped into a pitcher. Cotton balls on a stick enabled the crow to achieve her task while the pitcher was firmly anchored to the stage. The dog, in *The Dog and His Reflection*, handed the bone to the puppeteer and even thanked him for taking care of the bone while the Dog was talking.

Some props are hard to handle. A knotted kerchief is difficult to untie while one that uses Velcro or a slide can be removed more easily. Hats may need some extra assistance to stay on the puppet's head. The contents of a basket must fall out easily or stay

Dog carries his prize bone in his mouth for Aesop's "The Dog and His Reflection."

in firmly, depending on the needs of the play. The most important features of a prop are ease of use and appropriateness to the play and its action, so check the story's plot line and plan accordingly.

When you have chosen your props, practice with them to make sure that they are used properly and easily and that they add to, not detract from, the flow of the story. This will make your use of props both sensible and fun!

Engler, Larry, and Carol Fijan. *Making Puppets Come Alive: A Method of Learning and Teaching Hand Puppetry.* New York: Taplinger, 1973.

Punch and Judy

Mr. Punch and his wife Judy have had a long and prosperous career in England dating all the way back to the time of Samuel Pepys, the famed diarist. At that time, Punch was still Punchinello and closer to the *commedia dell'arte* of his origins. Over the years, Punchinello would cease being a marionette and become a hand puppet whose violent slapstick and eerie voice would become known throughout the world.

At first, Mr. Punch was a human actor standing outside the booth and commenting on the action, perhaps interpreting the squeaks of the *swazzle*, a curious reed vocalizer used by Punch and Judy "professors" to provide Mr. Punch with a voice. This incarnation interchanged with Punch-as-marionette for perhaps a century. Finally, at the turn of the nineteenth century, Mr. Punch gained his current incarnation as a hand puppet, for it is only as a hand puppet that Punch can indulge in all the slapstick and violence for which he is so well known.

It is this slapstick, so beloved of common people and children everywhere, which has gotten Mr. Punch into trouble and given him a bad reputation. Due to the violence of Punch and Judy shows, parents and educators have decried the shows and even asked for them to be banned. The violence is cartoon violence, but it is aimed at real people: the landlord, the Devil, the policeman, and Judy and Baby, Punch's family. It is probably because of this last that Mr. Punch has received his bad reputation. As we discover more about family violence, we don't want it held up to children as something to laugh at. The fighting and violence in Punch and Judy is something we now have trouble tolerating.

At the time of Mr. Punch's inception, however, the common people were beset by a host of enemies, and no one spoke up for them — except Mr. Punch. In every place where such slapstick farces have reigned, from the ancient Greeks to today's Three Stooges, they have been used as a way to vent anger and frustration at the problems of everyday life. Modern "professors" feel that there is no harm in Punch and Judy, that the violence is no worse than that seen in cartoons. As usual, it is an endless round of questions.

There are standard Punch and Judy plays and standard, expected characters which go along with them which makes it difficult for an inexperienced "professor" to put on a casual Punch and Judy show. Some of Mr. Punch's associates are Judy, his wife; Toby, the dog; the Baby; the Doctor; the Constable; the Clown; the Hangman; the Ghost of Judy; Mr. Jones; Hector, the horse; the Crocodile; and the Devil. Mr. Punch vanquishes all these formidable foes and remains supreme, drinking, fighting, even talking from the gallows after being hanged.

Mr. Punch, like Guignol, Karagoz, and all the rest of the descendants of ancient Greek new comedy and Roman attelian farces, is a man of the people: shrewd and tough, quick to anger, eager to join in any revelry, and resistant of authority. Because Mr. Punch takes the side of the common man, he remains popular despite all efforts to banish him. (*See also* Guignol; Karagoz.)

Baird, Bil. *The Art of the Puppet.* New York: Macmillan, 1965.

Puppet Gloves *see* Monkey Mitts and Puppet Gloves

Puppet Corners

The puppet corner is an area dedicated to puppetry established in a classroom, library, or other place where children are apt to gather or have services provided for them. The concept behind this, stated by Nancy Renfro in her *A Puppet Corner in Every Library*, is that all children should be able to benefit from the presence of puppets, that puppets contribute to the exercise of imagination, and that work with puppets increases linguistic and organizational skills in children.

Puppet corner from Nancy Renfro. A puppet tree creates a place for puppets in a library or school. The attraction of the tree is its ability to change with the seasons as the sample illustrations show.

A puppet corner can be made out of anything: a table with some puppets on it; a simple puppet theater with a tub of puppets nearby; or a clothesline, tree branch, or other hanging device with puppets hung from them and a theater set-up nearby. The theater need not be any more than a cloth strung on a clothesline and fastened in place. (*See also* Doorway Stages.)

A puppet corner can also have puppet-making materials available. These can be boxes of scrap materials, blank cloth hand puppet forms ready to be decorated, pages of finger puppets ready to color and cut out, or any other things that could safely be used to make puppets in a minimally supervised situation. The puppet-making materials could also be made available to parents who then agree to supervise their children while they work on making their puppets.

Supervising a puppet corner could be one of the duties of a teen volunteer or a member of your puppet club. Children who have had some experience making puppets can themselves teach other, younger children to make and use puppets in the puppet corner. This will provide the younger children with supervision and guidance, and it will provide an extra outlet for older children who may be experienced junior puppeteers. They will have an opportunity to pass on what they have learned and help younger children understand how to use puppets.

It sometimes happens that unsupervised children will start fighting with their puppets. Perhaps they are acting out, but it may also be that they just don't know how to use puppets. Supervision by an older child or a skilled adult will give these younger children some rudimentary skills in creating drama with puppets.

Puppet corners can also be places where a skilled adult can put on impromptu puppet performances if a few children gather there. Having puppets on hand in the puppet corner can make this possible, so have this in mind when you make puppets for your puppet corner.

Since young children will be using the puppet corner, try to make your puppets sturdy enough that they can stand a lot of wear and then be thrown into the washing machine and dryer. This is a good place for puppets made from stuffed animals and toys, especially when you replace the original stuffing with fiberfill. (*See* Stuffed Animal Puppets.)

A puppet corner has many possibilities for the classroom, library, or other space for children. It is a place where the imagination can run wild and language skills get honed. Drama with puppets becomes a real possibility for children who may have run from the idea of getting up on a stage. There's something about puppets that brings out the ham in all children. So establish a puppet corner for your children. You won't regret it!

Hunt, Tamara, and Nancy Renfro. *Puppetry in Early Childhood Education.* Austin, TX: Nancy Renfro Studios, 1982.
Renfro, Nancy. *A Puppet Corner in Every Library.* Austin, Tex.: N. Renfro Studios, 1978.

Puppet Gloves

With a puppet glove, your hand becomes the stage or backdrop; small characters, usually made of felt or pom-poms, stick to the fingers by means of Velcro buttons or squares. One commercially available variation is a furry glove called a Monkey Mitt.

Puppet gloves are great little mini-theaters for presenting nursery rhymes, simple stories, or children's action songs. Because figures can be added and taken away, puppet gloves can also be visual aids for teaching color recognition, spelling, beginning math, and story construction.

If you're not feeling terribly crafty, here are some shortcuts you can take to make a puppet glove from readily available materials.

Materials

• Cloth work gloves or gardening gloves for the regular puppet glove. For the furry type, look for a car washing mitt made of fuzzy material.

• Velcro dots or squares

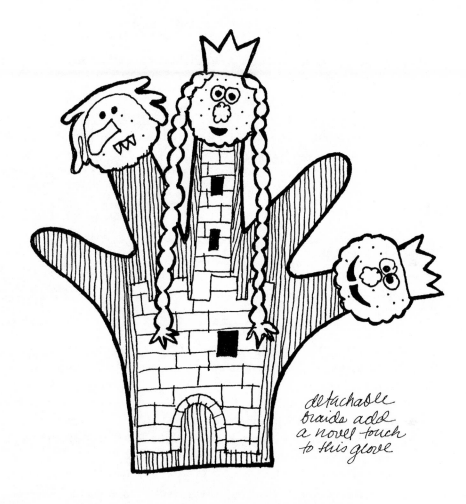

detachable braids add a novel touch to this glove

Monkey mitt or puppet glove from Nancy Renfro. This glove has the second act of *Rapunzel* with the Witch on the left, Rapunzel in the middle, and Prince Charming on the thumb. The tower where Rapunzel is imprisoned by the Witch can either be drawn directly on the glove or drawn on paper and attached.

- Hot glue, needle and thread. (The adhesive on the back of many Velcro dots or squares is not strong enough, so it's best to glue or to sew them on. Sewing is best with fuzzy material, since glue sticks to the fuzzy surface and not to the base material.)
- Felt scraps, pom-poms, thread or yarn, and notions to make puppets.

MAKING YOUR PUPPET GLOVE

- Attach the loop side of the Velcro dots or squares to the fingers of the work or gardening gloves or the car-washing mitt. Use hot glue or needle and thread to tack down and secure the Velcro. (See note under "Materials.")
- Make little figures out of the pom-poms and felt. Glue the other half of the Vel-

cro to the figures and try them out. Assemble enough characters so you can act out a nursery rhyme or put on a play!

You can also make a small hand-held puppet board instead of a glove. Picture the cardboard fans given out at political rallies and the like. Now imagine one covered with cloth or fur. You can attach Velcro dots and use them to hold small characters, just as you would with a puppet glove. The only difference is that you hold this board by the handle instead of putting it over your hand like a glove.

Hunt, Tamara, and Nancy Renfro. *Puppetry in Early Childhood Education.* Austin, TX: Nancy Renfro Studios, 1982.

Puppeteers

The American Heritage Dictionary of the English Language, Fourth Edition, 2000 defines a puppeteer as "one who entertains with and operates puppets or marionettes." In short, you!

The puppeteer is one third of the puppetry triangle outlined by Bil Baird when he said that "a puppet is an inanimate figure that is made to move by human effort before an audience." The puppeteer is the "human effort" which brings the inanimate figure not merely to movement, but to life.

The work of the puppeteer can be as focused as learning to move one kind of puppet, as with the Bunraku puppeteer who will choose whether to specialize in male or female figures or the Punch and Judy "professor" who masters many of the plays in the repertoire plus learning the use of the "swazzle," the reed squeaker which brings Mr. Punch's voice to life or the *dalang* puppeteer of Indonesia who must not only learn all the puppets and all the plays of the various cycles but also must conduct the *gamelan* and the singers as well. (*See* Bunraku; Punch and Judy; Wayang.) These puppeteers provide the human effort which brings the puppets to life. The modern American, Canadian, or European puppeteer or the puppeteers influenced by them must also select the story and write the script, make the puppets and their costumes, learn the lines and rehearse them, provide the background music, and print the fliers and sell the tickets. Whew! There is little that the modern puppeteer does *not* do!

It is this breadth of abilities which often calls people to puppetry. They can use writing skills and craft skills, as well as dramatic skills, to put on a performance which will touch the hearts and fire the imaginations of their audience. It is this combination of use of multiple talents plus the ability to touch people in a unique way which often inspires the modern puppeteer to embrace the art of puppetry.

Puppeteers of America

Along with UNIMA (Union Internationale de la Marionette) and UNIMA–USA, the Puppeteers of America are one of the leading professional organizations for puppeteers. While membership in this organization is not a necessity, it is a gateway to education and networking which can only work to your benefit as a developing puppeteer. The Puppeteers of America mission statement states:

> The Puppeteers of America, Inc., is a national nonprofit corporation founded in 1937. Its purpose is to encourage and promote puppetry as a means of communication, an extension of human expression, and as a performing Art; to enhance the proficiency of the Art of Puppetry, both professional and amateur, by publications, workshops, conventions or festivals, lectures, advisory services and any and all other means and methods.

Besides education and networking, Puppeteers of America offers a number of special programs and services for members. They have two publications: *Puppetry Journal*, a quarterly with a wide range of informative articles of interest to all puppeteers, and *Playboard*, their bimonthly newsletter. Once a year in April, Puppeteers of America sponsors the National Day of Puppetry, and they have an annual National Festival of Puppetry in July. Please see their web page for more information. (*See* National Day of Puppetry; National Festival of Puppetry.)

In addition, the organization has an audiovisual library with tapes on all manner of topics of interest to puppeteers. If you want to learn more about the history of puppetry, learn to make a particular type of puppet, or view performances from previous puppetry festivals, the AV library has something for you. For a nominal shipping and handling charge, you can have the best of puppetry come to you through the mail!

If this hasn't convinced you to join, think about their grants and scholarships, their information referral service, the classified bulletin board, and insurance for the self-employed professional. Most of all, think about the things you'll learn and the contacts you'll make if you become a member! Why don't you sign up today?

www.puppeteers.org/ Puppeteers of America web site.

Puppetools

Puppetools are an educational concept invented in the 1970s to add multidimensional use of puppets in the classroom, library, or anywhere children gather. Puppetools have now gone online with educational projects and continuing educational workshops. Contact them at www.puppetools.com.

Here is the 2001 mission statement from Jeffrey L. Peyton, founder, on the Puppetools web site:

To help you to become more creative, productive and fulfilled in your teaching.

To equip you with a unique set of communication tools and skills that enable you to reach young minds more meaningfully.

To transform the pages of your curriculum into a connective, visual, and hands-on experience easily, practically, and inexpensively.

To synthesize content and save you time by generating higher levels of interest, productivity, creativity, and cooperation in students.

To develop an ongoing resource and relationship with our network of creative trailblazers in education. Your teaching is alive — and what we share with you speaks directly to that life. For adults who use the power of play to reach and engage the young to process, deliver, and articulate information and feelings, the process of learning and communicating becomes a living thing.

More than anything else, we want to make it easy for you to access and experience the extraordinary power of the puppet medium in the classroom. With over 25 years of research and experience, we can confidently predict the impact which this powerful, untapped resource will have on you, your curriculum, and your students.

We invite you to grasp this new world — a unique dimension in which the art of puppetry has been re-defined and re-tooled to serve as a powerful mainstream communication platform for you and your students.

Puppetools believes that puppets, especially the Puppetool concept of puppet, can be used in education, therapy, creative activity — all forms of learning. However, the folks at Puppetools want to go beyond the concept of "puppet" as something which is only entertaining to something which is both a technique and a medium of communication between people.

I have used Puppetools in the library, not in a specifically educational environment, but as an aid to creativity. Their beginning puppet is made from a single sheet of paper folded the long way into thirds so that it fits around the fingers. Then the long sheet of paper is folded into a "W" shape and decorated in whatever way the children want. Sometimes I have used the preprinted facial forms found in the Puppetools workbook. At other times I have offered the children geometric shapes cut from construction paper plus strips of paper the children could use to create additional features for their puppets.

Puppetools is a great base upon which to build personal puppets and experiment with both abstract and concrete forms. It is also a great introduction to junk puppets without the weight of having to make something extraordinarily exciting the first time. (*See* Junk Puppets.) It is a wonderful warm-up to creative puppet making, especially if children have never been exposed to that kind of work before.

It is easy for children to build several puppets using the Puppetools form and then create a brief skit which the puppets can perform. Performance with Puppetools, especially creating a skit and then performing it, becomes easier since the children have been intimately involved in creating their puppets from their own imaginings. The exercise of creating the puppets and presenting a skit within an hour's time is possible in a small group of children.

Try out Puppetools and see if you like them. See if you can borrow one of the original manuals. Try interlibrary loan if your library doesn't own a copy. You may find that they can add another dimension to your classroom or library work in the telling stories and explaining concepts. Puppetools offer a doorway not only to puppetry for children but also as an avenue to creativity.

Puppets Defined

Bil Baird, in his monumental history of puppetry titled *The Art of the Puppet*, defines "puppet" in the very first sentences of his work:

> A puppet is an inanimate figure that is made to move by human effort before an audience. It is the sum of these qualities that uniquely defines the puppet. Nothing else quite satisfies the definition.

The Columbia Encyclopedia, sixth edition, defines "puppet" this way:

> A human or animal figure, generally of a small size and performing on a miniature stage, manipulated by an unseen operator who usually speaks the dialogue. A distinction is made between marionettes, moved by strings or wires from above, and hand puppets, in which the hand of the operator is concealed in the costume of the doll.

The American Heritage Dictionary of the English Language, Fourth Edition, 2000, defines "puppet" in this way:

> 1. A small figure of a person or animal, having a cloth body and hollow head, designed to be fitted over and manipulated by the hand. 2. A figure having jointed parts animated from above by strings or wires; a marionette. 3. A toy representing a human figure; a doll. 4. One whose behavior is determined by the will of others: a political puppet.

With all these definitions, I still prefer Baird's the best. In a few words, it says both what a puppet is—*an inanimate figure*—and what it does—*which is brought to life by human effort before an audience.* Baird goes on to point out that puppets are not clockwork figures nor are they dolls. Clockwork figures are automata made to go through mechanical motions to act out a scene over and over. In this light, one must wonder if anamatronics are puppets or merely automata? And is *claymation* animation or puppetry if figures are involved, a story is told, performed for an audience?

Neither are puppets dolls. Very small children may play with finger or stick puppets as if they were dolls. That's O.K. Very young children are just learning to put stories together and know how that thing called "story" works. So they may talk to their puppets and have them retell a story just for the child manipulator and that's just fine. It's part of the learning process. The moment they perform the story for a parent, sibling, or friend, however, it becomes puppetry because the audience is involved. (*See* Preschoolers' Puppets.)

I like Baird's inclusion of the audience as well. Puppeteers, especially beginning ones, may forget the audience in all their consideration of mechanics and construction. If it were not for the audience, though, there would be no theater. For puppetry is, first and foremost, an entertainment and part of the theater. It may be an overlooked part, but it is a part just the same. The *Columbia Encyclopedia's* definition implies an audience; the *American Heritage* leaves the audience out entirely. Only Baird's definition inserts the audience firmly up front.

For it is the triangle of puppet, puppeteer, and audience which makes puppet *theater*, after all. Tastes may change. One generation may prefer mechanical marvels and another subtleties of dramatic impulse and dialogue, but the triangle of puppet, puppeteer, and audience remains, and puppeteers must remember it.

Publications

There are a few publications in the field of puppetry which you should get to know and perhaps even subscribe to. Some come with a membership in an organization; others must be subscribed to individually.

The best known of these is *Puppetry Journal*, the quarterly publication of the Puppeteers of America. *Puppetry Journal* contains a wide variety of articles from history to how-to of interest to puppeteers and is indexed in *International Index to the Performing Arts-Full Text*. It is possible to purchase some back issues. Failing that, try your local library for Interlibrary Loan.

UNIMA-USA is now distributing *Puppetry International*, a twice-yearly publication serving the diverse theater interests of puppetry professionals, fans of puppetry, and theater people who might be interested in working with the world of puppetry. To quote UNIMA — USA: *As the lines blur among actors' theatre, mime, dance, masks and puppetry, Puppetry International is of interest to a continually expanding readership. Puppetry International* is distributed with the UNIMA — USA membership and replaces *A'Propos*, which is now a newsletter. Since *Puppetry International* has been published since 1994, you may be able to purchase back issues or find them through Interlibrary Loan. Check *International Index to the Performing Arts* to be sure.

The Internet is another great place for information about puppetry, and web zines are right there along with all other forms of information about puppetry. Start with the "Puppetry Home Page" by Sagecraft Productions. There are many links to web sites, stories, and all types of information about puppetry.

Journals, magazines, and e-zines are a great way to fill in the gaps in your knowledge about puppeteers and puppetry. Reading an article may inspire you to try something new on stage or delve into a new technique. Learning from others always expands your horizons in some way and provides some inspiration. It may be just the prompt you need to get the wheels turning!

PVC Puppet Stages

PVC or polyvinyl chloride plumbing pipe is a wonderful stage construction medium. Because it can be put together like Tinkertoys, puppeteers can have about any design of theater they like. The pipe can be glued together with PVC cement, which makes it sturdy and nearly indestructible. The material does have its drawbacks, but many puppeteers find that the PVC puppet stage is just what they need.

When making your puppet theater design, remember that PVC pipe is relatively inexpensive, so you can experiment with what you would like and work from there. PVC pipe comes in rods, curved sections, and "T" joints. Check with your local building supply place for further information about pieces.

PVC pipe is cemented in place with special PVC cement to make the joint permanent. The cement sets in about 20 seconds, so have your plan in mind and work flat on the floor on protective plastic sheeting. Make a drawing of what you want your design to look like and preassemble as much of your stage as you can. Considering the connective abilities of PVC pipe, you should be able to have just about any shape or combination of shapes you would like.

Walter Minkel, in his informative *How to Do "The Three Bears" with Two Hands*, has a design for a portable PVC stage and suggests using ½" to ¾" pipe, depending on whether the stage is for one or two puppeteers. However, he points out that the stage is a bit wobbly and not for use by children. If you plan to have a puppet club, you might want to use thicker pipe. Our library had a stationery puppet theater made with 1" pipe which had been extremely sturdy. However, it became brittle with age and in moving the stage from one branch to another, it cracked. The fact that PVC pipe is so inexpensive also makes it easy to repair or rebuild.

Walter Minkel offers these additional helpful suggestions:

Use Velcro for attaching the cloth sides of the stage. This will give a smooth fit and will make it easy to detach for transportation, washing, and any other cleanup.

Use bolts to attach a playboard, power strips, and perhaps fixtures for lighting.

Bolt on a length of yardstick for attaching Velcro. (Lath could be substituted for this, I believe.)

Insert ¼" doweling into the PVC pipe for hanging puppets.

If these hints aren't enough, go to your local building supply on a quiet morning and ask one of the local experts about how to handle this material and how to accomplish what you want to do.

PVC pipe is not for everyone. I have mentioned that I used sheet rock hangers to construct my stage, but it gets a great deal of kid use and it is not particularly portable. However, PVC pipe is inexpensive and easy to turn into all sorts of designs. You can have a closed or open proscenium, several activity levels, and a number of add-ons, depending on what you want to do with your puppetry. With the use of Velcro, you can add a shadow screen to your design with little trouble. Your stage can be portable or command a spot of distinction in your performance area. Give PVC pipe a chance as your first stage. You will find that it repays your effort many times over and discover why it is the frequent choice of beginning puppeteers.

Minkel, Walter. *How to Do "The Three Bears" with Two Hands: Performing with Puppets.* Chicago: American Library Association, 2000.

Record Keeping *see* Business of Puppetry: Record Keeping

Rehearsal

Rehearsal of a puppet play is not practice; it is the working out of the details of the elements of a play. Dialogue, cues, stage movement, choreography, and working with music are all parts of rehearsal. You may decide to record your dialogue, music, and other elements so that you have a seamless presentation for your audience as well as a lack of concern for voice failure, proper music cues, and so on. On the other hand, you may decide to do it all yourself, live — voices, music cues … everything! Whatever your choice of presentation, you need to rehearse.

If you are working out everything by yourself, you may want to begin creating the voices for your characters as soon as you have a good idea of how your story line will flow. Practice switching back and forth from voice to voice until it all sounds natural. When you have the dialogue worked out, begin rehearsing your lines without the puppets. See how the dialogue flows from one character to the other. Does it sound natural? Can you loosen things up a bit, make the dialogue flow more naturally?

After you have the dialogue worked out, begin blocking out the movements of your puppets. This means deciding where the puppets will be when they speak their lines and how they will move on the stage and interact with one another. You will want to know if there are places in the dialogue where you need to speed up, pause, or slow down in order to finish a piece of business.

If you have a multipart stage, blocking will help you decide when you move from one part or elevation to another. If you feel you need such a stage or an addition to your present stage, this is the time to build it. This is also the time to discover if you need any special equipment, special effects, or props to make the work of the puppets and the story flow more smoothly and effectively.

You will want to have stand-in puppets for rehearsal as you finish working on the puppets for the show. If the puppets you are using are generic ones, this may not be important. If your puppets are special ones created for this play alone, you may want to use stand-ins until you have the basics blocked out to your satisfaction. This will save wear and tear on your specially made puppets and permit you to make mistakes as you work on blocking out the action of the play.

After you have the dialogue, voices, and blocking worked out, you will want to consider music and choreography. (*See* Music.) Also, at this point, you need to think about prerecording the entire program. The plus is that you have everything ready, paced properly, and prerecorded so that all you need to do is push a button. If you get laryngitis, if it is a long play and your voice gives out, if you don't think you can keep one voice distinct from another throughout a long play or remember all your lines, then prerecording may be just the thing for you. If the play is a short one with few characters, as are most story time puppet plays, you probably won't need to prerecord. The downside of prerecording is that some spontaneity is lost and, of course, there are technical problems. Always have backup! Have an extra tape (or two) in case the tape jams. Have a second, stand-in tape recorder or CD player in case something happens to the first one.

If you feel that the prerecorded play will get ahead of you, remember that rehearsal is meant to help prevent such disasters. Also remember that disasters are part of show business, even if your actors don't belong to the Screen Actor's Guild or the American Guild of Variety Artists! Go over your blocking to see where there are problems which might get you into trouble and change or eliminate the problem elements.

Some professional puppeteers hire a director who has experience with puppets to help them correct deficiencies in their production. An experienced, objective eye can make suggestions, point out problems, and tell you when you've got it right. When your income depends on a professional performance, having professional assistance to get things right is absolutely necessary. This is true for any performance but doubly true if you're doing it all yourself. That impartial eye can be a lifesaver.

If you have a large enough company of players, you may want to have a stage manager who will maintain order and prompt cues just as a stage manager does for actors in live theater. The stage manager helps organize things back stage and makes events happen smoothly. The stage manager may also, in a large company, coordinate the efforts of music, lighting, props, and set changing. (*See also* Lighting; Props; Music; Scenery.)

The final element of rehearsal is time, and there is never enough of it. The rehearsals must be arranged into a schedule so that everyone knows what elements will be focused upon when. A large company will have the director and stage manager involved in this schedule. If you are a one-person company, you will organize the rehearsal schedule yourself, but it is important to approach rehearsal in an orderly manner so that you will cover all the bases and answer all questions before the curtain goes up on the opening night.

Do not skimp on rehearsal time, even if your play is just a simple story-time production for little toddlers. These productions are as important as all the others and may lead to bigger things. Good rehearsal habits with simple productions will create a foundation of good work habits for larger works to come!

Rehearsal is as important to puppet theater as it is to the theater with human actors. Puppet theater has the additional problem of manipulation, especially when marionettes or life-sized puppets are being used. Everything must be covered so that there are no problems (other than the 10,000 usual ones which occur on opening night). To help alleviate opening night nerves, make sure you take rehearsal time for a calmer stomach and a happier heart. Break a leg! And let the show go on!

Engler, Larry, and Carol Fijan. *Making Puppets Come Alive: A Method of Learning and Teaching Hand Puppetry.* New York: Taplinger, 1973.
Fijan, Carol, and Frank Ballard with Christine Starobin. *Directing Puppet Theatre Step by Step.* San Jose, CA: Resource Publications, Inc., 1989.
Lasky, Kathryn. *Puppeteer.* New York: Macmillan, 1985.

Rod Puppets

Rod puppets are any jointed puppets whose parts are manipulated by rods or sticks. They can be shadow puppets: thin, flat puppets made of leather, poster board, wood, or acetate and moved by means of sticks attached to arms, legs, body parts, or any other thing which will need to move. They can be three dimensional puppets constructed on a central pole with the arms manipulated by rods. They can be giant or life-sized puppets with the head held on a rod or placed on the head of one puppeteer like a mask; and the arms operated by rods by other puppeteers.

Movement differentiates the rod puppet from the stick puppet. Where the stick puppet is a drawing or a nonmoving figure mounted on a stick, the rod puppet's arms, legs, and head are expected to move to add emotion and personality through gesture. Depending on the complexity of the controls, a rod puppet can swim, hop, fly — do just about anything you can imagine.

Rod puppets have a long history and were first the national or regional puppet forms of Asian and Southeast Asian countries. The Wayang Golek and the Wayang Purwa rod puppets of Java in Indonesia date from the sixteenth century at least and were used to disseminate Islamic religious teachings. (*See* Wayang.) Along with the Wayang Kulit and Wayang Klitik, the shadow puppetry of Bali and Java in Indonesia, the puppetry of Indonesia is rich in the use of rod puppets.

India and China also had rod puppets, as did Japan. (*See* Bunraku; India and Puppetry.) It would seem that the rod form of manipulation was pre-

Miss Lucy, a rod puppet, has arms that are manipulated with bamboo skewer rods.

ferred by the people of Asia, and why not? The rod puppet is capable of great expression and can be manipulated by a single puppeteer if the right base is at hand for holding the rods of puppets which are not in use.

A wide variety of rod puppeteers exist in our modern world of puppetry. Still, it is the skill of the puppeteer in telling a story and bringing puppets to life, not the technological marvels available, which creates the wonder of puppetry.

Here are directions for making a large rod puppet.

MATERIALS:

- A half gallon plastic milk or juice container with a handle.
- 6 toilet paper tubes (7 if making feet)
- 2 paper towel tubes, if making legs
- A dowel rod which loosely fits the opening of the plastic container
- Two ¼" or ⅛" dowel rods to manipulate the arms or legs
- String
- Lightweight cardboard or poster board

- 2" masking tape
- Scissors
- Pencil
- Ruler
- Awl
- Tapestry needle

ASSEMBLY:

First, make the body of the puppet.
To make the shoulder:

1. Take a toilet paper tube and measure one inch from each end on the same plane. Mark these places with a dot.
2. Measure a second dot so that it is one inch from the first dot and one inch from the edge of the tube. You should now have four dots, two at each end on the tube parallel with one another.
3. Measure the center point of the tube on the same plane as each set of shoulder dots. Mark these places with a dot.
4. Pierce all six dots with the awl. You now have three parallel sets of holes with two holes each.
5. On the opposite side of the toilet paper tube from the first four dots, mark four new dots and pierce them with an awl. You now have 10 holes in all.

To make the hips:

1. Using a second toilet paper tube, measure 1" from each end of the toilet paper tube and mark with a dot.
2. Mark a second dot on each end of the tube, 1" from the edge and 1" from the first dot.
3. Pierce all four dots with the awl.
4. Make two identical sets of holes 1" from each edge of the tube directly beneath the first set of holes. Pierce with the awl. (The hole sets are approximately 3" apart, depending on the size of your tube.)

To make the torso:

1. Cut two 20" lengths of string.
2. Thread the string through the left lower hole set on the shoulder tube and the left hole set on the hip tube. Then thread the right set.

3. Adjust the strings so that the two rolls are approximately six inches apart and parallel with one another. Tie the strings in place. Set aside while you make the arms and legs.

To make each arm:

1. Measure 1" from the end of each of two toilet paper tubes. Mark the place and pierce with the awl.
2. Using a 10" piece of string, join the two tubes so the edges are 1" apart (approximately 3" from hole to hole). Knot the string securely and trim the tails to 1". This is the elbow joint.
3. Cut a hand from poster board and glue to the edge of one tube.
4. To attach the arm to the torso: On the tube without the hand, measure 1" in from the edge without holes and mark the place with a dot. Opposite that hole, mark another dot 1" in from the edge of the tube. Pierce both dots with the awl (these dots will be approximately 3" apart, depending on the size of your tube).
5. Take the second piece of string and thread it through the two holes you have just made in the arm tube.
6. Take the shoulder tube and thread the string through the two holes. Leave enough slack between the arm and the shoulder tubes for the arm to move freely. Tie off the string and trim the tails to 1".
7. Make the same assembly for the other arm. Make sure that when the arms are attached, the hands are placed correctly with the thumbs at the top of the hand.

To make each leg — if you need legs for your puppet:

1. Measure 1" from the edge of a paper towel roll. Mark and pierce with the awl.
2. Mark a second hole directly across from the first (1" from the edge and approximately 3" away from the first hole). Pierce this second hole.
3. At the opposite end of this tube, mark a place 1" from the edge of the roll and on the same plane as one of the upper holes. Pierce with the awl. There is no second hole on this end of the tube.
4. On one end of the second towel roll, measure a point 1" from the edge of the roll, mark, and pierce with the awl. There is no second hole across from this one.
5. With one piece of string, join the two tubes at the ends with the individual holes, threading the string through the holes. Keep the tubes about 1" apart. Tie off the string and trim the tails to 1".

6. With a second piece of string, thread through the two holes in one end of the hip tube and the two holes in the top of the leg. Space the leg and the hip about 1½" apart. Tie the knot securely and trim tales to 1".

7. Make the other leg and attach in the same manner.

   NOTE: Make sure that both legs are equal in length at this point.
   To make feet:

1. Cut a toilet paper tube in half to make two short tubes. In each, cut an even number of 1" slashes in one end, about ½" apart.

2. Bend the resulting tabs outward.

3. Cut an oval or foot shape from poster board (about 5½" to 6" long).

4. Put hot glue on the underside of the bent tabs and press the foot shape against them to attach foot. Allow the glue to dry.

5. Pierce a hole in the top of the tube at the front of the foot, 1" from the top edge of the tube.

6. Pierce a corresponding hole at the bottom of the leg, 1" in from the edge of the tube.

7. Tie the foot and leg together with the string. Make sure there is an inch between foot and leg for easy movement.

   NOTE: If you want less play in the foot, join the foot to the leg with a hinge made of two layers of masking tape. Make the first part of the hinge on the inside of the tube, joining the leg and foot at the front of the foot. Use two layers of masking tape. Make the second or front of the hinge on the outside of the leg and foot, placing the outside layers of tape at the front of the foot, covering the two inside layers of tape and making a stiff hinge for the foot.
   The head is made of a milk or juice jug. The handle will be the nose. Make a face on the jug any way you want. Then join the head to the body as follows:

1. Make 2 holes in the collar around the mouth of the jug.

2. Take the string and thread it through the two holes in the collar and the two holes in the top center holes of the shoulder.

3. Insert the dowel rod into the jug through the mouth collar. When positioning the head, remember to keep the handle of the container pointed to the front.

4. Take the hot glue gun and glue the dowel rod to the collar.

5. When the glue has set and the body looks all right, you are ready to dress your puppet.

Dressing the large rod puppet:

Because of the shape of the milk jug, this puppet's head can be dressed with a crown, a turban, a tall guardsman's hat, or piles of fruit or flowers à la Carmen Miranda.

If the character of the puppet is going to be sedentary, leave off the legs and dress the puppet in long, flowing robes.

Finally, attach the rods to the hands:

1. Cut a 4" piece of 2" wide masking tape.

2. Make a 2" cut in the tape so the bottom 2" of the tape make two equal strips.

3. Wrap the solid piece of tape around the dowel rod for the hands. Fasten the two strips to the palm of the hand.

4. Pinch a small space in the tape between the hand and the rod to create a little, flexible space between the hand and the rod.

Doney, Meryl. *Puppets.* New York: Franklin Watts, 1995.

Henson, Cheryl, and the Muppet Workshop. *The Muppets Make Puppets!* New York: Workman Publishing, 1994.

Lade, Roger. *The Most Excellent Book of How to Be a Puppeteer.* Brookfield, CT: Copper Beech Books, 1996.

Scenery

Scenery is the background of the puppet play. It can be nonexistent, with the action taking place outside of a proscenium arch and on top of the puppet stage. It can also be a simple black backdrop to provide contrast for the puppets and a place to hide the puppeteer, or the scenery can be a painted backdrop suggesting the place where the action of the play is taking place.

In the legitimate theater, scenery would include not only the backdrop, stairs, raised platforms, and other elements on the stage which would define a scene in a play; it would also include furniture which would make a setting more realistic and any other large thing — a tree, for instance, or the outline of a building — which would take up space on the stage and not be easily moved like a prop.

As with so many other stage elements, scenery in puppetry should be kept to a minimum. Objects jutting into the stage area are difficult to move around. A simple, straightforward backdrop is preferable.

However, there are times when special scenery is necessary, like it or not. The balcony scene in *Romeo and Juliet* is one instance of the need for special scenery. Any scene where the puppet must look out a window is another. Puppets popping out of holes, windows, nests, or other openings are times where specialized scenery must be used as well. Check the action of your story to determine what scenery is necessary for the presentation.

If possible, use a solid background for general puppet action. Story time can just as easily be acted out in front of a neutral background as any other. It is also possible to see the puppets more easily against a neutral background, unless the puppets are dark themselves. You may want to have a light and a dark neutral background for the purpose of contrast whenever necessary. The black background can be the basic ground and the lighter color fastened over it.

As with the apron stage, a number of basic backgrounds can be created and changed to suit the play. (*See* Apron Stages.) Some suggestions include the four seasons, a generalized town backdrop and a generic country one, and undersea landscape, a desert landscape, and a farm landscape. If you do a great many fairy tales, you might want to have a castle and a village scene. That's a total of eleven backdrops. You could also include a garden, a school scene, and a general store. Regional backgrounds could also be included, such as a ranch scene for out west and fishing boats at a dock for the northeast seaboard. Whatever you decide to do, make your backdrops easy to put up, take down, and store. If handled with care, they should last quite a while.

Remember when designing scenery to keep it simple. One always wants realism, but realism can catch strings, bump hands, and fall off during a performance. Keep design elements simple and in the background so that the scenery does not upstage the puppets. See what can be placed around the outer edge of the theater, out of the way of the puppets. Make sure that your scenery will not become a trap for your puppets but will add to the total atmosphere of the puppet play.

Baird, Bil. *The Art of the Puppet.* New York: Macmillan, 1965.
Currell, David. *The Complete Book of Puppetry.* Boston: Plays, Inc., 1975.
Currell, David. *Puppets and Puppet Theatre.* Wiltshire, England: Crowood Press, 1999.
Tichenor, Tom. *Folk Plays for Puppets You Can Make.* New York: Abingdon, 1959.
Watson, Nancy Cameron. *The Little Pigs' Puppet Book.* Boston: Little, Brown, 1990.

Scripts *see* Stories and Scripts

Sets of Basic Puppets

If you are just getting started in puppetry, you may feel as if you need more puppets than you will ever have. And even if you do have funds—say a grant to get started in your work—you may not know what puppets you will need. It seems that you need everything when you first begin.

An inexpensive way to build a puppet collection is to use stuffed animals. Go to the thrift store or to garage sales and purchase stuffed animals at low prices. Snip open the animal at the back base and remove some stuffing. Leave stuffing in the legs and tail, the ends of the arms, and the head. Stitch the legs and the ends of the arms (paws) shut. Take an old glove and use it to close off the head, making sure that two of the fingers extend into the head stuffing. Insert your hand through the back seam with two fingers into the head and thumb and fingers into the arms. (*See also* Hand Puppets; Stuffed Animal Puppets.)

Dolls made of fabric can also be used to make hand puppets. Prepare them in the same way you would prepare stuffed animals. If the dolls have skirts to hide their legs, the legs can either be dispensed with or left to hang. Fabric dolls can also be used to make simple marionettes by attaching strings to arms, legs, and head and using a simple control mechanism to make them move. (*See also* Marionettes.)

If you want to move beyond stuffed animals and converted cloth dolls, you may want to make your own set of puppets. If you are not a full-time puppeteer, however, you may require a shortcut to getting the puppets you need.

First, consider what types of stories you tell and the situations you tell them in. If you work with very small children, you may focus on animal stories. If you are a health worker, you may want puppets of people including lots of children. If you are a budding performer with ambitions to put on more-elaborate productions, you may want to consider working up a "troupe" of puppet characters you can use in a variety of situations and productions.

What stock characters do your stories contain? Make a list of those characters and make or buy only one of those puppets. Thus your cat character will work equally well for "Hey, Diddle-Diddle," "The Cat Went Fiddle-I-Fee," and "Belling the Cat." It might even work for a production of "Puss in Boots" with your cat in a jaunty hat to make him look cavalier. This interchangeable use of characters can extend to human beings as well. A queen in "Sing a Song of Sixpence" can also be a queen in "Pussy Cat, Pussy Cat, Where Have You Been?" The same is true of any other human character.

Try this list of characters to get started:

dog

cat

cow

pig

sheep

mice (2)

chicken

duck

fox

wolf

If you work with an African-American community or tell many African folk tales, you would want African animals:

elephant

lion

giraffe

rhinoceros

spider (for Anansi stories)

If you work with an American Indian community, consider the area of the country you live in and then choose:

sheep

deer

coyote

wolf

horse

salmon, fish, or killer whale

bear

If you tell many European fairy tales, consider this troupe of characters:

king

queen

prince

princess

peasant boy

peasant girl

peasant man

peasant woman

If you use mostly contemporary stories, think of the people in your neighborhood as you make your list of people:

mother and father

grandmother and grandfather

aunt and uncle (could also be mother/father for a second family and additional racial group)

girl and boy (enough children for all the families)

It is a good idea to have interchangeable heads and bodies for various characters. You might find that the grandmother head could also become a queen or an aunt or even an uncle! You just don't know until you try out wigs, beards, and bodies.

Remember to enjoy your puppets, and do not let them overwhelm you with extra work. It takes time to build a puppet collection, so go slow and make obtainable goals for yourself. See what is available to you in terms of time, money, and energy; then go for it!

Shadow Puppet Screens

A shadow puppet stage is the simplest kind of stage to create. For example, in India, shadow puppet screens are traditionally made by traveling puppeteers. A length of muslin or even a sari is attached to two bed frames, an oil lamp is lit behind the screen, and the play begins. The puppeteers have been using this method for hundreds of years, making it the most basic and portable of set-ups.

The same is true of puppeteers in Indonesia and Bali, where the shadow play is performed for special family occasions such as births, deaths, and weddings. The narrator-puppeteer comes into the family and sets up with whatever is available to support the screen material.

Table Leg Screen

Modern puppeteers can use the same screen method adapted to different materials or locations. The simplest way to set up a casual shadow puppet screen would be to use the legs of a table. If you have only one table, stretch cloth tight between the legs of the table and fasten the cloth to the legs making a tight, smooth screen. If you have two tables, you can invert one table over the other and fasten the cloth of the screen to the legs sticking up in the air. Again, make the cloth smooth and tight and without wrinkles which would snag the puppets and interfere with the evenness of the shadow. Shine a light behind the screen and place a shadow cut-out against the screen. Test the light source for brightness and its placement to avoid collisions and burns. Can you see the bulb? Test the thickness of the screen material.

Making a Doorway Screen

Another simple shadow puppet screen can be placed in a doorway. Check for the location of your power supply (plug or other outlet) to make sure it is convenient and located near the door. Make sure that the audience will have plenty of space for sitting and that the line-of-sight will be adequate so that everyone will be able to see well.

MATERIALS

- White or off-white material or paper 1' wider than your doorway
- Material, paper, or cardboard to make a "skirt" to hide the puppeteer in the doorway
- Light source: work light with reflector shield, flashlight, or lamp stand (*Do not use an open flame.*)
- Measuring tape or yardstick
- Pencils
- Scissors
- Masking tape

ASSEMBLY

1. Check the line-of-sight to make sure that everyone will have an easy time seeing the shadow screen.
2. Measure the width of the doorway and the length you wish to make the screen. Add an overlap of 6" on each side.
3. Tape the screen to the doorway, keeping the material tight and free of wrinkles.
4. Make a skirt of material, paper, or cardboard to hide the actions of the puppeteers.
5. Tape or hang the skirt to the doorway.
6. Test the light source. Test its placement to avoid collisions or burns. Also test it for the quality of the shadow it produces. Is it too bright? Can you see the bulb? Are the shadows it casts distinct?
7. Bring on the puppets, the audience, and have fun!

Cardboard Box Screen

A cardboard box is an easy and inexpensive alternative shadow puppet screen. It is especially useful if you are just trying out shadow puppetry or want to make a special craft time experience for older children.

MATERIALS

- Large cardboard box which will accommodate the size of your shadow puppets
- White or off-white material or paper to make the screen
- Strapping tape for fastening the screen to the box

- Box cutter or craft knife
- Scissors
- Pencils
- Ruler or tape measure

Assembly

1. Let the box sit on its bottom. Remove lid or cut off top of box.
2. Cut away part of one long side, leaving a 2" border all around. This side will hold your screen.
3. Remove the opposite side completely. The light will shine on the screen from this side.
4. Using the removed side as a pattern, cut cloth or paper for a screen.
5. Glue the cloth or paper to the screen side, attaching it to the remaining 2" border.

To use the theater, place a light source opposite the screen (so that the light shines from the back, toward the audience). Attach your puppets—which can be simple figures cut from paper — to wires or pipe cleaners. Working from the open top side of the box you will place the puppets gently but firmly against the screen, where the light will amplify and project the shadows as you tell the story.

You can also make a fancier shadow puppet screen using cloth and artist's stretchers.

Artist's Stretchers Screen

Materials

- Artist's stretchers (used to mount canvas for artists to paint upon)
- White or off white material to use as the screen including 6" of overlap all around
- Staple gun or tacks to fasten the material onto the stretchers
- Metal brackets to reinforce the stretchers
- Scrap lumber
- Pencil
- Scissors
- Measuring tape

ASSEMBLY

1. Decide the size you want your shadow screen to be.

2. Purchase two short sides and two long sides of an artist's stretcher set at an art supply store. Remember to purchase any reinforcing materials at the same time if the store carries them.

3. Measure the material to fit the stretchers, leaving 6" of overlap room.

4. Assemble the stretcher frame.

5. Screw in the reinforcing brackets.

6. Attach the screen material using a staple gun or tacks. You may need assistance with this.

7. Use scrap lumber to make legs to prop up the screen.

Lade, Roger. *The Most Excellent Book of How to Be a Puppeteer.* Brookfield, CT: Copper Beech Books, 1996.

Wisniewski, David, and Donna Wisniewski. *Worlds of Shadow: Teaching with Shadow Puppetry.* Englewood, CO: Teachers Idea Press, 1997.

Shadow Puppets

Shadow puppetry began in very ancient times and seems to be the preferred form of puppetry for the Middle East and Central Asia. Shadow puppets are easily transportable because they are flat and their rods small. It is easy to put on a shadow puppet play; all you need is some semi-transparent cloth, a lamp, and the puppets which are flat and made out of animal hide. These are all items which would have been available to the nomadic people of this area.

History

Shadow puppetry may be our oldest form of puppetry, dating from as far back as the fifth century B.C.E. or perhaps all the way back to cave paintings and ceremonies. The puppets involved with shadow puppetry are two-dimensional flat cutouts. The fifth century instance of such a cutout is a leather silhouette, created in the style of the Scythians, of a moose being attacked by a wolf.

The Chinese attribute the creation of shadow puppetry to Chiao-meng, an enterprising fellow living at the court of an emperor. The emperor's wife had died, and he missed her terribly. Chiao-meng created an elaborate silhouette of the emperor's deceased wife and projected it onto a back-lit cotton screen. The emperor took a great deal of advice from his "wife" before he discovered the hoax and had Chiao-meng executed. Still, Chiao-meng is credited with inventing shadow puppetry, and the screen is called the "screen of death."

Traditional Chinese, Turkish, Indian, and Indonesian puppets are created from water buffalo, camel, or donkey hide, beaten to make it thin, and painted with bright colors. The hide is usually pierced to indicate the puppet's features and clothing. Finally, the puppet is coated with a film of oil which dries, leaving the hide transparent. One or more rods are attached to the body of the puppet, giving it the ability to move and to facilitate fights, gestures, and other actions in the play.

A modern puppeteer can use these traditional puppets, but should be aware that they are part of cultures which extend back centuries. There are set plays and ways of presenting those plays which involve these characters. The traditional puppeteers study for years to master the art of presenting their puppets within an expected context. So I would hesitate before using a traditional puppet within a play, but there are many modern plays which have been written for the shadow puppet theater, some of which build on traditional folk stories. Many other stories have characters that can be adapted for use in the shadow puppet theater.

The screen in shadow puppetry must be "translucent enough to register a shadow and the light strong enough to cast a shadow." Ancient materials for the screen have included cotton, silk, parchment, and paper — any cloth "translucent enough to register a shadow."

Lighting

The final element of the shadow puppet theater is the light source. In traditional shadow puppet theater, this is an oil lamp which sheds a flickering light on the screen. The flicker and the dimness add to the mystery and illusory feeling imparted by traditional shadow puppetry. This is truly a place of wonders, of gods and demons where ordinary men and women become larger than life.

Due to safety concerns, modern shadow puppeteers use a regular light bulb fastened into some sort of clamp-on fixture. The light should be bright enough to illuminate the scene but not show the bulb. Experiment with various types of bulb: clear vs. frosted, different wattages, and so on. A specialty lighting shop may even have bulbs which flicker and thus replicate the flicker of the oil lamp without the danger of an open flame.

If there are any other safety concerns, such as working with children, a detached fixture could be used. The cover of *The Shadow Puppet Book* (Lynch-Watson) shows children working at a table top screen and using a lamp positioned behind them with a child to direct the placement of the lamp.

Making Shadow Puppets

If you are an artist or feel you can draw well enough to create silhouette figures, you can try your hand at creating your own shadow puppets. If you are not an artist, first check the books of shadow puppet plays, such as Judy Sierra's *Fantastic Theater*, which have the plays and figures for flannel board or shadow puppets.

Next, go to favorite picture books and see if there are figures you can sketch or turn into generic characters for the shadow puppet theater. Try the coloring pages presented on Jan Brett's web site. If you are a teacher or librarian, you can use the pictures there copyright free for non-profit organizations.

Shadow puppets can be articulated by dividing a limb, torso, or head into two parts, making each segment a bit longer to provide a joint, overlapping the segments, and joining the two portions of the limb. Fasten with string or brads and attach a rod to move the limb. (*See* Hinges.)

When you make your shadow puppet characters, remember that color can be added not only by painting and then oiling the puppets but also by using colored acetate. It's a bit like making a stained glass window or a paper cut-out where the spaces are filled in with transparent colored paper. Make the figure of poster board and then cut out the portions you wish to emphasize with color. Glue on the pieces of acetate and fasten the rods.

Clear acetate can also be used to make shadow puppets. Save the clear plastic serving containers used in the deli, wash well, and then use permanent markers to draw the basic forms of the puppets on the smooth acetate. Fill in with colored markers, cut out, and attach rods. Try clear plastic straws and clear strapping tape to attach the straws and make hinges. When the light shines through the clear acetate colored in by the markers, an additional dimension is provided by the stained glass effect provided by the transparent materials.

Scenery

Scenery in shadow puppet theater should be nonexistent or kept to a minimum. Just provide a hint to show that you are in the country or the town, in North America or on another continent, or in the past or the present. Sometimes the puppets and their clothing will provide enough information as to ethnicity or historical time period so that you can do without scenery. If you are making a piece of scenery for a character to enter — Cinderella's coach, for instance — either draw the coach with Cinderella already in it or make alterations in the design so that Cinderella can enter the coach and appear to be sitting.

Screens

A novel idea for the modern shadow puppeteer is to use an overhead projector. The puppet is placed directly on the glass platform of the projector and projected onto the wall. The puppets will be small, but can be used to good effect in a situation where setting up a stage may cause difficulty or distraction. The

Wisniewskis, in *Worlds of Shadow*, suggest this as the best method for a school classroom and they use it regularly.

Lynch-Watson, in *The Shadow Puppet Book*, makes a useful suggestion. Make a test screen for trying out new puppets or simple effects. Take a picture frame which will be big enough to accommodate most of the puppets you use. Cover it in the same material used for your shadow puppet screen. Use a light source similar to the one you normally use to provide the illumination. Use something such as a clamp, clay, or peg board, to prop up the puppets. You will have created a test screen very similar to your normal shadow screen. In fact, the "test" screen might be a more compact version of your usual screen, which will give you a second screen for use in more intimate or casual circumstances. (*See also* Shadow Puppet Screens.)

Flexibility

Shadow puppet theater is an alternative way to present stories and should not be eliminated from the repertoire of a general puppeteer just because it appears wildly different or doesn't seem to have the flash of other types of puppetry. Shadow puppetry is a wonderful medium to use to present the tales of the Near and Far East, its traditional home, as well as European or modern tales. Finally, shadow puppets are so easy and wonderful to make and use, you should give them a try!

Baird, Bil. *The Art of the Puppet.* New York: Macmillan, 1965.

Brandon, James R., comp. *On Thrones of Gold: Three Javanese Shadow Plays.* Cambridge: Harvard Union Press, 1970.

Currell, David. *An Introduction to Puppets & Puppet-Making.* Edison, NJ: Chartwell Books, 1992.

Flower, Cedric, and Alan Fortney. *Puppets: Methods and Materials.* Worcester, MA: Davis Publ., 1983.

Lynch-Watson, Janet. *The Shadow Puppet Book.* New York: Oak Tree Press, 1980.

Merten, George. *The Hand Puppets.* New York: Thomas Nelson, 1957.

Sierra, Judy. *Fantastic Theater: Puppets and Plays for Young Performers and Young Audiences.* Bronx, NY: H. W. Wilson, 1991.

Wisniewski, David, and Donna Wisniewski. *Worlds of Shadow: Teaching with Shadow Puppetry.* Englewood, CO: Teachers Idea Press, 1997.

Shelf-Sitter Puppets

Shelf-sitter puppets are a variety of rod puppet where the puppet's bottom is weighted so that the puppet easily and comfortably sits on the "shelf" of the puppet theater's playboard with its hands operated by rods. (*See* Cereal Box Puppets; Rod Puppets.) In this case, the activity of the puppet comes from the movement of its arms.

A shelf-sitter puppet can be used in any situation where you want a puppet that doesn't move from place to place yet has an interesting appearance. Little Miss Muffet is one such character. A puppet assistant might be another. (*See* Assistants.) An announcer or narrator puppet could be a third such character. Since you don't have to put on the shelf sitter as you do a hand puppet, it can remain in one place while it comments on the action or furthers the story through narration.

For instance, the shelf-sitter can have its own separate portion of the stage and a light which illuminates this separate stage when the shelf sitter is about to speak. When it is the shelf sitter's turn to speak, the puppeteer picks up the rods of the hands and arms, the lights go on, and the puppeteer speaks the puppet's dialogue. When that portion is completed, the lights go out on the little stage, the puppeteer puts down the rods and goes on to something else.

To make a shelf-sitting puppet, design the puppet as a complete figure with legs and feet as well as arms and hands. You may want to make the design of the bottom of the figure a bit larger than "normal" since you want some width to sit on that shelf! Before the puppet is completely stuffed, make a heavy weight of about three to five pounds. You want something with heft but also something with spread. Playground sand, lead shot, cat litter, or anything that fits the heft-spread qualifications will do.

Enclose the weight in a cloth sack. Sand should also be placed in a plastic bag. Place the sack in the bottom of the puppet and loosely close up the seam so you can try sitting the puppet on its shelf. Does the puppet sit easily and comfortably? Could you leave it alone and trust that it will not fall off the shelf? Does it need a little Velcro to assist in its shelf sitting and staying posed correctly? Are the arm rods the correct length?

When you have finished your shelf sitter, you will need to rehearse with your puppet to learn its special abilities. For instance, you will need to practice your arm movements so that they make sense within the context of that portion of the play. If you are the lone puppeteer, you will need to practice moving from the portion of the theater with your shelf sitter back to the main theater so the change is natural and easy. If you have another puppeteer creating the character the shelf sitter represents, you will need to rehearse the lines and cues with that person. If you don't have a separate stage for your shelf sitter, you will need to practice having the puppet enter and exit naturally.

A weighted puppet which can sit in one place, a shelf-sitting puppet, can be an asset in your work. This puppet can fulfill several roles and can expand what your puppets can do. Consider trying one out to see what they can do for your puppet plays. They can be easy to make and use. If you've never tried rod puppets before, this might be a good introduction. So don't sit on the fence; move to the shelf with your shelf sitter!

Henson, Cheryl, and the Muppet Workshop. *The Muppets Make Puppets!* New York: Workman Publishing, 1994.

Hunt, Tamara, and Nancy Renfro. *Puppetry in Early Childhood Education.* Austin, TX: Nancy Renfro Studios, 1982.

Renfro, Nancy. *Make Amazing Puppets.* Santa Barbara, CA: Learning Works, 1979.

Renfro, Nancy. *Puppets for Play Production.* New York: Funk & Wagnalls, 1969.

Shoe Box Theaters

The humble shoe box can become a boon to the puppeteer who works with young children. This theater can be placed in the lap and shown to a small group or classroom of children. It can contain an entire theatrical production within its small space and so become a part of a puppet corner. (*See* Puppet Corners.) It also can become a special play-time toy with each child having a personalized theater with which to act out stories.

The first thing you need to decide is what kind of theatrical experience will you present in your shoe box theater? Will it be a toy theater with scene changes and puppets on sticks? (*See* Toy Theaters.) Will it be a finger puppet theater where tiny finger puppets can act out stories? (*See* Finger Puppets.) Will you leave the action up to the child puppeteers, or will the theater have a theme such as a season or holiday or be a part of curriculum enhancement?

Let's say you decide to combine a diorama with the pop-up theater to create a dinosaur adventure theater. (*See* Dioramas; Pop-up Puppets.) First, each child must make a box for the diorama. (*See* Cardboard Boxes.) This activity includes measuring and simple geometry in the creating of right angles. Small-motor skills are used in cutting out the box, creasing the folds, and applying glue (unless you want to use the faster hot glue gun which an adult must operate). You may want to have an adult cut the slits for the stick puppets with a craft knife in the box's long side.

Art is involved in decorating the box, beginning with the choice of colors of poster board. Further art skills are involved in designing a decoration which will reflect the dinosaur theme. Math skills are involved in the design so that all elements are in proportion. The study of ancient animals and the prehistoric world in which they live is involved in the creation of the diorama itself. Finally, language arts are involved in creating a skit to be acted out by the young puppeteers. Creating such a small world is a great exercise for a classroom or puppet club. It involves many different skills directly applied from the curriculum or scaled to appropriate skill levels of puppet club members.

For presenting puppetry to a small group of youngsters in a story-time setting, the shoe box theater can become an enclosed world where each shoe box presents a single nursery rhyme or poem in an appropriate setting. Everything used in the presentation can be enclosed within the box and carried along as part of the program: scenery, stick or finger puppets, and the script for the poem or story if necessary. This kind of shoe box theater becomes an alternative to flannel board story presentations at a toddler story time.

Good things can come in small packages, and the shoe box theater is one of them. An entire theatrical production can be placed in a box to be used in a variety of situations. It can be a support to the curriculum, a new way of presenting a story or poem, or a free time toy for children. The creation and use of a shoe box theater involves many skills, from small motor exercise to art to math to language development as well as the vigorous exercise of imagination. By using this diminutive theater when you work with children, you will add to their learning experience plus giving them a gift we never have enough of: puppetry fun!

Making a Shoe Box Theater

Shoe boxes can be used to create all sorts of small, portable theaters. It must be remembered, however, that because of its size, the performance area in the shoe box must necessarily be small.

A shoe box theater can fit on your lap or hang from your neck, depending on whether you want to operate the little puppets from above or below. If you wish, the whole theater can be closed in the shoe box when the lid is put on, keeping its focus away from prying little eyes.

MATERIALS

- 1 shoe box, the larger the better (To make a box, *see* Cardboard Boxes.)
- Paper to cover the outside and inside of the shoe box (If you plan to have a scene across the back of your theater, and you will be having different kinds of plays in your theater, try to pick a scene that will fit many different kinds of plays.)
- Poster board
- Drawing or typing paper
- Craft sticks
- Markers or paints and paint brushes
- Pencils
- Ruler
- Craft knife
- Scissors
- White glue
- Optional stickers, metallic pens, and so on for decorating the outside of the shoe box theater

ASSEMBLY

1. If you do not have a shoe box the size you want, make one out of poster board. Decide whether you will need a lid or not.

2. Cover the shoe box both inside and out with either paint or paper. If you have made your box out of colored poster board, you can either skip this step or add more decoration with paint, markers, stickers and the like. Let the glue or paint dry thoroughly before going on to the next step.

3. If you want a backdrop (a scene on the back of your theater), make that now and glue it in place. If you will use the shoe box theater for a number of different shows, think of a generic scene that would serve as backdrop to most of them.

4. Cut one or two ½" wide slots in the bottom of the shoe box. Brace the box on a cutting surface if you need to. One slot should be slightly in front of the middle. If you have two slots, they should be at the ⅓ and ⅔ points in the box. The slots will allow you to insert puppets and their sticks and move them about a bit. Two slots provide a bit more choice in placement and movement. For instance, Humpty Dumpty could be sitting on the back slot while the King's horses and men would be in the front slot.

5. Use paper and poster board to create your puppets.

Mary, Mary, Quite Contrary

Shoe box theater to be used with children from Nancy Renfro. This little theater-in-a-box illustrates the nursery rhyme "Mary, Mary Quite Contrary." Such a theater is a great introduction to puppetry for young children.

6. Mount the puppets on craft sticks.

7. Insert the puppets into the shoe box slots, and try out the fit of the puppets and scenery.

8. Add anything you think would increase the character of your theater presentation.

9. Gather your audience and your puppets, and put on a play!

Hunt, Tamara, and Nancy Renfro. *Celebrate! Holidays, Puppets and Creative Drama.* Austin, TX: Nancy Renfro Studios, 1987.
Hunt, Tamara, and Nancy Renfro. *Puppetry in Early Childhood Education.* Austin, TX: Nancy Renfro Studios, 1982.

Slapstick *see* Comedy

Sock Puppets

The sock puppet, a much maligned member of the hand puppet family, is one of those early puppets of childhood. It is so easy to make! Take any sock, add some eyes and a wig, and there you have a perfectly serviceable character for a child's production of a first puppet play.

Sharri Lewis and her puppet Lambchop were big hits on television when I was growing up. Ms. Lewis was a skillful ventriloquist and comedian who played straight woman to Lambchop's sassy character. Later on, she would develop an "adult" program for night clubs as well as writing children's books. Somehow, though, the cuteness of Lambchop and the sock puppet became permanently entwined.

Lambchop was a simple but attractive puppet, a cartoon of a sheep. A contemporary sock puppet can either play up the cuteness angle or move toward a possibly more sophisticated interpretation of a character. Take a look at the photographs on page 88 and 89 of Cedric Flower and Alan Fortney's *Puppets, Methods and Materials.* On these pages, a light-colored sock with a cable pattern becomes a lion, deer, horse, bunny, bird, French artiste, snail, turtle, or funny fellow. Flower and Fortney emphasize the characteristics of the animal they are creating and don't worry about a mouth. As you may notice in these puppets, the hand is bent down with the fingers forming the long part of the face. A mouth really can't be seen and probably isn't necessary.

In Cheryl Henson and the Muppet Workshop's *The Muppets Make Puppets!* there is more emphasis on the caricature than there is in Flower and Fortney, who strive for more realism. Tommy "The Toe," a toucan, pig, baby, grandmother, dog, silly character, cowboy, rabbit, cowgirl, and dragon all have mouths and faces

Sock-puppet dragons Morris and Boris differ somewhat from other sock puppets in that the heel of the sock becomes the jaw of the puppet.

which face directly forward. The sock is brought forward in a fold which creates placement for the eyes as well as a mouth in several of the puppets.

In the Muppet book, the sock is placed on the hand with the fingers reaching into the toe of the sock and the thumb nestled into the heel of the sock. With your fingers and thumb making a "C" with the thumb underneath, press the sock back into the bend in the "C." The thumb nestled in the heel will naturally make a mouth for the puppet. By your knuckles, gather the loose material of the sock into a fold with the opening facing the ends of your fingers. This will become the eye line.

The sock puppet might never be called the most sophisticated creation on earth, but with some attention, the lowly sock puppet can become a wonderful addition to any general puppeteer's theatrical troupe. Each time you go into your local department or discount store, remember to walk by the sock counter. You may find it filled with future actors for your puppet plays!

Sock Puppet Dinosaur

MATERIALS

- 1 sock (Colorful is good in this case.)
- Felt to extend down the back of the sock (4"–6")

- Red felt for a tongue
- Black felt for eyes
- Needle and thread
- Scissors
- Pencil
- Compass
- Thread
- Pom-poms
- White glue or glue gun and glue sticks
- Newspaper

ASSEMBLY

1. Pull the sock onto your hand with the heel of the sock pointing downward. The thumb should fit easily into the heel area.
2. Gather the loose fabric together over the knuckles.
3. Make two newspaper balls and push them into this loose fabric.
4. Gather the sock around the balls and secure it with thread.
5. Cut two circles of black felt and attach them as eyes with hot glue.
6. Cut triangles out of the felt for scales.
7. Hot glue or sew the triangles in place down the back of the puppet.
8. Cut a tongue out of the red felt.
9. Glue the tongue in place in the back of the mouth.
10. Make some more sock puppets, put on a play!

Flower, Cedric, and Alan Fortney. *Puppets, Methods and Materials.* Worcester, MA: Davis Publ., 1983.
Henson, Cheryl, and the Muppet Workshop. *The Muppets Make Puppets!* New York: Workman Publishing, 1994.
http://www.legendsandlore.com/sockpuppets.html Good puppet making site for kids and adults. Lots of kinds of puppets to make.
http://www.pbs.org/totstv/english/puppetsock.html Good, kid-friendly site with instructions on making several kinds of puppets.

Sound Systems

Sound for puppet theaters used to consist of the puppeteer playing the fife and drum or clashing cymbals before a puppet show. Old pictures show some types of puppeteers playing the accordion or other portable instrument while they manipulated planchette figures or other small puppet displays. In the last century, elegant theaters might have had live musicians play for puppet plays. Today, things have changed considerably, and puppeteers will want to think of some of the choices they have.

First of all, this entry will not discuss large-scale theater sound systems. You will need a professional to analyze your situation and make suggestions. Instead, we will focus on the small puppet troupe of one to a few puppeteers who will need to consider some type of sound system and decide what will be best for their individual situation.

If you work alone, consider a portable microphone system. This will increase your projection without straining your voice. With most of the current systems, you can be mobile and walk around with your puppets. This can add a dimension of intimacy to your performance which you may consider desirable, or it may allow you to move about in front of a more elaborate set, interact with audience or puppets, come out from behind the stage at the end of a performance, and bring a feeling of immediacy to a larger audience.

If you have music as part of your productions, you will need some sort of tape or CD player with speakers suitable for your theater. While you won't have Surround Sound, you will want a high quality of sound reproduction for your music. You will have spent some time putting your tape together or recording music from an ensemble, and you don't want to waste this precious work with a tinny sound system. See if you can find a remote activating system so that you can operate your music from a foot switch or some other device.

Remember to keep your system in good repair and have a back-up system in case of problems. Things are always happening which you would never expect. Check with other puppeteers to see what they would suggest.

Music is important to a puppet play because it sets the mood and adds the dimension of sound to your performance. (*See* Music.) Good equipment purchased from a reliable dealer is a good investment. It will last you many years as well as adding to your performance. Talk with other puppeteers (the Internet puppet chats are good for this), check your bank account, shop around and compare, then make your purchase.

Currell, David. *Puppets and Puppet Theatre*. Wiltshire, England: Crowood Press, 1999.
Lasky, Kathryn. *Puppeteer*. New York: Macmillan, 1985.

Sponge Puppets

Soft sponges are much like foam rubber in that they can be manipulated in a number of ways to give them different facial characteristics. They can make easy, soft puppets for children. Sponges can be painted with acrylic paints, too, although it is easier to use the colors of the sponges as they are. Sponges can make a variety of humorous animal head puppets by trimming and gluing various pieces of foam together. Unfortunately, they cannot be sculpted as foam rubber can because of the large holes occurring in the sponge. Despite this, they can make interesting simple hand puppets.

To make a cellulose sponge puppet, the puppet's head will be the focal point, and your fingers will be needed to manipulate the mouth of the puppet. You can leave your arm exposed (remember that the children will be focused on the puppet anyway), or you can use a glove or cloth drape to cover your arm. You can also build a body which will hang down from the puppet's head and then manipulate the arms by rods.

Some sponges are difficult to manipulate, even though they may seem soft. You make an incision below the mouth opening and insert your fingers. Brace the puppet's chin against the heel of your hand and gently press your fingers downward. This should make your puppet's mouth move when speaking. Big movements aren't necessary; small ones are O.K. and more professional.

Sponges can be used to make animal puppets with bills or muzzles. Use two sponges and trim one to make a bill or snout. Attach with tacky glue or hot glue. If you find brightly colored sponges, try making an exotic bird or alien.

If you use two sponges to make a snout for an alligator, say, join the two parts with a fabric or tape hinge. (*See* Hinges.) Cut pockets in the upper and lower sponges for your fingers and thumb to manipulate the snout. Use a third sponge to create additional facial features for your puppet, attaching with hot or tacky glue. Make a body sleeve for the alligator out of green fabric or a long sock.

Remember to use natural sponges, too. These former sea creatures come in a variety of shapes and sizes which can suggest all sorts of creatures and animals. Make an incision in the sponge to accommodate one finger or a dowel to create a finger or stick puppet. Make a mouth, add some eyes, and you have a unique puppet!

Making a Sponge Puppet Alien

MATERIALS

- 2 soft cellulose sponges (the kind that don't dry out and get hard), preferably green
- Scissors
- Markers
- White glue
- 2 wiggle eyes, large in proportion to the alien's head
- 2 shiny chenille sticks and any other items which you think will make your alien even more special

ASSEMBLY

1. Using most of one sponge, draw the outline of an alien's head on the sponge and cut out the head. No one has actually *seen* an alien, so be as creative as you like!

2. On what will be the back of your alien's head, draw two horizontal lines: one for the mouth and one below it for your fingers.

3. Using your scissors, cut part way through the sponge to make alien's mouth open.

4. On the back of the sponge below where the mouth would be, cut part way through the sponge for the finger holes. Try this out to make sure that your fingers are comfortable and that the mouth works as you want it to.

5. If you want, use the other sponge to make additions to your alien to make it even more alien looking. For instance, you can cut an unusual nose in the style of Gonzo the Great from the Muppets and glue it onto your alien with white glue.

6. Glue on the wiggle eyes, or mount them on the chenille sticks and insert the sticks into your alien puppet. Try it out and see how you like your alien. It may need more eyes!

7. Add anything you think will make your alien puppet even more special. Remember to examine the puppet after each addition and see whether or not it was what you wanted.

8. It's show time! Make a bunch of aliens and invade Earth!

Henson, Cheryl, and the Muppet Workshop. *The Muppets Make Puppets!* New York: Workman Publishing, 1994.

Wallace, Mary. *I Can Make Puppets.* Toronto: Greey de Pencier Books, 1994.

Spring-Legged Puppets

A spring-legged puppet is a remarkable marionette found in *Imagination: At Play with Puppets and Creative Drama* by Nancy Frazier and Nancy Renfro, a book about the essence of puppetry. The spring-legged puppet is made from two sheets of paper, in any size, and can be an almost instant puppet, made while you are talking or telling a story.

The main part of the puppet is made from a single sheet of paper which forms the arms, legs, and torso. A second sheet of the same size of paper makes hands, feet, and head. Long thread loops form the controls and are attached to the head and hands of the puppet. Because the legs are loopy springs of paper, they will move on their own. You may find that the legs need weighting with a coin or washer to keep them extended, or you may have to make a fold at the hip line to keep the legs down properly.

Using two 8½" × 11" sheets of paper will make a puppet about 20" in height. Using two 11" × 17" sheets will make a puppet that is as tall as an adult and may have to be scaled down a bit to make a near-to-life-sized puppet that can still be operated without standing on something.

The advantage of the larger spring-legged puppet is that it can move with you. If you enjoy body movement, the spring legged puppet may be for you. Dressed in costume or in dark colors to fade into the background, you can dance with your puppet and tell your story in a new and wonderful way.

Materials

- 2 sheets of brown paper, construction paper, or watercolor paper of the same size
- Pencil
- Scissors
- Needle and thread
- Glue or tape
- Markers

Assembly

1. Fold each sheet of paper in half, one the long way and the other through the width.

2. On the long fold paper, beginning near the outside edge (not the folded edge), draw a spiral shape, staying about 1½" from the edges all around. Following along the spiral you've drawn, cut with scissors. Unfold paper. You should have a body-arms section which looks a bit like a "T" and a spiraling portion which will become the legs. Stretch out the spiral a bit; it will still spring back until you attach the feet/shoes and perhaps weight it a bit.

3. Take the second sheet of paper and cut it apart at the fold. One of these half-sheets will make the head and neck. The other half-sheet will make the hands and feet/shoes. Either draw and cut free-hand or make a pattern and cut out feet and hands. If you use this puppet style a lot, experiment with patterns for head, hands, feet and shoes to provide variety within the size of paper you use. Give the puppet personality by varying the hairdo, features, and facial outline.

4. Pierce or cut designs into the face to give more definition and emphasize personality.

5. Glue or tape the head and neck onto the torso and the hands and feet in their proper places.

6. Decorate your spring-legged puppet with markers if you want. If you want to leave the puppet in the simplicity of its silhouette, think about piercing or cutting decorations into the puppet. You can add clothes, but this will require more paper.

7. Cut about a yard of thread, and thread it on a needle. Pierce the head and hands (or fingers of the hands) with the needle and make a big loop with the thread. This will become the controls for your spring-legged puppet. (If the idea of handling the marionette threads directly is not comfortable for you, try making a simple control with a paper towel roll and a toilet paper roll. Tie the thread of the head and one hand to the paper towel roll. Tie the thread of the hand you will gesture with to the toilet paper roll so it will be able to move easily. (*See* Marionettes, Manipulation.) Keep two threads on one hand and one thread on the other. To free up the opposite hand for gesturing, move the head thread gently and smoothly from one hand to the other.

8. Test the height of your puppet if you are making life-sized puppets. If you will be making more than one, you will want to make notes or a pattern to let you know what to trim or what to add to make the puppet more manageable for you.

9. You can make two or three of these life-sized spring-legged puppets for a simple puppet show, or make just one dramatic one for the focus of your show. Whatever you do, gather your audience and your puppets and put on a play! Make your movements slow, graceful, and balletic. If you move too quickly, you will wind up tangling the legs and perhaps tearing something.

Frazier, Nancy, and Nancy Renfro. *Imagination: At Play with Puppets and Creative Drama.* Austin, TX: Nancy Renfro Studios, 1987.

Stages

Beginning puppeteers need a stage for their performances, but these stages do not need to be elaborate, expensive, or even time-consuming to make. Because they are somewhat ephemeral, basic puppet stages also give a puppeteer a chance to experiment and be creative with designs. Working out design ideas with inexpensive materials gives the puppeteer a chance to learn what works and what doesn't, what they like or don't like about a given design, and what they like as a puppeteer.

Basic Stages

The most basic stage for a puppeteer is the puppeteer's own lap. A puppet sits there and talks with the puppeteer, the audience, perhaps even talks to itself.

The puppeteer may be dressed in dark colors in order to fade into the background and focus attention onto the puppet.

Another version of this non-stage is the Apron Stage. (*See* Apron Stage.) This simple stage is made of dark cloth and is worn by the puppeteer, usually during story times or other times when children gather together. There are pockets on the apron in which puppets may be kept. Scenery can be buttoned onto the apron or appliquéd as part of the apron's over-all design.

In the world of professional puppetry, the simplest stages are found where puppetry is a part of folk life. Traveling puppet troupes may set up with the most minimal of stages to perform for village crowds. A white bed sheet stretched between two bed frames will be enough in some circumstances to create a stage and to put on a play. This kind of basic stage — sheets or curtains stretched between two supports — will also do for children first starting out in puppetry. Children can stretch curtains between the posts of a doorway or turn over a table and stretch material between the table's legs. Cardboard boxes are also excellent sources of material for making basic puppet stages. (*See also* Cardboard Boxes.)

Shorter and longer lengths of dark cloth and some heavy-duty clamps are useful things to have available if you are in a classroom or library situation. If you have easels, bookcases, or any similar sturdy items in your room, you can improvise puppet stages of various lengths whenever needed.

While it is wonderful to have an elaborate stage, it is not necessary in order to produce a great puppetry performance. This is especially true when beginning with puppetry or doing puppetry with children. A beginner hardly knows what to do with the puppets much less worry about an elaborate stage. Begin small and work up! That should be your motto. Find out what you want to do with your puppets first, then create a stage which will support your needs. You may discover that the best stage is no stage at all!

The Right Puppet Stage for You

Finding the right stage for you and your puppets is a process of learning about yourself as a puppeteer. What kind of puppets do you like to use? Do you have everything that you want in your present puppet stage? Have you experimented with different types of stages to see what might appeal to you and fit your circumstances? It isn't easy to find the right kind of stage, and depending on your puppetry style, you may not want one. A puppet held in your arms or sitting in your lap might be just the right thing, or you might want to use very large puppets so you can walk around with them and move with them, nearly dancing as you tell your story.

When I decided that I wanted to have a "real" puppet stage (as opposed to the jerry-rigged stage I was using), I was offered $500 to get my stage and was handed some catalogs. I knew that I wouldn't be able to afford what was in those catalogs. Ignoring the $1,200 price tag, one of the catalogs showed a huge and showy stage which would accommodate both hand puppets and marionettes. Super! Just what I wanted!

With that in mind and a dreadful little sketch, I went to the local lumber store and talked to one of the people there. I came away with sheet rock hangers, bolts, and a little lumber. With the hardware, curtain material, and curtain rods, it all came in just under $500. My boss couldn't stand to see me laboring in vain over this project, so he and another staff member took the project over and put it together. They made a few changes in the design which made it sturdier and dubbed the whole thing "the 'Fallout Shelter,' because it was so sturdy it won't be blown away by anything!"

The design itself is a cube with the performance side divided in half and the back side open. The upper and lower halves each have a set of curtains so that whatever unit is not being used can be closed off. I usually use the upper, or hand puppet, portion. I have put on simple marionette shows to good effect using the lower portion. Some of our puppet club members have used both halves when putting on a play. It has plenty of room for two people to work in the stage, but three is snug. More than that and we're in puppet club territory where *every*one wants to be behind the stage!

This stage has two small performance areas and room for two or more puppeteers. The upper stage is for hand puppets and shadow puppetry. The lower stage is for simple marionettes.

If you are thinking of building a more-permanent stage, try to get a look at as many different kinds of stages as possible. (*See* Apron Stages; Box Stages; Chinese Bag Puppet Theaters; Doorway Stages; Finger Puppet Theaters; Greeting Card Theaters; Hanging Stages; Hanging Toy Theaters; Paper Bag Theaters; PVC Puppet Stages; Shoe Box Theaters; Table Top Stages; Toy Shadow Puppet Theaters; Toy Theaters; Whirling Disk Puppet Theaters.) Contact as many puppeteers as possible and ask to look at the stage setup they are using. Talk to traveling theater troupes and see what they are able to do with minimalist stages. In short, get as much input as possible before committing to any particular stage set-up.

Consider these problems, too:

Will you need to transport this stage? If you work for a school, library system, or public health information facility, will your stage be in one space or will it move from place to place?

Will you have an assistant, or will you be working alone? This is a major consideration, especially if you are a body language person and move around quite a bit. On the other hand, I have seen a small hand puppet stage which nicely accommodates two people sitting on folding chairs.

How large will your audiences be? Are you going to be seen by a large number of people and, therefore, need to have large puppets? Will you primarily have smaller, more intimate performance spaces?

Do you intend to focus on one kind of puppet, or do you want to have the ability to use many kinds? Focusing on hand puppets may let you have a simpler stage set-up, while marionettes usually require a more elaborate one.

How much money do you have for a stage? A small budget need not be a hindrance, and a big budget is not a guarantee of success. It's careful planning and a fair idea of what you want to do with puppetry which will make things work for you.

Are there people who can help you with construction work? Is there someone on your staff or Friends of the Library or PTA who would be able to help you with the construction details of your project? Perhaps there is a Scout troop looking for a public service project like this.

Will you want to own this puppet stage or let it belong to your facility? You may find yourself wanting to be a full-time puppeteer and take your stage with you. Building it yourself will be critical in this case. On the other hand, by letting someone else build your first stage, you get to experiment and see what is right for you.

When you have an idea of what you would like in a stage, make a mock-up from cardboard or foam core board and try out the size and workability of the space. Even paper, suspended from ceiling tile supports, can give you an idea of the working room you will have. If you continually run into problems, you will want to reconsider your design. Another reason for making a mock-up and using it for a while is that you may discover a desire to try something you had not thought of when you were still planning on paper.

A stage of your own is a wonderful thing to have. It permits you to experiment even as it limits other considerations such as space. Most of all, a stage of your own says you are taking your puppetry seriously. You may never go on the road with your puppets and plays, but you will take another step toward professional status by staking your claim to your own performance space.

Currell, David. *The Complete Book of Puppetry*. Boston: Plays, Inc., 1975.
Currell, David. *Puppets and Puppet Theatre*. Wiltshire, England: Crowood Press, 1999.
Hunt, Tamara, and Nancy Renfro. *Puppetry in Early Childhood Education*. Austin, TX: Nancy Renfro Studios, 1982.
Minkel, Walter. *How to Do "The Three Bears" with Two Hands: Performing with Puppets*. Chicago: American Library Association, 2000.
Watson, Nancy Cameron. *The Little Pigs' Puppet Book*. Boston: Little, Brown, 1990.

Stereotyping

Every country has a conventional way of seeing people. Let's call them "types." There is a pretty girl type, a handsome man type, a business type, a child type, an elder type, and so on, and these may vary from country to country. In each country and culture, people expect these characters to look as well as act a certain way.

When we visualize a heroic warrior, for instance, we expect him not only to be strong and brave and good but also to be handsome with a noble appearance. When we think of a villain, we not only expect him to be nasty, scheming, and crafty but also to look a bit like a melodrama villain with thin fingers and a pinched, narrow face.

To some extent, stereotyping plays into this visualization. We expect a princess to be dressed in fine clothes, to be beautiful and pleasant, and to act in a gracious and regal manner. When we see characters acting out of type — Robert Munsch's *Paper Bag Princess*, the rambunctious in Babette Cole's *Princess Smartypants*, or the princess and Plane Jane in Jane Yolen's *Sleeping Ugly*— we know that there is some important reason for this unusual behavior. The castle has been burned down by a dragon in *The Paper Bag Princess* and there are no clothes left; independence is the characteristic of *Princess Smartypants* who does not want to get married under any circumstances; *Sleeping Ugly* is making the point that beauty comes from within.

Stereotyping takes our normal cultural expectations and applies them to people and places. When we think of a fairy tale princess, for instance, we not only think of the attributes mentioned previously but also usually think of her as European ... and blonde. Here is an anecdote which may illustrate this stereo-typical thinking. When the movie *The Princess Bride* was made, Whoopie Gold-berg applied for the role of Buttercup, and the director and all his entourage fell out of their chairs. What was so funny to them was the idea of an African-Amer-ican woman applying to play the role of a European fairy tale princess. Stereotypes did not allow for this to happen, and the movie was cast with a blonde hero and heroine. In fact, there are no African-Americans in any part of *The Princess Bride.*

Take a look at some of the older books on puppet making and you will see what I mean. The faces of people of races other than the European are not only caricatured, they are stereotyped. This leads to assumptions about what people are and what kinds of people they can be. If a famous actress like Whoopie Gold-berg is barred from playing certain roles because of her color, then what roles may she play?

Children's books like to play with stereotypes and break them all to pieces. Perhaps the first children's book to do so was William Steig's *Shrek*, an anti-fairy tale book which broke every stereotype while maintaining the conventions of the fairy tale. If you haven't read *Shrek* you should. It is nothing like the movie and will leave you laughing and rooting for Shrek to win his, er, beautiful princess.

In the stereotype-breaker fairy tale *Sleeping Ugly*, the princess is beautiful but mean tempered while Jane is sweet and kind but also unattractive. The witch is elderly, but conventionally dressed, so she doesn't "look" like a witch. The prince who comes along to waken all the sleeping women must choose: whom will he awaken first? Fortunately, he is a bright and good-hearted young man and makes the right decision.

Stereotyping is bad manners. It is making fun of or putting down someone for something they cannot control. To engage in stereotypical portrayals in pup-petry is to betray the goal of puppetry as stated by UNIMA (Union Internationale de la Marionette): to bring about peace and understanding through puppetry. As our world grows smaller and our populations more diverse, we must find new ways of portraying our characters which convey their inner selves. The old types may no longer hold. By applying ingenuity and respect, we can have a puppet world which leads the way in showing the rest of the world a better way of living.

To give you some ideas of what *not* to do, try these titles and examine their chapters on character creation and faces.

Ackley, Edith Flack. *Marionettes: Easy to Make! Fun to Use!* New York: Lippincott, 1929.
Fling, Helen. *Marionettes: How to Make and Work Them.* New York: Dover, 1973.

Stick Puppets

A stick puppet is the simplest of puppets. It can be a picture or object mounted on a single stick or a figure drawn *on* a wide stick, such as a tongue depressor or flat, wooden ice cream spoon. The figure does not move but is paraded onto the stage and perhaps jiggled a bit when its voice is speaking to indicate focus.

One kind of stick puppet is a picture of a person or other character mounted on a stick. Figures can be cut from magazines or coloring books and glued to construction paper for reinforcement before taping or gluing to a straw or craft stick. Simple pictures of animals and birds can be copied onto colored paper and mounted on chenille sticks to create dancing or flying puppets that can teach colors or numbers. Favorite children's book characters can be drawn and turned into stick puppets.

A more individual stick puppet can be made by using scraps of felt, pompoms, lace, and other notions to build characters on a paint stirrer or tongue depressor. Paint can also be used to draw and paint in figures of characters, although this technique creates a more two-dimensional effect. Nursery rhymes, Aesop's fables, and other simple stories can be told this way to a small group. A group of unrelated stick figures can be created, and older children can create a play using these characters.

Small figures can be mounted on a stick and become stick puppets. The figures themselves can be quite complex, such as a many-tentacled sea creature, a small human figure, or a star or planet. The figures do not move except as the stick is moved, although I have seen Griane MacGregor of Ivy Vine Players use

These three stick puppets are the wise elders of their village.

small human figures which whirl and dance and fling their arms and legs about when their stick is twirled. Other than that, there is no movement of any part of the Ivy Vine figures.

Puppets made of items which naturally come mounted on a stick, such as wooden spoons, kitchen whisks, tooth brushes—any kind of brush, really—can become stick puppets as long as they are not made more complex. This is pushing the outer limits of the stick puppet, really, because it takes very little to make these stick puppets into the more-complex rod puppet. (*See* Brush Puppets; Rod Puppets; Wooden Spoon Puppets.)

There is one feather duster which is even advertised as a puppet on its cardboard sleeve. The picture on the sleeve shows a pair of eyes, a beak, and two little bird legs attached to the feather duster with the feathers on top of the duster forming the body of the bird and the handle of the duster becoming its operating stick. As long as the puppet stays at this level and does not acquire wings which move independently, it is a very fancy stick puppet.

In this same vein, a wooden spoon can be given arms and hands, a costume, wig, and facial features. As long as the arms do not move, it is a stick puppet. If rods are attached to one or both of the arms, it becomes a rod puppet.

A moving mouth is somewhat ambiguous. Because some part of it moves, by definition it is not a stick puppet. But if nothing else on the puppet moves.... Well, I'm not so sure. I have seen mask puppets where all that moves is the mouth and that not much. Are they stick puppets? I am tempted, but I say no, it's a rod puppet. Rod puppets can have one rod and a very complicated system of controls enabling the puppet on the rods to do some quite amazing things! Hobie Ford of Goldenrod Puppets has such a group of rod puppets, but there is only one rod and some complex control mechanisms involved.

Stick puppets are wonderful, simple things. They can be used to illustrate nursery rhymes, simple stories, and some curriculum materials. They can become a child's early introduction to puppetry. Toy theaters are based on this principle of the stick puppet and can be quite elaborate. (*See* Toy Theaters.) However, the puppets themselves are still stick puppets. The stick puppet can also be used to introduce a small puppet into the general action, sometimes only for a brief period of time, sometimes longer. A small, swimming sea creature, a shooting star, a bouncing baby bird can all be mounted on a stick and given their turn on the stage. Although the stick puppet is simple, it can be used to great effect in the right circumstances. Don't count them out because stick puppets are a puppeteer's good friend!

Bauer, Caroline Feller. *Leading Kids to Books through Puppets.* Chicago: American Library Association, 1997.

Henson, Cheryl, and the Muppet Workshop. *The Muppets Make Puppets!* New York: Workman Publishing, 1994.

Hunt, Tamara, and Nancy Renfro. *Puppetry in Early Childhood Education.* Austin, TX: Nancy Renfro Studios, 1982.

Storage

Puppets take up space! They also need special care and handling so that they will not receive more wear in storage than they do during a performance. Also, some materials need special handling to prevent deterioration, so storage of puppets becomes an important element of managing your puppet inventory — as important as creating the puppets themselves.

It would be wonderful if every puppeteer had plenty of room in which to store all puppets in the correct manner and at the correct temperature! Short of opening a museum, however, there is little possibility of that for most puppeteers, so the puppeteer must make the best of what is available.

The goal is both to protect the puppets and to have them easily available for use when needed. Additional goals may be to keep marionette strings from becoming entangled or to keep fine costumes from becoming wrinkled. If you have foam rubber puppets, they must be prevented as much as possible from deteriorating. Regular inspections should take place, making sure that the puppets are still in good working condition.

Bags are a common method of protecting puppets, but take care when choosing the material for the bag. Avoid plastic, even though it is easy to see what puppet you have in the bag. Plastic doesn't breathe, so you must leave the bags open, which invites dirt and dust. Lightweight muslin bags are the preferred material. Ordinary puppets can be carefully folded up into the bag. Special puppets can be hung from their rings with the bag gathered around it. Attach a photograph of the puppet to the bag to identify it, and write its name on the bag in ink that won't smudge.

The beauty of muslin bags is that they are inexpensive, breathe well, and can be made to any size. This is especially necessary with marionettes and rod puppets which are often tall. Rods should be secured and the puppets hung in the bag from their feet or shoulders. The rod puppet should not be allowed to sit upon itself. Flat rod puppets can, of course, be placed flat in an artist's portfolio. The rods should never be folded in with the puppet as they might crease or bend the puppet in some way. If the rods are attached to the puppet, make sure that the rods and the puppet are wrapped in order to protect them.

An alternative for frequently used hand puppets is to mount them on stands and perhaps cover them with a protective muslin cloth. Stands can be made from scrap wood and dowels, if you have a woodworker handy. If not, try a shoe rack, placing the puppets where the shoes would go. A third and perhaps the cheapest storage alternative is to fill 16- or 20-ounce drink bottles with play sand, cap the bottle, and place the hand puppet on the bottle. Cover all the puppets with a muslin cloth to keep out the dust.

The strings of marionettes should be tied off at the control, then carefully wound around the control and the marionette inserted into the bag. The bag should be tied beneath the control and a cord on the bag used to hang the bag in its proper place.

Foam rubber puppets should be stored in a climate controlled environment, but this is rarely possible. First, keep your foam rubber puppets away from light. Then keep them away from heat. One puppeteer friend has all her linen closets and clothes closets filled with foam rubber puppets.

Space is an important part of puppet protection, too. You need to have a place with enough space to protect your puppets. Chiefly, you need hanging room for marionettes and for more elaborate hand puppets. You also need room to keep all the characters in one play together. Sadly, there never seems to be enough room, but with careful planning, what you have will be enough.

Protecting your hard-won puppets is a necessity. Children love to handle them, and dust and dirt will take their toll. Heat, too, is a problem as well as sunlight. All in all, the protection of your puppets may take as much time and thought as making them did, but it will be worth it when you can remove a puppet from its bag a year after use and find it in as wonderful a condition as you did at the beginning.

Fling, Helen. *Marionettes: How to Make and Work Them.* New York: Dover, 1973.

Stories and Scripts

Stories and scripts for puppet plays can be found in books in libraries everywhere. In the back of this book is a bibliography with many puppet plays suitable for school or library and for various age ranges.

Story Sources

The puppeteer is always looking for stories to turn into puppet plays. Do you always want to do fairy tales? They are the best known of children's stories but are they always the best to turn into puppet plays? Here are some additional story sources for puppeteers.

My favorite puppetry author is Aesop for several reasons. First of all, there are usually no more than a couple of characters in these vignettes, and the stories are compact. They usually contain animals, always a favorite with children. The stories are easily adaptable to what puppets you have at hand. Finally, you don't have to emphasize the moral statement at the end. You can incorporate the moral into the story rather easily. On top of that, the moral is pretty obvious, so you needn't belabor the point.

Beatrix Potter, who wrote *The Tale of Peter Rabbit*, can be another source of simple animal stories for children. Peter Rabbit, for instance, usually has only one or two characters on stage at one time. This is not true for all her tales, so you must be careful and read thoroughly before saying, "Yes! I'll do that one."

Wide reading of children's literature is another way to find stories to perform. Most picture book authors try to keep the number of characters in their books small which can work to your advantage if you are a lone puppeteer. Talking to children you know is another good source of stories. What stories do they like? Which ones do they gravitate to or want to read repeatedly? Sometimes children's book authors go through a period of popularity, then wane, that doesn't make them any less desirable as potential puppet plays. If they were popular at one time, there was a reason. Hook into that.

Which brings us to another subject: copyright and permission. If you are connected with a school or library, you may get a break on copyright restrictions, but you may not. It always pays to check. Write to the copyright department of the publisher involved if you have any questions at all.

One reason puppeteers use fairy tales—other than the magic created by the tale—is that fairy tales are in the public domain. That is, you don't have to pay for the permission to turn the tale into a play and present it to the public. If you find a story you think would work as a puppet play, check on its copyright. Fairy tales are always being redone by contemporary authors and illustrators, and it may be the illustration, not the story, which is copyrighted. Here's another problem: you may think an author is dead and the copyright in the public domain, but heirs and family members may have renewed the copyright, and it may still be theirs.

How about a popular character such as Harry Potter or Pokemon or The Hobbit? Most of these characters will be protected by copyright, but you may be able to create a similar situation or character for a puppet play.

There are an endless number of story sources for puppeteers. If you include adult sensibilities in your considerations, you may take story ideas from any source: books, films, or the newspaper. But for those puppeteers who cater to children, becoming familiar with children's literature is a must. Fairy tales now include tales from many lands and cultures as well as the newfangled fractured fairy tale. Get down to your library and do some research. You may be surprised at what you find!

Tragedy

Tragedy, in classic terms, was a type of drama that allowed the audience to feel sorrow and catharsis through the observation of the actions of the great persons in the story. They had great flaws to match their high station in life and suffered the tragic consequences of their errors. The audience watched this suffering, felt sorrow, and underwent catharsis. Usually the hero of the play died as a result of his errors, although occasionally the result was banishment or exile. The grief felt by the audience was supposed to be as great as the hero's suffering.

Tragedy in puppetry is a thing which needs to be used carefully, since most puppetry is aimed at children. Loss is common to almost all children, however, and this is one of the tragic themes which can be used to good effect if it is not dwelt on too greatly. The odd kid out is another useful theme, as is *the personal problem*. Let's take a look at each of these in puppetry for children.

Loss is something which is experienced by many children. The loss of a toy or the loss of privileges fall within the common realm of most children and are manageable by them. Sadly, many children also will have experienced much larger losses: the loss of a loved one, the loss of their home, the loss of friends. When tragedy strikes, no one is spared. In children's stories, however, loss is often something removed from a contemporary child's experience. Jack's loss of his cow in *Jack and the Beanstalk*, the cobbler's near ruin in *The Shoemaker and the Elves*, and near-starvation in *Hansel and Gretel* are also distant losses for most small children. If they know the stories, they know these tragedies as plot devices, and they know that everything will work out for the best. At the time of the telling of these stories, however, these tragedies were all too real, and we have seen similar things in the United States: the loss of family farms, homelessness, and starvation. Can these tragedies of modern life be incorporated into a puppet play?

The odd kid out is often expressed by the dummling stories. *The Golden Goose* and *Jack and the Beanstalk* are the ones which most readily come to my mind. In these stories, a not-too-bright kid is able to save the day through pluck, luck, and good-heartedness. How does it feel to be a dummling — the youngest of the family, the brunt of all the jokes, and one who is not expected to do much with his life? How does it feel to be picked on this way and how does it feel to triumph in the end?

Personal problems are everywhere in children's stories. Some of the problems are life-and-death sized as in *Little Red Riding Hood* or *The Wolf and the Seven Little Kids*. Others are personal problems to be overcome or dealt with as in *Beauty and the Beast* or *Goldilocks and the Three Bears*. How do fairy tale characters deal successfully with these personal problems? Or do they?

Whenever you decide to deal with tragedy in a children's drama, do it lightly, but don't skip over it. Children will understand, for instance, a bullying or teasing scene in *The Golden Goose* where the dummling is shown to be the brunt of bad treatment from his brothers. Then the boy's kindness which gives him the golden goose and the means of making something of himself becomes a greater triumph. The teasing needn't be belabored; a taste will be enough, but it needs to be established just *why* the kindness of the youngest brother is important enough to grant him a triumph.

When our puppet club did *Jack and the Beanstalk*, they cast it in a contemporary setting. Instead of trading in the cow, they had to trade in the family car. You can do the same with a fairy tale to give it more immediacy. *Jack and the*

Beanstalk can address themes of poverty, homelessness, and family economic loss in the same way by making the setting contemporary. Again, don't make it heavy handed. A touch will do to get the point across.

Another traditional tale which can be given a contemporary treatment is *The Three Billy Goats Gruff*. The troll can become the school bully. Maybe the three brothers can be three friends who need to get into the gym to practice for a crucial basketball game or out onto the field for soccer practice. There is a door or gate which the troll-like bully controls. "Give me your lunch money, crumbs, or you're not going anywhere!" The three need to come up with a solution, preferably one that doesn't involve fighting.

The one tragedy I have no real solution to is the community tragedy where a city or area has been struck by a tornado, flood, or some other natural catastrophe. Of course, there are the national tragedies of the Oklahoma City bombing or the destruction of the World Trade Center in New York. If your community is struck by such a disaster, consult with counselors or public health professionals and ask them if they think a play about the situation would help. Listen to their suggestions, and see where you can go from there.

If you live in an area where natural disasters happen regularly, you may find that your state's commission on the arts may be open to having you present programs in disaster-struck areas, especially if it includes workshops for teachers or classes on using puppets to work through the fear or grief brought on by the disaster. You may find you have a new calling here.

Because puppetry is part of theater, it has the option of using tragedy in its plays, although puppetry seems to gravitate towards comedy instead. Tragedy can be presented with a lighter touch, especially since the bulk of the audience at puppet plays are children. One method is distance, the method used by fairy tales. By casting a play in the past, it seems more emotionally remote to the audience. The other method, which makes the tragedy more immediate, is to set the play in the present. In either case, if the story is well known, the audience knows that everything will work out for the best. Either method can be used by the puppeteer to incorporate tragedy into the puppet play.

Creating a Script

What about creating your own puppet script? How do you go about taking a story and adapting it or writing an original play for your own puppets and situation?

In adapting an existing story for your puppet theater, begin with a story you enjoy and would like to tell to others. If you tell the story out loud several times, you may find yourself eliminating certain scenes or pieces of business which were not memorable to you. Perhaps you didn't understand them, or perhaps you felt they didn't advance the story sufficiently to remember the detail.

After becoming well acquainted with the story, begin to plot it out in storyboards or in flowcharting steps, whichever feels most comfortable to you. This should break the story down into its component steps with each element covered along the way. Remember that a good story has a beginning, a reason for the action to start; it has a middle, where the concerns about the action are worked over, and an ending, where all the questions are answered and problems resolved. The flow of the story is something like a lopsided, right-leaning curve where the story starts, builds to a climax, and flows to the finale or denouement. Your stories may not build up a great deal of tension, but there will be questions to be answered and actions to be resolved.

Cartoonists and movie makers use storyboards to give them an idea of how the story should flow, and you can, too. Usually they use pictures, and you can if you wish. You could also make collages and word descriptions—anything which helps get the flow and the steps of the story down on paper so you can see the whole.

Next, you need to do two things: begin to write the script based on the storyboards, and begin to design the puppets for your play. Try to get an idea of what you want the puppets to look like. As you write out the script, try to see these puppets in action. You may discover that the hand puppets you originally envisioned giving way to rod puppets or shadow puppets. While working with the script, make any notes you may have about scenery, props, and music. Next, begin to make your puppets and firm up the script. (*See* Rehearsal.) Then start promoting your play. (*See* Business of Puppetry; Advertising and Marketing.)

If you work for a library or health service, you may develop scripts for the specific messages you want to get across: reading is fun, brush your teeth, take care of your library books and return them on time, wash your hands before eating and after using the bathroom, visit the doctor and dentist for regular checkups. Since you will be trying to present a message, don't be heavy handed. Sometimes the best messages are encased in a story which presents the message without really stating it. Try an Aesop's Fable with and without the moral at the end. You still get the message while enjoying the story. You can look for specific stories focusing on your message and adapt those, or you can create a troupe of regularly appearing characters and write plays for them on various specific topics. If you decide to look for stories, treat them with some of the same care you'd use for the full-blown play production treatment discussed previously. You will already have your puppets, so that part of the preparation process is taken care of. Remember that in a generic story, animals can substitute for humans (as they have been doing it for millennia), and the story can be massaged to match the puppets you've already got. So what if a star fish is talking to a cat! The kids don't care, and it's the message that's important anyway.

If you want to write your own story, you can follow an abbreviated form of the play production outline given previously. Try flowcharting or outlining the story to see if it flows the way you want it to. Try recording the story or telling the story to someone else to see if the story hangs together. Make note of any "business" you want your puppets to do, any props they need to rehearse with, or any scene changes you need to rehearse.

Teacher's use play writing for puppets as a great language arts exercise, try it yourself! You may discover a real interest in writing these little gems. If you are concerned enough about your skills, you can seek out a course in playwriting at a local college or through online continuing education. Play writing is fun! It's another great skill you need to learn to be a puppeteer. And again — you may find you really like it!

Long, Teddy Cameron. *Make Your Own Performing Puppets*. New York: Sterling/Tamos, 1995.
Minkel, Walter. *How to Do "The Three Bears" with Two Hands: Performing with Puppets*. Chicago: American Library Association, 2000.
Renfro, Nancy. *Puppetry and the Art of Story Creation*. Austin, TX: Nancy Renfro Studios, 1979.
Watson, Nancy Cameron. *The Three Little Pigs' Puppet Book*. Boston: Little, Brown, 1990.
http://www.legendsandlore.com/puppetscript.html Legends and Lore is a great puppet site. This portion offers some good, general ideas for kids and adults about writing puppet scripts.

Stuffed Animal Puppets

Stuffed animals and dolls with cloth bodies can be turned into puppets, and you can build up a stable of puppets without spending a great deal of money or time. If you are a flea market shopper or enjoy going to thrift stores, this is a great way to get lots of puppets cheaply and in a short time and is a favorite method of children's librarians everywhere.

The basic method for turning a stuffed animal or doll into a puppet is to carefully slit open the back of the animal or doll and remove as much stuffing as you feel is appropriate. The idea is to leave the head and legs filled with stuffing in order to hold the shape of the animal or doll and have access to the arms and head. The legs can either be hidden behind the theater or can sit on the edge of the playboard, whichever seems best to you. The hand inserts through the back of the animal or doll and the fingers reach up into the head and arms to manipulate them. The slit in the back should be hemmed to prevent raveling.

The problems with such puppets are that the stuffing shifts and falls out, and you may not know where to put your hand into the head. If so, you can make a simple pocket for your hand which will close off the stuffing and provide a place for your hand. Use muslin or a remnant of some firm fabric. Sew a generous pocket which will hold two of your fingers. Leave flaps of material at the bottom so that the whole looks like a "T" standing on its head. The pocket for your fingers

Stuffed animals as puppets from Nancy Renfro. Three methods for turning old cloth, rubber, or plastic toys into puppets are shown.

can be inserted into the midst of the stuffing for the head, and the flaps can be tacked into place around the head stuffing.

Another way to turn stuffed animals or dolls into puppets is to affix rods or strings to the toy and turn it into a marionette or rod puppet. A traditional form of marionette found in northern India only uses a single control thread for an animal puppet. The thread runs from the head to the rump of the puppet and is long enough to be held and manipulated by the puppeteer. You might consider this method for turning stuffed animals into marionettes. (*See* Marionettes, Simple Controls.) They would be easy to manipulate and would be easy enough to produce. If you don't like the single loop method, try attaching the control thread to a paper towel tube or paint stirrer.

When you are just starting out, especially if you work with children in a day-to-day situation such as a library or classroom, you won't have a great deal of money to spend on puppets. You will want to show your parent's group or friends of the library that you are serious about puppetry before you ask them for money for special materials or for more-advanced puppets. Give these bargain basement puppets a try, and see if they don't reward you generously!

Hunt, Tamara, and Nancy Renfro. *Puppetry in Early Childhood Education*. Austin, TX: Nancy Renfro Studios, 1982.

Styrofoam Puppet Heads

Styrofoam comes in many sizes and shapes and can be used as the base for creating a puppet head. It can have materials molded over it, or it can be carved into shape with knives or simple carving tools.

The most basic head is a bare Styrofoam ball or egg with hair added and a few facial features painted on. A hole is bored into the ball, and the ball is placed on the index finger. The hand can be covered with a glove or a simple cloth throw.

A step up from the plain Styrofoam head is the one covered with one or more layers of papier-mâché. (*See* Papier-Mâché.) The head still remains smooth; the features are only painted on. A hole is bored into the ball and a tube inserted and glued into place to become the neck of the puppet. The neck as well as the head is covered with papier-mâché, making a ridge at the bottom of the neck in order to attach the body more easily to the head. When dry, the papier-mâché is painted and hair and features are added to complete the character. A body is added to the head, and the puppet is complete.

The next Styrofoam head is built up to form a face. Either layers of tissue- or papier-mâché or papier-mâché mash are used to create features. Remember to cover the neck tube as well and add the ridge at the bottom. As above, when everything is dry, the head is painted and hair and features added. Finally, the body is attached and any accessories added to complete the puppet's character.

If you analyze the human face, you will see that the features either sink into the head or extend out of it. Eyes sink in a bit. Noses protrude, as do lips and ears and chins. Cheeks can either sink, be level, or puff out. The next Styrofoam head uses sculpting tools (a knife) and papier-mâché mash or tissue-mâché to create a face with more features. The eye sockets are gently dug out, and the nose and lips built up. Cheeks can be padded, either with papier-mâché mash or additions of Styrofoam. Remember to add the neck tube with the ridge for attaching the body. When the sculpture is finished, cover the whole with gesso and add the features and wig.

Styrofoam is a lightweight base upon which to build puppet heads. The ball and egg shapes can be used by themselves as simple puppet heads, or they can become the base for a more elaborate sculpture. Styrofoam saves time, too, since you don't have to go through the clay mold making or the sawing and reconstruction steps for making a traditional papier-mâché puppet head. Try working with Styrofoam as a base for puppet heads. You may find that you like or even prefer it to traditional methods.

Allison, Drew, and Donald Devet. *The Foam Book: An Easy Guide to Building Polyfoam Puppets.* Charlotte, NC: Grey Seal Puppets, Inc., 1997. Second printing, 2000.
Currell, David. *An Introduction to Puppets & Puppet-Making.* Edison, NJ: Chartwell Books, 1992.
Flower, Cedric, and Alan Fortney. *Puppets, Methods and Materials.* Worcester, MA: Davis Publ., 1983.

Table Top Stages

The table top stage is a basic stage and is similar to the cardboard box stage but is made with a folding screen of cardboard. (*See* Box Stages.) This screen can be cut down from a cardboard carton, made from foam core board, or purchased as a three-part cardboard screen at office supply stores, craft stores, or office supply departments of grocery stores, drug stores, or discount stores. An opening for the stage is cut in the center panel of the screen, and a back curtain is suspended from a dowel or cord hung towards the back of the two side panels.

Like the cardboard box stage, the table top puppet stage is a great beginner's stage and fine for informal performances. It is also a good craft project for older children or for members of a puppet club. An added advantage of the table top puppet stage is that it can be used for either hand puppets, marionettes, or shadow puppets (with the addition of a paper or cloth screen, especially if you use the large, three-fold cardboard screen). (*See* Shadow Puppets.) With the proscenium opening at the top, you can use hand puppets; with the proscenium opening at the bottom, it becomes a stage for marionettes.

MATERIALS

- Cardboard box at least 22" tall *or* 2 large foam core board panels *or* a three-part cardboard screen
- Paints and paint brushes, markers, contact paper, construction paper or other things to use in decorating your stage
- Ruler, yard stick, or tape measure
- Scissors, craft knife or box cutter
- Pencils
- If using foam core board: strapping tape or two 4" wide cloth strips plus glue to join the sides of the foam core board to the central panel
- 1½ yards of 45" material in black or a dark color
- Needle and thread or sewing machine and thread
- Dowel or cord the width of the center panel plus 6" to hang the back curtain

ASSEMBLY

1. If you are using a cardboard box, cut away the top, back, and bottom, leaving only the widest side and the two shorter sides of the box. (If you are using two foam-core-board panels, cut one panel in half and join these two half panels to the long side of the remaining panel with strapping tape or 4" wide cloth strips dipped in glue.)

2. On the widest panel of the cardboard box or the center panel of the three-part screen, measure and draw a square or rectangle 2" from the top and side edges of the center panel and 18" tall.

3. Cut away the center of the middle panel, using the cut lines you have just measured.

4. Decorate your stage in any way you like with the materials you have.

5. To make the back curtain, first cut slots or holes in the top and bottom of the sides of the stage 2"–3" from the back of the stage sides. These slots will hold the back curtain dowel rod. Make sure that the ends of the dowel stick out beyond the edges of the stage side panels.

6. Sew a rod pocket in the curtain.

7. Thread the curtain on the dowel rod and hang the curtain.

8. Bring out your puppets and put on a play!

Lade, Roger. *The Most Excellent Book of How to Be a Puppeteer.* Brookfield, CT: Copper Beech Books, 1996.
Watson, Nancy Cameron. *The Little Pigs' Puppet Book.* Boston: Little, Brown, 1990.

Tajikistani Puppetry *see* Islamic Puppetry

Teeth

Teeth are one of those things that add to the character of a puppet. Theoretically, most beings have teeth, but not all of them show their teeth. A sweet girl or boy would not, nor would a fairy tale princess. A monster would show its teeth, and so would a dragon. Some animals would. An angry person might very well show his or her teeth.

There are also some puppets designed to show children how to brush their teeth. These look like a set of false teeth and force the puppet to be a really wide-mouthed one. The opportunity to show children and interested adults how to effectively brush and floss their teeth is worth the distortion of the face.

Teeth can be made from the tines of a plastic fork. Considering the varied colors plastic utensils come in these days, you could have puppets with yellow, purple, or blue teeth. Because of the tendency to get tangled if placed on both jaws, attach the teeth to either the upper jaw (the usual place) or the lower jaw (an unusual place).

Plastic cups can also be cut down to form sharp, jagged teeth. The rim offers a bit more support and sometimes a contrast in color. You may be able to use just one cup, cutting it in half; or you may have to overlap more than one cup's worth of teeth depending on the size of your puppet's mouth.

Teeth can also be made individually from Styrofoam meat trays, felt, ricrac, craft foam, or Naugahyde. Hot glue the individual teeth into place in the mouth, or tape the teeth together and glue the whole denture into the mouth.

Make sure that the teeth are not damaged by the mouth action when you operate the mouth. If you want to close the mouth completely and with less damage to the teeth, try using soft sponge or craft foam for the teeth.

Other items can be used to make individual teeth: beans, beads, Styrofoam packing pieces, and pom-poms. If your puppet is very big, the bowl ends of plastic spoons, ice cream wooden spoons, Styrofoam packing peanuts, or egg crate carton cups might be just the thing.

Remember that the teeth of your character should support its personality. Teeth are not a necessity for a puppet, though the lack of teeth itself gives your puppet a "toothless" character. If this is the character you want, great! If not, try out some teeth to expand the personality of your character and give it some bite!

Henson, Cheryl, and the Muppet Workshop. *The Muppets Make Puppets!* New York: Workman Publishing, 1994.

Lade, Roger. *The Most Excellent Book of How to Be a Puppeteer.* Brookfield, CT: Copper Beech Books, 1996.

Renfro, Nancy. *Puppets for Play Production.* New York: Funk & Wagnalls, 1969.

Theaters *see* **Stages**

Therapy through Puppetry

Puppets are extensions of the self. For the puppeteer, this is a great feature as it provides an avenue for creative self-expression as well as a platform for wider issues if they are important. It is this very characteristic which can allow the puppet to assist in the therapeutic process as dolls and toys can. By allowing the puppets to express inner conflict, the therapeutic process is advanced. This article in no way seeks to cover the wide ground of the use of puppets in therapy, but for children who are not attracted to dolls or stuffed animals, puppets may offer a viable alternative.

In everyday use, however, the puppet can assist children in social and emotional growth through expression of emotions and self-concept; resolution of conflicts, especially in a group situation; and working through any number of normal, childhood events. Going to the doctor or dentist, going to the hospital, having a new baby in the home, and dealing with the bigger problems of grief can all be dealt with through puppets.

In a group situation, talking through the puppets can work out a theme problem: going to a first sleep over, moving, or staying with a baby sitter. The whole class can work on one of these problems, either by acting out a story they have had read to them or by creating a story on their own. The children will have to explore their own fears and concerns, working through them in a positive way to create such a story.

Individually, children can learn the names of various feeling states and how to express those states concretely. Using an emotions chart of facial expressions drawn on felt circles and a flat puppet figure, children can dress the figure and give it a feeling state as well. They can even talk or write or draw about the feeling they have given their puppet to explore the feeling some more. For children who cannot write yet, they can talk to the teacher or speak into a tape recorder, handing their tape to the teacher to be transcribed later.

Another possibility for therapeutic use, especially in a classroom setting where tensions may build up over the day, is to have one or two large puppets in class which the children can curl up with and talk to about whatever they want. At this point, the puppet becomes more of a doll or stuffed animal rather than a puppet. The teacher may even want to initiate ideas of conflict resolution by working with these life-sized puppets in the classroom. Children need to learn to identify emotions, especially feelings of anger, and be taught how to work with those feelings to resolve the tensions and resentments they produce.

Puppets have a great value as therapeutic tools, especially in group situations where concerns and feelings can be brought up in a more diffused situation. No one is pointed out or put on the spot, but everyone can contribute to working on the resolution of the problem, whatever it happens to be. Let puppets help with learning about feelings and emotions, self-concept, and conflict resolution. Your children will enjoy the puppets and learn something about themselves at the same time. (*See also* Stories and Scripts: Tragedy.)

Hunt, Tamara, and Nancy Renfro. *Puppetry in Early Childhood Education*. Austin, TX: Nancy Renfro Studios, 1982.

Peyton, Jeffrey L., *Puppetools: Introductory Guide and Your Specialized Applications Manual*. Richmond, VA: Prescott, Durrell, 1986.

Tissue-Mâché

Tissue-mâché is like papier-mâché but made with tissue paper. Tissue paper's pliability makes it easy to work with and its light weight makes it perfect for large projects where weight could become an issue. An armature is used as a base on which to form the sheets of tissue into the desired shape.

An added advantage of tissue-mâché is the ease with which an older child might use it instead of the clay-form process to make a simple puppet head. In this way, it could become part of your puppet club activities to introduce older children to a more complex creative technique within a limited amount of time and ability.

Making a Tissue-Mâché Puppet Head

MATERIALS

- Cardboard tube or a Styrofoam egg or ball shape (this will be the base form)
- Newspaper to make at least one layer of harder papier-mâché
- Colored tissue paper to make the skin of the puppet head and its molded features
- White glue and water to thin it
- Fabric to make the body of the puppet
- Wig material
- Paints and paint brushes
- Felt, craft foam, or cardboard to make hands
- Hot glue gun and glue sticks

Fred and Ted have tissue-mâché heads on cardboard-tube bases. The tissue paper molds easily and wrinkles interestingly.

ASSEMBLY

1. Cut the cardboard tube ½" longer than your longest finger, or cut a finger hole in the Styrofoam ball or egg.

2. Tear the newspaper into rough 1" squares.

3. Thin a tablespoon of white glue with one teaspoon of water. Stir to mix thoroughly.

4. Dip the base paper into the glue mixture or apply the glue mixture to the paper with a brush.

5. Paste the base paper to the base form. Make at least two layers.

6. Since the cardboard tube will be wet by now, it must dry out. If you used a Styrofoam base, it can still be worked. It can also be allowed to dry overnight.

7. Tear the tissue paper into 1" and 2" × 2½" pieces. Use enough layers of the larger pieces dipped in the white glue mixture to create the skin color you desire and

to cover the base layers (made in step 4). Use the 1" pieces to create a smoother top layer.

8. Using the larger pieces of tissue paper, dip them in glue and form a nose, eyebrows, ears, and so on. Do not press the tissue to wring out the glue but gather it together lightly. Attach to the head by pressing lightly.

9. Using the smaller pieces of tissue paper, form a smooth layer over the attached pieces to ensure that they adhere to the head. Allow the head time to dry thoroughly.

10. Paint any features.

11. Attach the wig.

12. Make the body of puppet.

13. Hot glue the body to the head.

14. Gather your puppets and put on a play.

Flower, Cedric, and Alan Fortney. *Puppets, Methods and Materials.* Worcester, MA: Davis Publ., 1983.

Toy Theaters

The toy theater is a miniature, portable Victorian parlor or nursery entertainment in which a small box contains all the makings for an elaborate theater presentation including actors, script, and scenery. Everything in the toy theater can be kept in one box, although many plays could be presented in the same toy theater. The class of toy theater can include the diorama and the peep show in which a tableau is created but no movement happens. (*See* Dioramas; Peep Shows.)

The toy theater's origins may lie in the eighteenth century theater broadsides and souvenir sheets engraved with one or two characters from a play. These sheets could be colored in, the figures cut out, and a stick puppet made from the decorated figure. Sometimes scraps of material or other notions could be used to decorate the figures and make them more realistic.

As time passed, more-elaborate sheets were created that included several characters, some scenery, and eventually the script of the play. A theater was made and decorated with pictures representing the interior of a real theater. The scenery was colored and mounted on thin cardboard. The cut-out actors were placed in special wire holders so they could be moved about. The script was recreated for the toy theater, and the whole could be enacted by one person doing all the characters and voices. Engravers in the nineteenth century vied to be the first with a theater production on sale after the opening of a new play.

At first, theater scripts were written for adults and not for children, but the engravers were soon writing plays and pantomimes especially for children to perform. The toy theater was not only considered to be a pleasant pastime but educational as well.

The popularity of the toy theater lasted for over a hundred years and ceased in England only with World War II when many of the historic engraving plates were destroyed. Today, some of the old plates have been recovered, and the theaters, complete with actors, scenery, and scripts are once again available for purchase. Performers are touring again as they did once in the late nineteenth century. Perhaps you can find a toy theater in your local book store!

Almost anything can become a toy theater. As mentioned, dioramas and peep shows can be toy theaters. Pop-up puppets are made with a decorated cup or container with a stick or rod puppet that pops up to act out a scene. (*See* Pop-up Puppets; Stick Puppets.) Paper bag theaters are decorated small brown paper bags with a puppet inserted or created especially for the theme. (*See* Paper Bag Theaters.) Holidays are very popular for the paper bag theater and pop-up puppet. Another toy theater is the greeting card theater or finger puppet theater. (*See* Greeting Card Theaters; Finger Puppet Theaters.) A contemporary toy theater can be made from a small box. Traditionally the puppets are stick figures which are inserted through the side of the theater. The scenery is mounted on rods that hang from the top of the box. I have also heard of toy theaters that hang around the puppeteers' neck with the stick puppet actors inserted through the bottom of the theater. In theory, you can also make a toy theater from a large carton with the scenery and actors approaching the size of puppets and marionettes; at this point, however, it loses its "toy" or miniature feeling and begins to become a kind of enlarged stick or rod puppet theater.

Making a Basic Toy Theater

MATERIALS

- A small box, such as the ones kitchen-counter appliances come in
- Poster board for constructing scenery
- Skewers or thin dowels for hanging the scenery and using as rods for the puppets
- Ruler
- Pencil
- Eraser
- Craft knife
- Scissors
- Tape or glue

- Paints
- Markers
- *Optional*: small, lightweight clip-on lamp or flashlight

ASSEMBLY

1. Remove the top of the box. Mark the right and left sides in thirds and make notches there at each third.

2. On the same right and left sides make a notch at the back of the theater, right up against the back wall, and at the very front of the theater against the front wall. You will have a total of four notches on each side. These notches will be used to hold the skewers or dowels from which the scenery is hung. Using notches at various places creates a feeling of depth with the scenery placement.

3. On the front of the box, cut out a proscenium arch through which the audience will view your play. Give yourself as much room as you can, but try to include cardboard representing curtains, a valance, etc.

4. Decorate around the proscenium arch with markers or paints to make your theater look more professional and to create a theater atmosphere.

5. If you want to operate your puppets from the side in the traditional manner, you must cut out an opening in part of the right and left sides of the theater so the puppets can be inserted from the sides and moved around.

6. Decide on your play and create scenery for it on posterboard. Draw, color, and cut it out.

7. Cut the dowels to extend slightly beyond the box width.

8. Tape or glue the scenery to the skewers or dowels.

9. Hang the scenery using the notches in the sides of the box for appropriate depth.

10. Draw, color, and cut out your rod puppets. (*See* Rod Puppets.)

11. Note: If you want to operate the puppets from above, mount the rods on the backs of the puppets and have the rods coming out of the top of the puppet. If you want to operate your puppets from the side, add a base to your puppet figures and use that to attach the puppets to the rods.

12. Clip your light source onto the back of the theater. Turning on the light will signal to the audience that the play is about to begin.

13. Check that the light is not too overwhelming but illuminates the entire scene. (*See* Lighting.) If you cannot find a light which is suitable and the room light or natural light is sufficient, dispense with the artificial light source.

14. Stand in back of the theater and insert the puppets with both hands. Move

the puppets with short, sharp little movements to create focus for the puppet which is talking. (*See* Focus.)

Transformational Puppets

Transformation is the art of changing one thing into another, seemingly by magic. In puppetry, transformation can turn a puppet from one thing into another. At the end of the nineteenth century, it was the stock in trade of most puppeteers. Puppets which came out looking like one thing would seemingly fall apart and reassemble themselves into something or someone else. Today, puppeteers needn't be so dramatic. Occasionally, however, transformational puppets are useful tools, and the puppeteer should give them some consideration.

You have most likely seen a sleep–awake doll. On a single torso are two dolls: one whose eyes are open and one whose eyes are shut. They may be dressed alike or in reversible daytime–nighttime outfits, with a long skirt. To transform the doll from asleep to awake or vice versa, simply turn the skirt inside out so that you reverse the doll.

Multiple transforming figures can be achieved with a little planning. One commercially made puppet/doll has Little Red Riding Hood and Grandma done in the same way as the asleep–awake doll. To achieve the third character, the Wolf's head is sewn onto the back of Grandma's and is hiding behind Grandma's kerchief.

The four figures of *Goldilocks and the Three Bears* takes some ingenuity, there is a commercial example of this as well. Goldilocks reverses with Mrs. Bear; Mr. Bear is sewn on the back of Mrs. Bear's head and his legs hang down over Goldilocks'/Mrs. Bear's skirt. Baby Bear is a miniature, attached to a cord, and fits in Mrs. Bear's pocket.

In *Puppeteer* by Kathryn Lasky, a dwarf puppet changes into the evil magician in *Aladdin*. The head of the magician puppet is contained in the bundle carried on the dwarf's head. When the wrappings fall away from the head of the magician, they drape around the dwarf and conceal him from view. A puff of smoke and a pulled string is all it takes.

In Jim Gamble's video of *The Nutcracker*, his Sugar Plum Fairy transforms into a Christmas tree by pulling on the tree's mechanism. The tree is the skirt of the Sugar Plum Fairy turned inside out. The head of the Fairy puppet is now concealed within the cone of the tree. The skirt–tree is reinforced and stiff enough to stand on its own.

As you are planning out the story and designing your puppets, consider where the transformation could take place. It should fit naturally within the flow of the plot line. To make a transformation possible, you must visualize one shape within the other: for instance, the Christmas tree within the Fairy's skirt. The transforming shapes needn't suggest themselves. The shape of the tree and the shape of the skirt match well, but the dwarf and the magician is more of a stretch to the imagination. You simply need to see the possibility.

Once you have seen the possibility, make a mock-up of the transforming puppet and its machinery. How will you effect the transformation? Will you need to use some kind of transforming puff of smoke, or will the switch fit nicely in the flow of the story? And what will the mechanism of the transformation be? You will need to practice to make the transformation a smooth one.

Finally, have someone from the outside take a look at your presentation. If the transformation doesn't seem natural or doesn't support the story line, don't hesitate to throw it out. There will be a chance to try it again in another play, perhaps one you can write to center around the transformation much as the Nutcracker centers around the Christmas tree in the parlor which grows to fill the entire stage.

Transformation is a nice effect which the puppeteer can use if a way can be found to incorporate it smoothly and naturally into the play. It is a way to make a dramatic statement or to move the story along in a mysterious or wonderful manner. While transformation used to be part of the stock-in-trade of the marionette shows of the nineteenth century, contemporary puppeteers need more than flashy showmanship. Every element of the puppet production should fit within the flow of the story line, just as it would in the legitimate theater. So try transformation, but use it with care.

Baird, Bil. *The Art of the Puppet.* New York: Macmillan, 1965.
Bell, John. *Strings, Hands, Shadows: A Modern Puppet History.* Detroit: The Detroit Institute of Arts, 2000.
Lasky, Kathryn. *Puppeteer.* New York: Macmillan, 1985.

Turkish Puppetry *see* Karagoz

UNIMA and UNIMA–USA

UNIMA, the *UN*ion *I*nternationale de la *MA*rionnette, is the international organization of puppeteers (not just marionettes). It unites member puppeteers in a search for peace through the universal language of puppetry in accordance with the United Nations Declaration of Human Rights.

The fifth annual meeting of Czechoslovakian puppeteers met in Prague, Czechoslovakia, on May 20, 1929 and at that meeting proposed an international organization of puppeteers. Members from Europe and the Soviet Union attended and agreed to found such an organization. Sadly, World War II began, putting an end to meetings in Czechoslovakia and making meetings elsewhere in Europe exceedingly difficult.

During World War II, the members met in secret, keeping in touch with one another under the most trying of circumstances. Following the war and the division of Europe into East and West, meetings began again in the 1950s but under the political stresses of the Cold War. In spite of everything, the puppeteers of UNIMA strove to keep their ideals alive not only in Europe but everywhere in the world.

In the 1960s, there came a period of reaching out and creating national chapters which would carry on the work of UNIMA. UNIMA–USA was founded in the United States by Jim Henson, who became its first president. The mission statement of UNIMA–USA is as follows:

> The organization's mission is to promote international understanding and friendship through the art of puppetry. UNIMA–USA fulfills its mission in a range of formal and informal ways, but especially by encouraging and providing contacts to North American puppeteers traveling throughout the world and providing the same courtesy to international puppeteers traveling in North America.

Like its parent body, UNIMA–USA seeks to implement the humanistic ideals found in the original charter of UNIMA. In addition, it strives to uphold excellence in puppetry as well as to promote worldwide understanding and communication through puppetry.

Both UNIMA and UNIMA–USA hold conventions and festivals, award prizes for excellence, and promote puppeteers and puppetry wherever they can. They encourage contact and cooperation between puppeteers in all countries. Recently, UNIMA has been elevated to the status of a nongovernmental organization affiliated with UNESCO. If you are considering a career in puppetry or simply wish to support the work of puppeteers worldwide, you are urged to join UNIMA or UNIMA–USA.

http://www.unima.org/ UNIMA website.
http://www.unima-usa.org/ UNIMA–USA website.

University of Connecticut's Puppetry Arts Program

The puppetry program at the University of Connecticut's Department of Dramatic Arts is the premier degree-granting program in puppetry in the United States. Begun under the auspices of Dr. Frank W. Ballard, the university offers B.F.A., M.A., and M.F.A. degrees in puppetry. The program began offering classes in puppetry arts in 1964 and soon outgrew its facilities. Eventually, it became the education standard in the United States for learning and teaching about puppetry.

The puppetry department not only has its classes and theater, it also has a renowned museum, the Ballard Institute and Museum of Puppetry (BIMP) at the Depot Campus of the University of Connecticut. Through the permanent collection and visiting displays, the museum strives to teach the public about the history and the impact of puppetry.

Students who want to enroll in the program are urged to present a portfolio of their artistic, dramatic, and puppetry work to the chair of the department as well as a brief presentation in their field of strength. Not everyone entering the program at the graduate level need be a drama or sculpture major, although those are certainly welcome. The program includes students with undergraduate majors in many fields. The audition process strives to maintain a high level of quality within the program.

Not everyone will be able to go to the University of Connecticut to participate in their puppetry program, but you may be able to create a college program for yourself which will give you a foundation for your puppetry goals. The University of Connecticut undergraduate program can serve as a model for puppeteers wishing to enhance their education with a college degree or college courses. You can make the best of what you have at hand by looking at the course requirements from the University of Connecticut program and adapting them to your needs and your college or university. Check with your college's art or drama department, and let them know of your interests. See if there is a way to create an interdisciplinary degree or to acquire a combination of courses and electives which will match your goal.

Here is a general overview of the courses required by the University of Connecticut's puppetry arts program. For exact information on courses and schedules, write to the University for a catalog or see their online catalog. At the undergraduate level, you will need to take introductory courses in costuming, lighting, management, scenery, and fundamentals of theatrical design. More advanced courses include introduction to acting, directing, masterpieces in dramatic literature, scenery construction, lighting design, scene design and painting, costume history and design, voice and diction, and theater history. There are also several courses specifically in puppetry which are not likely to be at any other college or university but which you might be able to adapt with the assistance of your theater or art department. Courses in art could include drawing, design, color theory, and sculpture.

Even if you only have access to a junior college in your immediate neighborhood, you can take courses from the list given for the university's requirements as they are offered at your college. Even distance learning now offers courses in art, writing, and theater which might suit your needs. The point of all this is to educate yourself as widely as possible.

The University of Connecticut was the first university in the United States to offer undergraduate and graduate degrees in puppetry. Since then, it has gone on to educate several generations of puppeteers. Not everyone can pull up stakes and move to Connecticut, but that program can serve as the basis for a personal program of education in puppetry arts.

http://www.sfa.uconn.edu/Drama/Puppetry/HOMEPAGE.HTML University of Connecticut's Puppetry Arts web site.

Voices

It would be great if every puppeteer could provide a different voice for each puppet. That way, grandpa could have one voice, the queen another, and the baby a third. Unfortunately, the ability to make varied voices depends on the flexibility of the individual who possesses the original voice, and we are not all gifted with the ability to vary our voice range and quality.

Various television puppeteers, such as Burr Tillstrom and Bob Clampett, limited themselves to just a few voices and, therefore, to just a few puppets. They performed live so that whatever they did depended on the voices they could produce. They also had a more intimate relationship with their puppet characters and the one or two adult actors who worked with them.

You may be in the same situation, the sole puppeteer performing all the voices. In that case, you need to practice creating voices just as you practice assorted puppetry moves. Create the various voices of a family — mother, father, grandmother and grandfather, and the children — and read or tell a story using those voices. Then try modifying these voices so that mother becomes a queen, father becomes a pirate, and so on. If you have a base of voices to work from, you can expand into other types of characters. Your little girl or boy voice may become that of a bird, grandfather or grandmother voice become that of a turtle, and your dad voice could also be the voice of the Biggest Billy Goat Gruff.

If you have never tried accents before, obtain a recording actors use for practicing various accents and try it out. If you can do even one accent convincingly, you will have an added dimension for your characters. Dad's voice plus a Scottish accent might make a more convincing pirate than dad's voice alone. So try out these vocal flourishes and see if they don't add something to your repertoire.

When you are doing a large production, you may want to prerecord your presentation to have everything just right. This may take on added urgency if you have a number of characters of various ages and throw in a few accents as well. My voice can just make it through a twenty-minute presentation with five regular characters. Nerves make my voice tight and my throat dry. I don't always remember to breathe. I don't have time to take even a mouthful of water. So twenty minutes is the absolute outer limit for my voice. You may be more fortunate, perhaps not. However, do consider prerecording your dialogue for a long, theatrical stage presentation. You will have enough things to worry about without worrying about how long your voice will last.

Although movement is the most important element in presenting puppetry, puppetry is most like mime, and a puppetry skit should be presented in mime and make sense, nevertheless, audiences want to hear the puppets speak effectively as well as move effectively. By practicing voices and creating a stable of voices you can produce easily and automatically, you will add an important dimension to the characters of your puppets. An appropriate voice given to a puppet character can add as much depth as giving it a proper costume. Practice your voices along with your manipulation exercises, and you will see your puppetry flourish even more brightly than before. (*See also* Practice.)

Putting "accents" "actors" into a web browser produced a number of book titles and CDs for assisting actors with creating accents. Since I have not reviewed any of these titles, I cannot list them or recommend them. Try the search for yourself and see what you might like. If you don't want to invest in an untried book, try interlibrary loan from your local library.

http://www.sagecraft.com/puppetry/using/character.html "Creating a Puppet Character" by Bill Woodburn.

Wayang

Wayang is an Indonesian word which means "shadow" and is applied to almost all theatrical presentations in Indonesia and Bali. The puppet theater of Indonesia — Bali and Java — is ancient, over a thousand years old. It represents the battle between good and evil and often presents religious themes. Shadow or rod puppets are used by the puppeteer, along with singers and a percussion orchestra. These plays are the soul of the area and represent the highest moral aspirations of the people. There are three types of puppet presentations in Bali and Java, Indonesia: *wayang kulit*, shadow puppets made of leather, operated by rods, and portraying characters from the Hindu epics; *wayang golek*, wooden rod puppets which act out both the Hindu and Moslem epics; and *wayang klitik*, flat wooden puppets which act out the epics of the Javanese Majapahit Empire heroes. Besides these larger, general styles, there are several local theatrical forms and styles of figure which vary from country to country.

The Dalang

The *dalang* is the puppeteer, conductor, choreographer, and master of ceremonies for a puppet play. He must know a great many plays and lines of dialogue as well as the music appropriate to each play. As the medicine person, he is the medium between the people watching the play and the gods who participate in it.

A puppet play may be given to fulfill a vow, to celebrate a life passage, or to contribute to the well-being of the community. A puppet play is open to everyone. In a shadow play, the men sit with the dalang and watch the action of the puppets while the women sit on the opposite side and watch the shadows. Men may move back and forth to watch whichever side they want. The puppet represents the physical side of the character, while the shadow represents its soul.

Wayang Kulit

The puppet plays of Bali and Java date from at least the tenth century A.D. and are assumed to have migrated from India. However, the use of Javanese terms and characters in the plays indicate the existence of an oral and perhaps theatrical tradition indigenous to Java before the arrival of immigrants from India. These indigenous characters are clowns, servants, and subordinate figures. The plays also deal with the land and its fertility, balance and harmony in the culture, and local spirits of the land. Some scholars theorize that these characters are the old gods of Bali and Java, reduced in size and power as European brownies and elves became.

The master of ceremonies, the dalang, is not only the puppeteer but the leader of the gamelan orchestra, the coordinator of the singers, the voices of many of the characters, and the shaman who intercedes between gods and men. He is a semi-sacred figure, and the puppets he uses are also considered sacred and filled with power. Some puppets are considered extremely powerful and are rarely used. They are kept wrapped separately from the other puppets but must be available for a set of puppets to be complete and effective. Once the dalang begins a performance, it may not stop until the completion of the cycle some seven to ten hours later. Ideally, the play begins around 9:00 P.M. and continues to daybreak.

The puppets come in sets. A village may have a hundred shadow puppets or sixty-five rod puppets on hand at all times to put on their plays, while palaces might have as many as five hundred shadow puppets. In addition, there needs to be a gamelan, a percussion orchestra of xylophones, marimbalike instruments, gongs, and drums which will take thirty to forty musicians to play. There are one to three singers, one female and the rest male, and the dalang.

The shadow puppets are made from deer, buffalo, or goat hide and may take as long as ten years to cure to prevent warping. There are patterns or templates used to make the puppet parts and used as guides for the piercings which enrich the puppet. The limbs are jointed with metal, bone, or bamboo hinges, and bamboo or horn sticks are split and used as the main stick to hold the puppet. Rods are attached to make the limbs movable.

Wayang Golek

The rod puppets of the wayang golek are made in large, extended-family workshops. The head of the family carves the faces of the puppets as this feature will embody the character and the essence of the puppet. The younger family members make the rest of the body. Often, a village will have only one puppet-making family. A palace might have a vast workshop of artisans making a wide variety of puppets.

The wayang golek plays are either the Hindu religious epics— the Mahabarata or the Ramayana — or the Javanese cycles of plays, which may be historical or Islamic. If the play is from the Hindu cycle, the puppets will be dressed in the style favored by the shadow puppets. If the puppets are enacting the Javanese cycles, they will be dressed in the local fashion with Javanese hair and clothing styles. Since these are rod puppets, they can be used in the day or at night and of course do not use a screen.

Wayang Klitik

Wayang klitik puppets are carved out of wood in low relief and painted as the leather puppets are. Limbs are made of leather and jointed like the wayang kulik puppets. Because they are heavy, the sets of wayang golek and wayang klitik puppets are kept to a minimum of sixty-five to seventy puppets to a set and puppets may have to play more than one character. The performances are given during daylight hours without a screen, but the role of the dalang is the same as for shadow puppet performances.

A large, pierced, fan-like object is also used in the play. Called a *genungan*, it is used in the introduction of the play and its characters and the opening and closing of each act. Its motion can indicate the mood of the act to follow. The leaf shape may indicate the heart or a tree, perhaps the tree of life symbol popular in Indian classical art.

The puppets are introduced with the good characters on the right, the bad ones on the left. The main support sticks of the puppets can be inserted into a banana leaf stalk so that the dalang can continue with other action of the play.

Baird, Bil. *The Art of the Puppet.* New York: Macmillan, 1965.
Bell, John. *Strings, Hands, Shadows: A Modern Puppet History.* Detroit: The Detroit Institute of Arts, 2000.
Doney, Meryl. *Puppets.* New York: Franklin Watts, 1995.

Whirling Disk Puppet Theaters

The whirling disk puppet theater, as described in Lyndie Wright's *Toy Theaters*, is a complete puppet show in a theater no bigger than a large greeting card. This is, of course, another form of toy theater, and it takes very few materials to make! (*See* Toy Theater.) You will want to make a mock-up first to ensure the proper placement of materials and openings.

MATERIALS

- 2 sheets of plain construction paper or card stock
- Paper fastener or brad
- Compass with pencil
- Paints and paint brushes or markers
- Pencils
- Kneaded eraser
- Ruler
- Craft knife
- Scissors

ASSEMBLY

1. Find the center of one sheet of paper. You can do this by lightly drawing two intersecting lines which are centered in each side of the paper and are perpendicular to one another. Mark the center with a dot. (This is where you will fasten the disk to the paper.)

2. Draw a smaller rectangle whose base starts ½" above the center point. The rectangle should be approximately 4" wide × 3" high and centered from right to left on the paper. This will be your theater's "stage."

3. Decorate your stage any way you like by drawing footlights, curtains, a frame and so on. If you draw curtains, make sure that they are in the upper third of the stage opening so they will not obscure the puppets.

4. Using your compass, lightly draw a circle with a 3½" radius on the second sheet of paper.

5. Without raising the compass point, draw a second circle with a ½" radius within the first circle.

6. Cut out the outer circle.

7. Draw the characters for your play within the space between the edge of the inner and outer circles, leaving the inner circle blank. You should have room for 6–8 tiny characters on your disk. If two characters need to be on stage at the same time, you must take that into account when planning your design.

8. Color in the theater and the characters on the disk.

9. Attach the disk to the theater with the brad at the center mark of the first sheet of paper and the center mark of the circles. Test the disk to make sure that it moves easily.

10. If you want, you can fold the sides of the theater back so it will stand but the

disk can still move easily. You needn't do this if you don't want; you can just hold the theater in your hand or on your lap.

11. As you tell the story, move the disk back and forth to bring the characters to the front.

Wright, Lyndie. *Toy Theaters.* New York: Franklin Watts, 1991.

Wigs *see* Hair and Wigs

Wooden Puppet Heads

Carved wooden puppets have been the standard for European puppets until modern times. This technique is certainly the best way to make a lasting puppet of the European style. Pinocchio, as you may remember, was carved out of wood by Gepetto. Today, puppets may be made from all sorts of materials, but you still may want to try carving your own puppet or puppet head out of wood.

If you have not carved before, you may want to practice carving on clay, Styrofoam blocks, or the like. Check with your craft or hobby store for carving materials and tools. While carving tools to be used with clay or Styrofoam will be made of wood or plastic, wood carving tools are made of steel. Remember that carving tools are cutting tools and should be kept sharp and used with care.

Juan, a fisherman puppet from Portugal, has a carved wooden head. Fur was used to make his hair, and his hands are felt mitts.

Check with your craft shop or hardware store for advice on the maintenance of blades and carving tools.

When you decide to make your wooden puppet head, begin with a light, soft, easy-to-carve block of wood such as pine or even balsa wood, although the latter is not of great quality. The dimensions should be between 5" and 6" long and 3½" to 4" square. Vary these dimensions depending on your needs. Draw the complete, individual views of the head on each side of your block of wood. You may want to draw these on paper first and transfer the drawings to the wood with graphite paper which should also be available at your hobby shop.

The front of the drawing will have all the details of the face, neck, and ears, a view of the head from straight on. The sides will have the outline of the head and neck, the face and its details, and the ears. The top of the block will have the outline of the head, nose, and ears. The bottom of the block the neck, chin, and the bottom of the ears and perhaps the bottom of the nose. The back of the block will have the outline of the back of the head, the neck, and the back of the ears. The bottom will also mark the place for either a finger hole for a hand puppet or a screw for a marionette. If the head is for a hand puppet, the neck will need a 1" hole drilled into it for your finger. Use a brace and bit to make the hole rather than an electric drill, which would be too powerful. (*See* Hand Puppets; Marionettes.)

Slowly begin cutting away the parts of the head from the back, cutting away from you with your tools and gently rounding off the scull and the neck as you go. Work toward the front, following your diagram. If you should make mistakes, remember that it takes a *long* time to learn to carve well.

When the head is complete, sand it to smooth out any rough spots using progressively finer sandpaper. Finish with gesso and paint with acrylic paints. Attach a wig if one is called for, and add the body and costume to your puppet. You will have a puppet you can be proud of, made in the tradition of the great European puppeteers.

Ackley, Edith Flack. *Marionettes: Easy to Make! Fun to Use!* New York: Lippincott, 1929.
Fling, Helen. *Marionettes: How to Make and Work Them.* New York: Dover, 1973.
Flower, Cedric, and Alan Fortney. *Puppets, Methods and Materials.* Worcester, MA: Davis Publ., 1983.

Wooden Spoon Puppets

Wooden spoons have been used to make dolls as long as there have been little girls and wooden spoons! It doesn't take much to move from the wooden spoon doll to the wooden spoon puppet — just imagination and an audience. The wooden spoon puppet is a simple rod puppet which can become more complex depending on what you would like your puppet to be and to do. (*See* Rod Puppets.)

At its simplest, the wooden spoon puppet needs some wire, rope, or heavy cord to become the armature for shoulders, arms, and hands. (*See* Armatures.) Attach some hair; paint or draw on some features, and dress up your wooden spoon puppet. Make more than one (packages of wooden spoons usually come in small, medium, and large — an entire family) and put on a play!

Spoon puppets can become much more complex, though. Make the arms move by adding rods. If the spoon is small enough, plastic forks can become both the hands *and* the rods by attaching the hands to the wire arms and using the handles of the forks as the rods. Finally, you can make a moveable mouth by attaching a ponytail holder manipulated with a string attached to the lower part of the "mouth." (*See* Ponytail Holder Moveable Mouth) See! Your plain old wooden spoon puppet is now talking, gesturing — you won't be able to stop!

So what are you waiting for? Get your puppets, get your audience (get some assistance if you have many rod puppets), and put on a play! Get going!

Henson, Cheryl, and the Muppet Workshop. *The Muppets Make Puppets!* New York: Workman Publishing, 1994.
Renfro, Nancy. *Puppets for Play Production.* New York: Funk & Wagnalls, 1969.

Wrist Puppets

Wrist puppets are simple puppets strapped gently to the wrist with elastic, ribbon, or a strap with Velcro fasteners. A wrist puppet allows children or adults with motor control disabilities to participate in puppetry. Wrist puppets are also ideal first puppets for very young children. In addition, they can permit informal puppetry encounters in a library, school, or other place where children and adults interact.

A wrist puppet can be any form which can be mounted on a strap and fastened around or tied to the wrist. It can be a flower, insect, or even a little doll which could lie across the wrist. Beanie Babies and other little stuffed animals made to lie flat make ideal wrist puppets. All you need to do is hand sew or hot glue the stuffed toy at its stomach area to a strap which fastens around the wrist with Velcro closures. (There are plenty of Beanie Baby imitators on the market at lower prices.) You might even be able to find patterns for that style of animal toy.

If you work with special children or have such a child who comes to your story times, consider making wrist puppets, wrist shakers or bell bracelets for them to use in your programs. Make sure that everything is attached firmly to the strap so it can't be pulled off. Nancy Renfro has a number of patterns in her books which can be turned into wrist puppets. *Puppetry in Early Childhood Education* has an entry under "Bracelet Puppets" on page 151. Check further in her book for patterns which can be used flat on the wrist. All children can be included in puppetry experiences, and the wrist puppet makes that a possibility for many children.

Informal puppetry encounters are wonderful moments in libraries, doctor's offices, health clinics, schools, religious schools, summer camps, and other places where children and adults interact. The wrist puppet can be used like the puppet assistant, or it can just hang around, waiting for someone to comment on the puppet sitting on your wrist. (*See* Assistants.) A wrist puppet is a good conversation starter, especially if the child seems frightened or shy. Children love to interact with puppets, and this is just another way in which puppets can be used to good effect.

Try a talking flower, Mr. Happy Tooth, any little animal, or a lady bug or butterfly. You might want to keep Mr. Tarantula in your pocket for that tough guy who hates "girly stuff" though. I saw a very personable tie-dyed spider at the Durham, NC, Museum of Life and Science which could be easily turned into a wrist puppet. Think about it! Snakes, snails, and puppy dogs tails (with the dog attached, please). That's what little boys might like.

If the puppet seems awkward tied onto the wrist like a wristwatch, try moving it around to the back of the wrist for puppet play or kid interaction. Just make sure that it's right-side-up when you move it around.

Hunt, Tamara, and Nancy Renfro. *Puppetry in Early Childhood Education.* Austin, TX: Nancy Renfro Studios, 1982.

Annotated Bibliography

Ackley, Edith Flack. *Marionettes: Easy to Make! Fun to Use!* New York: Lippincott, 1929.

An old favorite! I used it to make my first marionette. This is a good overview of creating, dressing, and using a marionette. The marionettes presented are of a traditional, more complex character than the ones being offered in more contemporary books. The stereotyping present in the creation of character is something to be aware of, however.

Allison, Drew, and Donald Devet. *The Foam Book: An Easy Guide to Building Polyfoam Puppets.* Charlotte, NC: Grey Seal Puppets, 1997. Second printing, 2000.

The art and technique of creating polyfoam puppets by the Grey Seal Puppets. Whether you are a beginner or an experienced puppet maker, you can benefit from this book. It is one of the standards in the field.

Baird, Bil. *The Art of the Puppet.* New York: Macmillan, 1965.

The history of puppets and puppetry by a master puppeteer. There are many old lithographs and photographs illustrating that history. A few traditional plays— Punch and Judy; Commedia dell' Arte — are included in the text. An essential reference.

Bauer, Caroline Feller. *Leading Kids to Books through Puppets.* Chicago: American Library Association, 1997.

Simple puppets and one-person puppet plays tie puppetry and children's literature together in effective presentations for library or school. The focus in on the plays; resources for making puppets are given in the bibliography.

Baumann, Hans. *Caspar and His Friends: A Collection of Puppet Plays.* New York: Henry Z. Walk, 1969.

These German plays involve Kasperl, the equivalent of the English Punch. There are two brief introductions about the history of Kasperl. The violence in the stories has been toned down a bit for use in schools. There are no directions other than the play and a few stage instructions.

Bell, John. *Strings, Hands, Shadows: A Modern Puppet History.* Detroit: The Detroit Institute of Arts, 2000.

This catalog of the Paul McPharlin Collection of Puppets and Theater Arts is a wide-ranging history of modern puppetry arts. Through photographs, sidebars, and the hundreds of puppets and props now owned by the Detroit Institute of Arts, John Bell tells the history of modern puppetry and all its sources and influences. A must-have for puppetry collections.

Boylan, Eleanor. *How to Be a Puppeteer.* New York: McCall, 1970.

This book strives to instruct young children in how to be puppeteers without being too heavy handed and didactic. Instruction is also given in making puppets and puppet theaters, and scripts are provided for several one-person puppet plays. Over all, a very good introduction.

Bradley, Virginia. *Is There an Actor in the House? Dramatic Material from Pantomime to Play.* New York: Dodd, Mead, 1975.

Puppeteers need to know how to act, and this is a good collection of skits and short plays. Some can be adapted for puppets.

Brandon, James R., with Pandam Guritno, eds. *On Thrones of Gold: Three Javanese Shadow Plays.* Honolulu, HI: University of Hawaii Press, 1970/1993.

This may be the only book of its kind to present three major Javanese shadow plays—*The Reincarnation of Rama, Irawan's Wedding,* and *The Death of Karna*—in English. There are wonderful notes about the history and performance of the plays, with photographs taken from a live performance.

Brown, Jerome C. *Puppets & Mobiles.* Belmont, CA: David S. Lake, 1983.

Instructions are given for a variety of junk puppets for elementary grades. Instructions for simple puppet theaters are also given. The mobiles don't seem to fit within the theme of the book.

Buchwald, Claire. *The Puppet Book: How to Make and Operate Puppets and Stage a Puppet Play.* Boston: Plays, 1990.

Good information is hindered by a lack of illustrations. There are a number of good hints, but the long blocks of text and inadequate patterns and illustrations make the puppetry half of the book disappointing. The six plays are pretty good. Several can be performed by a single puppeteer. The production notes at the end of each play are also quite good.

Buetter, Barbara MacDonald. *Simple Puppets from Everyday Materials.* New York: Sterling, 1996.

The text gives a great many ideas for making "junk" puppets. Fans of that genre of puppet may find lots of ideas here.

Carlson, Bernice Wells. *Play a Part.* New York: Abingdon Press, 1970.

This book includes a group of skits, short plays, and a few puppet plays for use in elementary school dramatics. Adaptations could be made for reader's theater as well.

Cheasebro, Margaret. *Puppet Scripts by the Month.* Nashville, TN: Broadman Press, 1985.

Puppet plays for Christian education. Each month of the year has two scripts with a theme and a Biblical reference.

Coudron, Jill M. *Alphabet Puppets: Songs, Stories, and Cooking Activities for Letter Recognition and Sounds.* Belmont, CA: Fearon Teacher Aids, 1983.

This is a wonderful book for classroom use or for extended use in a library. Patterns traced upon a grid for enlarging are included along with rough drawings for the puppets. Imagination will have to be used in getting from the drawing to the finished puppet. An alphabet treasure box or set could be created from these puppets. A great deal of effort would be involved in creating all the puppets; so consider the effort versus the payoff.

Creative Teaching with Puppets: Resources for Seven Integrated Units. Tuscaloosa, AL: The Learning Line, 1981.

Although this book is supposed to be a classroom resource, there is much that can be used by librarians. The patterns are easy to follow for those with sewing experience and are meant to create puppets to be used by adults.

Currell, David. *The Complete Book of Puppetry.* Boston: Plays, 1975.

This text lives up to its title. It includes history, the use of various kinds of puppets including "junk puppets," building stages and using stage materials, and finally the philosophy of puppet performance from two leading English puppeteers of the day. Filled with valuable information of all sorts, this book should be available to every puppeteer.

_____. *An Introduction to Puppets & Puppet-Making.* Edison, NJ: Chartwell Books, 1992.

A wonderful introduction to making basic types of puppets— shadow puppets, hand puppets, rod puppets, and marionettes— including the use of modern materials such as wood compounds instead of carving wood. Simple stages and tips on production and performance are included. An excellent addition to a puppeteer's library.

_____. *Puppets and Puppet Theatre*. Wiltshire, England: Crowood Press, 1999.
An updated and somewhat abbreviated version of his earlier classic work, *The Complete Book of Puppetry*. The focus here is on construction and manipulation of puppets as well as production (scenery, music, lighting, and so on) with more up-to-date equipment. The information is still the same solid background as before. Recommended.

Doney, Meryl. *Puppets*. New York: Franklin Watts, 1995.
This work provides patterns and instructions for making puppets from eleven countries which have a long history of puppetry. A few hints about making stages. No plays. The photographs are great.

The Educational Puppetry Association, A. R. Philpott, ed. *Eight Plays for Hand Puppets*. Boston: Plays, 1968.
A group of puppet plays for use by schools. At least one can be produced by a single person. Stage direction is somewhat sketchy, and there is no information about lighting or scenery design.

Engler, Larry, and Carol Fijan. *Making Puppets Come Alive: A Method of Learning and Teaching Hand Puppetry*. New York: Taplinger, 1973.
A text on hand puppet manipulation and an excellent introduction to the essence of puppetry. Each chapter is filled with exercises and improvisations. There are special chapters on mouth puppets, puppet voices, and movement when speaking. Essential for hand puppeteers.

Feller, Ron, and Marsha Feller. *Paper Masks and Puppets for Stories, Songs, and Plays*. Seattle, WA: The Arts Factory, 1985.

Instructions on how to make colorful sculpted masks and use them in dramatic presentations.

Fijan, Carol, and Frank Ballard with Christine Starobin. *Directing Puppet Theatre Step by Step*. San Jose, CA: Resource Publications, 1989.
A textbook on directing puppet plays for large and small groups. Excellent if you've never directed before. Good for one-person productions as well.

Finch, Christopher. *Jim Henson: The Works: The Art, the Magic, the Imagination*. New York: Random House, 1993.
This volume came out after Mr. Henson's death and served both as biography and eulogy. Some material will be of service to the puppeteer. The best elements are Mr. Henson's philosophy, both personal and professional. The idea puppeteers can carry away with them is: have a vision of what puppetry should be for you and strive to manifest that vision. Listen to everyone, and learn from everyone whenever you can.

Fling, Helen. *Marionettes: How to Make and Work Them*. New York: Dover, 1973.
This is an old work, revised and republished by Dover Publications. The information in this volume presents a European-styled, realistic marionette rather than the simplified marionettes presented currently for use by children. There is an assumption of adult supervision rather than work accomplished completely by youngsters. *Cautionary note*: Examples of faces reinforce racial stereotypes.

Flower, Cedric, and Alan Fortney. *Puppets, Methods and Materials*. Worcester, MA: Davis Publ., 1983.
An encyclopedic overview of puppet construction. All types of puppets are covered as well as all types of controls for more advanced puppets. Advice is given about manipulating all types of puppets. For those who think a sock puppet must always look like Lambchop, take a look at pages 88–89.

Frazier, Nancy, Nancy Renfro, and Lori Sears. *Imagination: At Play with Puppets and Creative Drama.* Austin, TX: Nancy Renfro Studios, 1987.

Another excellent text on making puppets come alive, with an appendix on puppet construction condensed from other books from Nancy Renfro Studios. The exercises given in this book can be completed individually or in a group and will teach the puppeteer the essence of creating a puppet character.

Gates, Frieda. *Easy to Make Puppets.* NJ: Prentice-Hall, 1976.

An extremely basic introduction to different kinds of puppets. For someone with a lot of imagination, this would make a fine outline.

Geertz, Armin W., and Michael Lomatuway'ma. *Children of Cottonwood: Piety and Ceremonialism in Hopi Indian Puppetry.* Lincoln: University of Nebraska Press, 1987.

Some of the tribes native to what are now called the Americas used puppetry in religious ceremonies. This scholarly work focuses on the Hopi and how they "respected things artificially made."

Henson, Cheryl, and the Muppet Workshop. *The Muppets Make Puppets!* New York: Workman Publishing, 1994.

A great manual for making junk puppets! Covers everything from devising the character through building the puppets to creating a puppet play. If you like whimsical puppets and well constructed, artfully conceived junk puppets, you'll really enjoy this book.

Hunt, Tamara, and Nancy Renfro. *Celebrate! Holidays, Puppets and Creative Drama.* Austin, TX: Nancy Renfro Studios, 1987.

A useful book full of month-by-month celebrations for library or classroom. The focus is on imaginative play, with many of the puppets useful for individual as well as group drama. Every library and elementary classroom should have access to this book.

_____. *Pocketful of Puppets: Mother Goose.* Austin, TX: Nancy Renfro Studios, 1982.

An idea book for classrooms and toddler times. The small scale of the puppets make them suitable for small groups of children. They are also wonderful as craft ideas for individual dramatic play.

_____. *Puppetry in Early Childhood Education.* Austin, TX: Nancy Renfro Studios, 1982.

Highly recommended as a text for those working in the classroom. There are also excellent ideas for the children's librarian in the "Puppetelling" chapter. A fount of wonderful ideas.

Jagendorf, Moritz Adolph. *Puppets for Beginners.* Boston: Plays, 1966.

Although the pictures are dated and stereotypical in some instances, beginners can get basic information from this book. The most interesting information comes from the realization that anyone wanting to make a puppet can simplify the mechanisms enough to make them manageable by the one-person puppeteer.

Jenkins, Peggy Davison. *The Magic of Puppetry: A Guide for Those Working with Young Children.* Englewood Cliffs, NJ: Prentice-Hall, 1980.

This includes ways to use puppets in the classroom or in other settings where children will be together for some time. Exercises are given to develop the skills of puppeteers. Suggestions are made for puppet corners, boxes, and so on. Excellent for classroom and library.

Kohl, Mary Ann F. *Making Make-Believe: Fun Props, Costumes and Creative Play Ideas.* Beltsville, MD: Gryphon House, 1999.

This book encourages imaginative play! Chapter 3 has puppets and theaters. The whole book is wonderful for encouraging the kind of imaginative work that can make the best puppet plays. Recommended!

Krisvoy, Juel. *The Good Apple Puppet Book: Over 100 Projects — Puppets to Make, Stages, Plays, Songs, Poems, Games.* Carthage, IL: Good Apple, 1981.

This book is filled with lots of interesting ideas for the beginning puppeteer.

These ideas could also be used with classroom or library puppet projects. The biggest drawback to this book is its lack of good patterns or illustrations. The patterns are only suggestions, and the illustrations are not realistic.

Lade, Roger. *The Most Excellent Book of How to Be a Puppeteer*. Brookfield, CT: Copper Beech Books, 1996.
A great book for the beginning performer. It is like having a textbook in outline. This may be one of its limitations, of course. Written for a young audience, it may give too little information to the serious adult. On the other hand, if you are just beginning in full-scale puppetry, this could be just the sort of outline book you could use.

Lasky, Kathryn. *Puppeteer*. New York: Macmillan, 1985.
Lasky highlights the work of Paul Vincent Davis, the puppeteer for Boston's Puppet Show Place. Mr. Davis's performance life is discussed in detail through the development of "Aladdin and the Wonderful Lamp" from first concept to final performance. Mr. Davis is a one-man theater, hiring outside help for direction, costume design, and music. An excellent view of how a professional develops an idea from conception to performance.

Long, Teddy Cameron. *Make Your Own Performing Puppets*. New York: Sterling/Tamos, 1995.
This is the most original puppetry book I have seen written with children in mind. Rather than presenting the puppets (here is a sock puppet, here is a mouth puppet, here is a rod puppet) and then offering plays or suggestions for making a script, *Make Your Own Performing Puppets* offers the puppets in context.
A rainforest theme has a stage in a doorway and puppets dressed up as characters from the rainforest made from the performers' own hands. "Santa's House" has paper bag puppets and a table top theater. "Outer Space" has marionettes and a changing backdrop. Children (and adult beginners, too) need some guidance, and

this book gives a framework in which to try out various kinds of puppets and theater situations. Highly recommended.

Luckin, Joyce. *Easy-to-Make Puppets*. Boston: Plays, 1975.
This book has patterns for several basic puppet types, including a basic marionette of papier-mâché. There are also puppet patterns for shape puppets.

Lynch-Watson, Janet. *The Shadow Puppet Book*. New York: Oak Tree Books, 1980.
A complete text on creating and performing with shadow puppets. Included are creating the screen, using lighting, and adapting stories on your own. Examples of contemporary shadow puppeteers and their backgrounds are given. The history of shadow puppetry is also included. Highly recommended.

MacLennan, Jennifer. *Simple Puppets You Can Make*. New York: Sterling, 1988.
This has basic patterns for finger puppets, five-finger puppets (animals whose legs as well as arms move), and three-finger puppets (traditional glove puppet). Good patterns.

Mahlmann, Lewis. *Puppet Plays for Young Players: 12 Royalty-Free Plays for Hand Puppets*. Boston: Plays, 1974.
The first in Mahlmann's series. Good for a serious puppetry program for older children.

_____, and David Cadwalader Jones. *Puppet Plays from Favorite Stories: 18 Royalty-Free Plays for Hand Puppets*. Boston: Plays, 1977.
Similar to *Puppet Plays for Young Players*. These are good works for teachers and librarians who are establishing a puppetry program for older children and who expect to put on more professional work.

_____ and _____. *Plays for Young Puppeteers: 25 Puppet Plays for Easy Performance*. Boston: Plays, 1993.
Each play calls for several puppet actors, so there is a need for a large cast and many puppets. Scripts are simplified and plays last about twenty minutes, a good length

for presentation. Attention should be paid to the stage directions and what your puppets can do.

Marks, Burton, and Rita Marks. *Puppet Plays and Puppet-Making: The Plays, the Puppets, the Production.* Rev. ed. Boston: Plays, 1985.

This is an interesting beginner book. It starts with the plays, then gives instructions for making the puppets shown in photographs illustrating the plays. Finally, there is information about making stages and props. This book does all that it promises and can be a quick introduction to simple play production. Unfortunately, it doesn't give enough information to take you further.

Mauriello, Barbara. *Making Memory Boxes.* Gloucester, MA: Rockport Publishers, 2000.

Details and patterns for making all sorts of boxes. While this is not a puppetry book, you may discover techniques you can use to create interesting, small-scale theaters.

Merten, George. *The Hand Puppets.* New York: Thomas Nelson, 1957.

While this book touches on many puppet types, the focus in on the conventional hand puppet with a papier-mâché head. The materials used are old-fashioned and some, like asbestos powder, are dangerous. Other than that, the instructions are wonderful, especially those for the glove and shadow puppets. A great many puppets are covered in some depth including glove, rod, marionette, and shadow puppets. Sections on history, shadows and silhouettes, and toy theaters are also given.

Milligan, David Fredrick. *Fist Puppetry.* New York: A. S. Barnes, 1938.

An early entry in the field of nonsports recreation, this is a first book for schools, libraries, hospitals, and other places wanting to put on puppet plays. There is a little bit on everything with not much depth but a great deal of breadth. Check the "topper" stage for wheelchairs and hospital beds. Ten plays are given in outline form.

Mills, Winifred H., and Louise M. Dunn. *Marionettes, Masks and Shadows.* Garden City, New York: Doubleday, 1928.

This is another classic of puppetry with a history of puppets and masks as well as information on how to use them in education and work with groups of older youths. It attempts to cover everything, creating more of a text than a children's book. There is not as much stereotyping here as in other works of the era. There seems to be some realization of how puppets and masks are used in other societies. What is exciting is to realize what professional productions can be realized by young teens.

Minkel, Walter. *How to Do "The Three Bears" with Two Hands: Performing with Puppets.* Chicago: American Library Association, 2000.

A text for the lone puppeteer covering puppetry technique; script writing and adaptation; stage, scenery, and props; and performing the one-person program. Construction of puppets is not included, but the manipulation of the most common types is included.

Owen, Cheryl. *Making Decorative Boxes for Gifts, Storage and Display.* Newton Abbot, Devon, England: David & Charles, 2002.

Methods for making and covering boxes of all kinds may help you create small puppet theaters for finger puppets and stick puppets.

Packham, Jo. *Glue Crafts.* New York: Sterling Publishers, 1995.

This is an excellent, nontechnical introduction to various types of glues through various projects with materials appropriate to the glue. If you ever wanted to discover how and in what sort of situation a particular glue could be used, this should give you the answer.

Painter, William M. *Musical Story Hours: Using Music with Storytelling and Puppetry.* Hamden, CT: Library Professional Publication, 1989.

A core text for the subject of musical story hours. The focus is on music in this work and how to integrate music into story times and puppet plays. Different types of programs are covered, showing how to choose appropriate music for different topics.

_____. *Story Hours with Puppets and Other Props*. Hamden, CT: Library Professional Publications, 1990.

Painter gives detailed instructions for twenty-one themed story times using visual aids. He also discusses making and acquiring puppets cheaply and using puppets and props in story telling workshops.

Pels, Gertrude. *Easy Puppets: Making and Using Hand Puppets*. New York: Crowell, 1951.

This is an interesting book when viewed in the light of the developing recreation movement (see Milligan, *Fist Puppetry*) of the 1950s. It begins by using various vegetables for puppet heads and moves on from there. This is a book to be used with adult assistance although it does not say so.

Peyton, Jeffrey L. *Puppetools: Introductory Guide and Your Specialized Applications Manual*. Richmond, VA: Prescott, Durrell, 1986.

This work focuses on the use of quickly made puppets for group situations at school, during therapy, or at home. Focus is on puppetry as a transpersonal or whole person activity.

Pflomm, Phyllis Noe. *Puppet Plays Plus: Hand Puppet Plays for Two Puppeteers*. Metuchen, NJ: Scarecrow Press, 1994.

These are plays for librarians offering puppet time at the library. The plays are for two people and should be pretaped. Many of the plays could be performed by one person in a carefully orchestrated production.

Poskanzer, Susan Cornell. *Puppeteer. What's It Like to Be a ... Series*. Mahwah, NJ: Troll Associates, 1989.

A book for very young children which talks about the basics of putting on a puppet play. There is not too much information for more than a five- or six-year-old.

Rasmussen, Carrie. *Fun-Time Puppets*. Chicago: Children's Press, 1952.

An introduction to puppetry meant for children and supervising adults. The activities are more complex than the brief instructions would imply. There are some good ideas in here, including a paste formula and a formula for sawdust molding compound.

Renfro, Nancy. *Make Amazing Puppets*. Santa Barbara, CA: Learning Works, 1979.

This book should be in any junk puppeteer's library. The puppets are divided into types of materials: paper plates, cups, boxes, rod puppets, and so on. There are sections for stages, special effects, and so on.

_____. *A Puppet Corner in Every Library*. Austin, TX.: Nancy Renfro Studios, 1978.

Renfro covers the many ways in which puppets can be used in libraries: as mascots, as educators, and of course as part of story times. Scenery, props, and stages are covered. Patterns are given for making puppets. This is a book with a wealth of ideas for any librarian interested in using puppets.

_____. *Puppetry and the Art of Story Creation*. Austin, TX: Nancy Renfro Studios, 1979.

This work focuses almost equally on story creation and puppet making with useful additions for teachers of disabled/special-needs students. Focus is, as usual, on the "junk puppet" turned out in so many inventive, creative ways. For kids and beginners, this is an excellent overall introduction to the creation of puppets and scripts to fit them.

_____. *Puppets for Play Production*. New York: Funk & Wagnalls, 1969.

Renfro shows how to make innumerable "junk puppets" that are inventive and stylish. Problems for skits are presented that could be interesting to the budding amateur as well as to children. Putting on an actual play is presented in an outline form more useful to a person with some experience. Pictures are in black-and-white.

Romberg, Jenean. *Let's Discover Puppets: Arts and Crafts Discovery Units.* West Nyac, NY: Center for Applied Research in Education, 1976.

For use in libraries and schools, this book concentrates on "junk puppets" using ordinary materials. The discoveries break into units; materials and steps are provided. There are some great ideas on how to present a discovery unit as well.

Ross, Laura. *Hand Puppets: How to Make and Use Them.* New York: Lothrop, Lee, Shepard, 1969.

This is an excellent beginner book with extensive patterns for the puppets planned. There is a complete set of shadow puppet patterns for "Peter and the Wolf," paper bag patterns for "Rumplestiltzkin," and papier-mâché puppets and a script for "Punch & Judy."

_____. *Puppet Shows: Using Poems and Stories.* New York: Lothrop, Lee, 1970.

This collection of short plays focuses on well-known poems like nursery rhymes, "A Visit from St. Nicholas," and other familiar items to create simple and effective puppet presentations. Little emphasis is given to making puppets, although hints are given.

_____. *Scrap Puppets: How to Make and Move Them.* New York: Holt, Rinehart, & Winston, 1978.

Here is a baker's dozen of scrap puppets. Like so many of the puppet books of this era, these are definitely for older children or for children using adult assistance. The instructions include patterns for shadow puppets and instructions on marionette stringing.

Sierra, Judy. *Fantastic Theater: Puppets and Plays for Young Performers and Young Audiences.* Bronx, NY: H. W. Wilson, 1991.

This complete book on shadow puppet theater provides history, theater design, and most importantly, patterns for shadow puppets. An excellent book for anyone interested in getting started in shadow puppetry. Highly recommended.

_____. *Mother Goose's Playhouse: Toddler Tales and Nursery Rhymes, with Patterns for Puppets and Feltboards.* Ashland, OR: Bob Kaminski Media Arts, 1994.

Though most of the patterns used in this book are for flannel board figures, they can easily be converted to stick puppets. Try enlarging the puppets for better theater size. Excellent.

_____. *Multicultural Folktales: Stories to Tell Young Children.* Phoenix, AZ: Oryx Press, 1991.

This collection of folk tales is planned for the flannel board but can easily be transferred to shadow puppet theater. The book includes patterns for puppets. Excellent.

Sullivan, Debbie. *Pocketful of Puppets: Activities for the Special Child with Mental, Physical and Multiple Handicaps.* Austin, TX: Renfro Studios, 1982.

Sullivan and Renfro promote the idea that puppets are useful tools in all classrooms and that those who are developmentally challenged should not be excluded from the fun of puppets. Patterns and improvisational ideas are all included. This is another great book from Renfro Studios.

Switzer, Ellen. *The Magic of Mozart: Mozart, The Magic Flute, and the Salzburg Marionettes.* New York: Athenaeum, 1995.

The story of *The Magic Flute*, an opera composed by Mozart, is told through the wonderful Salzburg Marionettes. The book is broken into three parts, Mozart's life, the story told by *The Magic Flute*, and the Salzburg Marionettes—the history of the company, of puppets in the city of Salzburg, and the hopes for the future of the company. This is an affectionate look at one of the world's great puppet companies.

Tichenor, Tom. *Folk Plays for Puppets You Can Make.* New York: Abingdon, 1959.

Directions for five plays from fairy tales are given along with directions for making puppets, scenery, as well as production and action instructions.

Wallace, Mary. *I Can Make Puppets.* Toronto: Greey de Pencier Books, 1994.

Directions for making terrific puppets from everyday materials. Has simplest control for marionettes (String King) as well as instructions for making simple puppet stages.

Watson, Nancy Cameron. *The Little Pigs' Puppet Book.* Boston: Little, Brown, 1990.

An outline of puppetry basics filled with good advice. Instructions for making three easy puppets. Good, basic advice for writing the script and rehearsing and for making a stage and scenery. It is one of the few books kids could really use without adult supervision or more than occasional assistance.

Winer, Yvonne. *Pocketful of Puppets: Three Plump Fish and Other Short Stories.* Austin, TX: Nancy Renfro Studios, 1983.

These short plays are for use in the classroom or with a young acting troop. Stories could also be used at story time with participation from children in audience. Patterns are included for great puppet craft ideas. The more I use this book, the more uses I find for it.

Wisniewski, David, and Donna Wisniewski. *Worlds of Shadow: Teaching with Shadow Puppetry.* Englewood, CO: Teachers Idea Press, 1997.

This is the book teachers and librarians should use if they are interested in shadow puppetry *with* children or for use in the classroom or in workshops. The use of an overhead projector keeps children from accidental contact with any hot light bulbs and is an easy platform for them to use. Special effects are easy and nifty. "Sagging puppet syndrome" is eliminated. Another "must-have"!

Woods, Geraldine. *Jim Henson: From Puppets to Muppets.* Minneapolis, MN.: Dillon Press, 1987.

This brief biography covers the life and philosophy of Jim Henson, master puppeteer. Although on the abbreviated scale of most juvenile biographies, Woods manages to cover Henson's philosophy of puppetry and of life as well as the facts of his life to that point.

Wright, Denise Anton. *One-Person Puppet Plays.* Englewood, CO: Teacher Ideas Press, 1990.

Lots of scripts for the one-person puppeteer. The book includes patterns in the back for puppets and ideas for puppetry crafts.

Wright, Lyndie. *Masks.* New York: Franklin Watts, 1990.

If you want to know how to make various types of masks from the simplest to the most complex, Lyndie Wright's *Masks* is just what you need. These are basic yet stylish masks which can be used to enhance a performance or become puppets by themselves. The materials used are commonly found in the home or classroom and do not require extensive outlays of money or use of new techniques or tools.

_____. *Puppets.* New York: Franklin Watts, 1989.

Puppets is another, good, all-in-one book which gives a brief introduction to the basics of making puppets. Beginning with painting your open hands to make a face or figures and continuing on through a simple marionette, *Puppets* concentrates on creating interesting puppets and giving them good places in which to work. It has nothing on creating characters for the puppets or writing scripts, but this is a fine introduction to creating simple puppets.

_____. *Toy Theaters.* New York: Franklin Watts, 1991.

Toy theaters are an old European puppet tradition. The idea of having an entire theater — scenery, actors, and all — within an area as small as a shoe box is entrancing. Not only is it possible for a child, teacher, librarian, or even a small group to put on a puppet play, the making of a toy theater calls for all possible talents to be engaged in the construction of the theater, its actors and the presentation of the play. In *Toy Theaters*, we learn to make a diorama, spinning wheel theater, shoe box stage for finger puppets, miniature shadow puppet theater, and of course, a toy theater.

Yerian, Cameron. *Puppets & Shadow Plays.* Chicago: Children's Press, 1974.

This book focuses on basic puppet making and play production. Instructions for puppets, stages, props and even a couple of plays are given. Content is divided between puppets and shadow plays. An interesting twist is the use of live action in shadow plays rather than puppets.

Young, Ed. *The Rooster's Horns: A Chinese Puppet Play to Make and Perform.* New York: HarperCollins+World, 1978.

The story of the rooster's horns is told with instructions for making a shadow puppet theater and patterns for making the rooster and the dragon. This is identical to "The Camel, the Horse, and the Deer," a folk tale from the Asian country of Tuva.

Index